Praise for *The Un-Chosen Body*

"Ilana Szobel's The *Un-Chosen Body* offers a compelling analysis of disability culture in Israel, revealing the vivid brilliance of disabled poets, artists, and filmmakers whose work deserves our attention. Szobel grapples forthrightly with state violence and social inequality—and makes a powerful case for the political urgency of thinking critically with disability."

—Julia Watts Belser, author of *Loving Our Own Bones: Disability Wisdom and the Spiritual Subversiveness of Knowing Ourselves Whole*

"Exploring the provocative work of disabled creators and subjects who refuse to stay on the margins, Szobel claims Israeli art as a powerful form of political protest. *The Un-Chosen Body* is an exhilarating analysis of the flourishing creativity of Israeli disability culture."

—Rachel B. Gross, author of *Beyond the Synagogue: Jewish Nostalgia as Religious Practice*

"In her nuanced study of cultural production and performance by disabled artists in Israel and Palestine, Ilana Szobel delineates a vital, original, and diverse creative force. Keenly attuned to the sociopolitical context of this art and critically engaged with factors that intersect with disability—gender, sexuality, ethnicity, race, economic status, national identity—Szobel's *The Un-Chosen Body* makes a compelling case for social and political justice by inviting readers to think in new ways about Israeli culture."

—Karen Grumberg, Stiles Professor of Humanities and Comparative Literature, University of Texas at Austin

"Szobel brilliantly analyzes how artists in Israel/Palestine represent and mobilize disability. Her account is especially powerful because it is not always one of triumph or progress; it dwells in moments of pain, violence, exclusion, and nonrecognition as well as focusing on the art and artists who provide models for rethinking accessibility. Szobel carefully considers a broad spectrum of forces, from the intimacy of desire for a specific body to complexly related identities including gender, sexuality, and age to geopolitical power relations and the Israel/Palestine conflict. The result is a book that both sits with the complexity of disability in our world and pushes its reader to imagine new futures."

—Sarah Imhoff, Jay and Jeanie Schottenstein
Chair in Jewish Studies, Indiana University

"In this remarkable study, Ilana Szobel attends to the unique linguistic, geographic, and historical influences that have shaped Israeli disability culture from the twentieth century to the present day. 'Who has a right to speak for another?' pulses at the heart of this book, a question that Szobel explores with deep attention and unflinching honesty."

—Adriana X. Jacobs, associate professor of
modern Hebrew literature, University of Oxford

The Un-Chosen Body

The Un-Chosen Body

DISABILITY CULTURE IN ISRAEL

Ilana Szobel

WAYNE STATE UNIVERSITY PRESS
DETROIT

ISBN 9780814351833 (paperback)
ISBN 9780814351826 (hardcover)
ISBN 9780814351840 (ebook)

Library of Congress Control Number: 2024948223

On cover: Raida Adon, *Woman Without a Home*, 2014. Used by permission. Cover design by Elke Barter.

Publication of this book was made possible through the generosity of the Bertha M. and Hyman Herman Endowed Memorial Fund.

Wayne State University Press rests on Waawiyaataanong, also referred to as Detroit, the ancestral and contemporary homeland of the Three Fires Confederacy. These sovereign lands were granted by the Ojibwe, Odawa, Potawatomi, and Wyandot Nations, in 1807, through the Treaty of Detroit. Wayne State University Press affirms Indigenous sovereignty and honors all tribes with a connection to Detroit. With our Native neighbors, the press works to advance educational equity and promote a better future for the earth and all people.

Wayne State University Press
Leonard N. Simons Building
4809 Woodward Avenue
Detroit, Michigan 48201-1309

Visit us online at wsupress.wayne.edu.

To my father, Peter Miguel Szobel Deutsch, who taught me the art of thinking through language.

CONTENTS

ACKNOWLEDGMENTS

One of my favorite aspects of writing is that the solitude it requires is made possible through the support of a community, one writer's weight buoyed by the many waters of their social sustenance. I can only maintain the silence and concentration necessary for writing thanks to the wonderful distractions and noise that my loved ones provide me. It is the small and everyday moments with others that have enabled this book to be written: walks with friends, family visits, conversations with colleagues, shared meals, and countless WhatsApp messages filled with pictures of cats and loved ones, not to mention the creative captions that accompanied them. While it is well known that there aren't many tangible benefits that come from publishing books, one of the greatest pleasures for me is the opportunity to express my gratitude to the wonderful community that has created this "blessing noise" in my life and supported me so generously throughout the years of writing *The Un-Chosen Body*.

Hannah Naveh, without whose blessing I would not dare to publish a word, has read selected chapters over the years. Although her notes were not in the colored pen and handwriting that I so cherished as a student, they were as sharp, precise, and insightful as ever, and I am as moved as I am grateful. My brilliant friend Michal Ben-Josef Hirsch, who helps me bear the burdens of life with humor, and other friends near and far—Irit Dekel, Talya Meltzer, Einat Grunfeld, Merav Opher, Nitsa Kann, Edith Pick, Dana Bar-El Shwartz, Miriam and Avi Hoffman, Kimberly Stewart, and Taly Ravid—have all enriched my life in immeasurable ways these past few years. Every conversation, every swim at Walden Pond, every walk around Fresh Pond, and every visit to the Museum Berggruen in Berlin wrapped me up in the regenerating comfort of your wisdom and support. Aren't I the lucky one? My friend Karen Grumberg, thank you not only for reading chapter 4 and providing such wonderful comments but also for your unwavering support. I'm not sure how you do it, but every idea always feels more vibrant after we talk about it. You wield a special kind of intellectual magic. Julia Watts Belser, who read the same chapter and provided thoughtful feedback, I am learning so much from every interaction with you and your writings. Orian Zakai, Nadav Linial, and Efrat Bloom, thank you for including me in your wonderful poetry group, which has provided me with a much-needed creative and supportive space.

At Brandeis I am privileged to be surrounded by brilliant feminist colleagues: ChaeRan Freeze, Gannit Ankori, Sue Lanser, and Bernadette Brooten. Thank you for fostering a nurturing environment of genuine authenticity where we can openly discuss and embrace our truths. I am also grateful to Jonathan Decter, Eugene Sheppard, Darlene Brooks Hedstrom, Yuval Evri, Alexander Kaye, Lynn Kaye, Laura Jockusch, and Shayna Weiss for their unwavering assistance and advice. This gift of reinforcement comes from nearby but also from different campuses around the world: I deeply appreciate the encouragement and guidance of many role models, including Chana Kronfeld, Hannan Hever, Yael Feldman, Nili Scharf Gold, Naomi Seidman, Ofra Yeglin, Mikhal Dekel, Maya Barzilai, Tamar Hess, Ranen Omer-Sherman, Adriana X. Jacobs, Shira Stav, Irit Aharony, and Slava Greenberg. As always, I had the profound privilege of learning from my students, particularly in my course "Disability Cultures: Art, Film, and Literature of People with Disabilities." The life experiences and insights of the students, along with the contributions of Deborah Feingold and Shirah Malka Cohen, then doctoral students and teaching assistants, greatly enriched the writing of this book.

Many artists whose work is featured in this book generously shared their thoughts, invited me backstage, and provided photos: Tamar Borer, Victoria Hanna, Rona Soffer, Limor Ashkenazi, Shiri Oved, Tamar Kay, nili Broyer, Nataly Zukerman, and Iddo Gruengard. Without your groundbreaking talent and extraordinary contributions, this book would not have been possible. And Sandra Korn, the talented and exceptionally generous acquisitions editor at Wayne State University Press: from our very first email, I knew this book would come to fruition with your sensitive and thorough guidance. Thank you for your vision and dedication to Israel/Palestine studies, which align so seamlessly with queer, gender, and disability studies. I also extend my gratitude to the manuscript's anonymous reviewers for their precise and helpful suggestions. A special thank-you to Mikayla Zagoria-Moffet, the word artist, who meticulously edited each chapter of this book. With a magician's touch, she polished every linguistic error and posed insightful questions that clarified and refined my arguments. I am indebted to her for transforming my imperfect English into a polished and eloquent text.

While working on the book, I was fortunate enough to conduct my research at two prestigious institutions during the 2023–24 academic year. I want to express my heartfelt gratitude to Hadassah-Brandeis Institute (HBI), especially its gifted and devoted director, Lisa Fishbayn Joffe, and the entire HBI team—Debby Olins, Amy Sessler Powell, and Terri Brown Preuss—for warmly welcoming me as HBI Scholar in Residence into the scholarly community you are creating with such great effort and sensitivity. I am also deeply grateful to the Center for Jewish Studies at Harvard University, especially to its esteemed director, Derek Penslar, and its wonderful team: Rachel Rockenmacher, Sandy Cantave Vil, Maura Kohl Gould, and Osnat Aharoni, for your generous hospitality during my time as a visiting scholar.

Chapter 4, "Choreographing the Disabled Body: Performing Vulnerability and Political Change in the Work of Tamar Borer," was previously published in the *Journal of Jewish Identities* 12, no. 1 (2019): 55–74. I thank the publisher for granting me permission to include it in this book.

Here is that same truth again: the work I have been able to do issues from the essential work that others also do, which is something I do not take for granted. I offer my profound gratitude to Marilyn Reid, head of Willow Hill school (WHS), Mark Hall, director of student services, and the rest of the amazing teachers and staff at WHS. Your dedicated care of my child makes them skip with joy and has allowed me to return to being a woman who writes.

It's difficult to convey how grateful I am for the friends, colleagues, family and other loved ones I name above and below, having just stacked my thanks in a bundled list of acknowledgments. Though this catalogue is nothing if not insufficient, it gestures to the ways that this book has been a collaboration between myself and the many people who have endowed me with the gift of their encouragement. This is nowhere more real than when it comes to my relatives: I feel blessed by the many circles of support from my family—my parents, siblings, their partners, and children—whose love is a constant and undoubted presence in my life. I am also immensely thankful for the endless support of my partner, and for our children, the apples of my eye, for the countless laughs and hugs, for the unexpected ways you animate my life.

INTRODUCTION

Cripping Accessibility

Contradictory Positionings

Some time ago, my child Elisheva surprised me by asking me to schedule an appointment with a speech therapist for them, in hopes that they could get help with their stuttering. The request took me off guard, not because I was unaware of the stuttering, but because the stutter has never struck me as something in need of "fixing." We have never tried to conceal or obfuscate the fact that Elisheva is autistic—from them or from anyone else, for that matter. Despite the advice of "friends" we are (unsurprisingly) no longer in touch with, that because Elisheva can often pass as neurotypical, we should be more discreet about their diagnosis, we have always been open and up front about the matter, and as far as I can tell, they deal with questions related to their identity in a positive, constructive way, befitting the smart and curious teenager they are.

So to me, my child's stuttering was trivial and unconcerning: simply put, that is how they speak sometimes and all we need to do is wait a bit before their words are understood. But their request for professional speech therapy revealed the obvious: an individual's experiences of their own self and their disabilities will be unique to them, and therefore different from the perceptions of those around them, no matter how supporting or loving that network might be. But for all of its obviousness and all of the work I had done to internalize these realities as the parent of an autistic child, I felt momentarily oblivious, despite the fact that they have shared with me, for years, the fact that none of us can really understand them or know what they experience or how they feel as the only autistic person of an otherwise neurotypical family.

So why was I so surprised? And, to be absolutely transparent here, why was it not only a surprise to me, but also a bit of a disappointment? I asked myself then: why do I, a woman who does not stutter, feel uncomfortable with this request and their desire to speak more fluidly—in a more "typical" way? Could it be that one of the major themes of the current book (which I had just finished when my child approached me with their request) dealt with the creative possibilities living with stuttering opens up or enables? And why would a child be so driven to "fix" their stuttering, especially in the context of a supportive network of family and friends, as well as a school environment that warmly embraces and accommodates neurodiversity and disabilities? Why, for a teenager who speaks openly and explicitly with their many friends about their myriad disabilities, friends who wholeheartedly accept them and each other, would this be such a significant concern?

I can't—and don't want to—speak on behalf of my child here. If they so choose, Elisheva will find a way to communicate and tell their story by themselves, in their own way. But I found this to be a marked example, on such a personal level, of the contradictory positioning of disability explored in so many ways throughout this book. There is the acceptance and even celebration of the disabled (in this case, autistic) identity on one hand, but the desire to minimize other aspects (in this case, stuttering) on the other. *The Un-Chosen Body* deals at its core with Israeli disability culture—a space that, by definition, is full of contradictions and confusion. It is a disability culture that functions and exists in an area of the Global North (Israel) that on the surface celebrates and highlights certain aspects of disability; simultaneously, however, that same Global North holds so many traditional and ableist social expectations and regularly excludes people socially, politically, and economically; many are neither entitled to nor even receiving rights that would be (theoretically) perceived of as basic in other Global North areas such as the United States and the United Kingdom.

While we live in the United States, the emotional Janus-faced duality my child expressed in their request reflects the central position in contemporary Israeli disability culture: attempting to create innovative crip cultural spaces that stem from lived experience(s) of disability while grappling with proper integration into Israeli society and its mainstream (ableist) culture. This tension is related to the complicated relationship between the authors and artists discussed in the book—many of whom are women of different origins and backgrounds—and the environment in which they create, but also concerns their enormous dependence on what Israel (as a state with a relatively comprehensive social welfare system in which health and education are still largely not privatized) is theoretically supposed to provide them, such as, but not limited to education, medical care, decent income, security, and a sense of belonging and worth . . . to name a few.

It is hard to overemphasize the social, cultural, ethnic, gendered, and economic marginalization of most of the authors and artists who dwell at the core of artistic disability culture in Israel. The first book publisher I approached in an attempt to publish the current manuscript rejected it with the argument that the American readership does not know the artists and authors whose work I explore in the book. And to be precise, what I wanted to clarify with that editor was that, other than a few exceptional cases, the spectacular works of these poets and artists are hardly known outside of the disabled community—even in Israel. This lack of visibility is inherently linked to these aforementioned social barriers. Some of the artists featured in this book lack the financial means to market their art; in Israel, most cases of individuals receiving general disability benefits bar those same individuals from working. Some of the poets never received a formal education due to an ableist system that blatantly failed to provide them with the legally mandated education they were entitled to by virtue of the Israeli Compulsory Education Law (1949) and the Israeli Special Education Law (1988). Furthermore, in Israel the army (specifically the mandatory military service) serves as a central base for networking and therefore plays a central role in determining the social and economic status of groups and individuals (which explains, among other things, the massive inequalities when it comes to things such as gender, ethnic, and national disparities in Israel). A significant number of the artists in my book were unable to enlist in the Israeli Defense Forces (IDF) due to their disability and are therefore now without connections that might have paved their way to more established positions within the Israeli art world. In addition, some other poets or filmmakers come from backgrounds that make it difficult, if not impossible, to relay their unique and intersectional position in public (regarding, for example, the sexuality of disabled women) without risking family or community support networks they rely upon to survive. It is not difficult to understand: it is lack of access and lack of support that have kept so many disabled artists secluded from more mainstream Israeli artistic communities.

The artists often share an adherence to the mainstream, trust in the mechanisms of the state, and belief that the discourse of rights resulting from it will be upheld. At the same time, there is a body of artistic works that radically depart from, and often contradict or confront, these assumptions and loyalties. This creates a tension, often examined in the context of disability studies, that is incorporated into mechanisms of "inclusion" or "accommodation," and crip theory and politics that can instead "signal a refusal of social and bureaucratized systems of classification, and that . . . tend to recognize the limitations and exclusions of rights-based claims on the state."[1] In the Israeli context, this separation is not unambiguous; it requires a deep attention to the nuances of friction created from passions and ideologies that do not always align with each other. *The Un-Chosen Body*, therefore, examines what grows out of a disability culture influenced by the discourse on disability originating in Anglo-American contexts but existing in a non-Western space that is not part of the Global South. As I will discuss later in this introduction, there are many complicated shifts when discussing paradigms of power and identity and location, and the questions these engender are not as simple as they might seem at first.

Accessibility and Disability Justice

Rona Soffer's short film *Please Stand Up* (2010) focuses on the character of Gady (Itay Ganot), a Jewish soldier who was wounded during his army service. The film takes place during the Memorial Day for Israel's Fallen Soldiers at the Alyn Hospital in Jerusalem. During a physical therapy session, the siren blares in memory of the IDF fallen soldiers, and Gady struggles to stand, as is customary.

At first glance, it seems that the film expresses identification with Zionist ideology. After all, despite his injury Gady tries with all his might to honor those fallen in battle. However, a closer look reveals a different interpretation of the film that might stem from the director's life experience as a disabled woman (even the hospital setting is one familiar to the director, who was hospitalized there with severe injuries after a car accident at the age of fifteen). The expectation that one will stand during the siren is a symbolic requirement that celebrates and commemorates the nation—an action meant to identify, appreciate, and respect the lives of fallen soldiers. In Rona Soffer's film, the expected symbolic standing of a nation is literally placed upon a wounded soldier, someone who is unable to stand *because* of his participation in that which is essentially national. In this way, the movie subverts conventions, shifting the conversation from the values associated with commemoration of the fallen (patriotism, sacrifice, and comradeship) to instead focus on the daily reality of soldiers who survived. Rather than the fantasy of the immortalized and perfect fallen soldiers, the viewer instead sees the daily reality of so many soldiers who survived the war, only to be pushed to the edges of society as disabled and therefore "damaged."

The expectation that the soldier will rise to stand is symbolic of an expectation that a soldier will overcome injury and disability to assimilate seamlessly back into their previous life, all for the sake of a national narrative. The injury is not only physical but also cultural; the soldier is expected to neutralize any subversive potential of injury or disability, as those events and investigations might provoke questions about the Zionist project and/or the necessity for war and violence. An injury may change a life but not a worldview, so that the soldier's rehabilitation process becomes a metaphor not only for the physical but simultaneously the national: the soldier gains back physical mobility and rehabilitates a sense of national pride (if in spirit only), to remain a loyal citizen of the nation.[2]

Please Stand Up is a film that challenges this demand to "overcome" or "move past" disability, in order to merge back into line with the ideals of Zionist national discourse. During the siren, Gady finds an overwhelming sense of motivation, then manages to stand and even walk a few steps across the physiotherapy room. He fulfills his role as a soldier supporting the national agenda in that moment, but after a few seconds,

Gady collapses and sits down. On the surface, this is simply because of his injury. But with further consideration, Gady's act of sitting while an entire country stands in memory of the fallen dead becomes a form of protest. Gady refuses to erase both his injury and his resulting disability, and simultaneously disrupts the discourse that glorifies the fallen and continues the justification for war. It is a moment that invites us to focus on the experiences of the living and injured, the disabled and the traumatized, rather than on the immortalized perfection of the fallen soldier and the national agenda that this image perpetuates.

Thus, while most scholarly interest in the experience of disability in Israel addresses disability as a condition of personal deficit and misfortune, Rona Soffer's artistic articulation renders disability as a starting point for radical sociopolitical change. In line with that, *The Un-Chosen Body* explores the work of writers and performers who have reinterpreted disability as a fact of life, a form of human variation, and a mode of political force. By discussing representations of and by women with disabilities, *The Un-Chosen Body* not only analyzes the roles and stereotypes of disabled figures in Israeli culture but also celebrates the alternative self-representations of writers and artists with disabilities. Following disability scholar Alison Kafer's call to create "accessible futures," the book examines the ways in which various Israeli performers, authors, and film directors make and imagine a more accessible future for people with (and without) disabilities.[3]

While this book sometimes grapples with the desires (both subversive and overt) appearing in art to "fit in" to more mainstream Israeli culture (to "fix" the proverbial stutter, to return to my opening example), it does not focus on the integration of disabled artists into Israeli society as part of a narrative of normalization. Rather, *The Un-Chosen Body* portrays disability culture in its fullest as a cultural space where dancers, poets, and filmmakers with disabilities challenge hegemonic norms as they create and celebrate their own culture. The book thus refers to the disabled bodymind as a source of creative material that generates its own form of crip aesthetics.[4]

Although disability culture is not a new phenomenon in Israel, it has developed significantly in recent decades.[5] Accordingly, the book focuses on Israeli disability culture from the 2000s onwards. The flourishing of Israeli disability culture in the beginning of the twenty-first century can be explained by the influence of American discourse on the topic. In the 1990s, important studies such as David Mitchell and Sharon Snyder's documentary about disability culture, *Vital Signs: Crip Culture Talks Back* (1995), and Carol Gill's article "A Psychological View of Disability Culture" (1995) were published in the United States and shifted the focus from "Disability Rights to Disability Culture," to use the language of Paul Longmore from his pivotal 1995 talk carrying this title.[6] Although somewhat delayed, a more distinctive and apparent disability culture developed around this time in Israel as well. Netta Ganor's mouth painting, Nataly Zukerman's performances *35 Steps but Who Counts?* (2010) and *The Other Body* (2013), Ido Gruengard's *Metamorphosing* (2014) and *Playback Paralysis* (2016), *It's Not About Ebisu* (Sign Language Theatre for Deaf and Hearing Alike, directed by Atay Citron, 2016), and Elad Cohen's documentary *The Sign for Love* (2017) are just a few examples of works by artists with (in this case, physical) disabilities, who have taken active roles in the Israeli disability culture that has developed significantly in the last two decades.

While each of the artists discussed in this book builds their creative practice around and alongside their experiences of disability and difference in their own unique ways, the project as a whole is an endeavor to crip our conversations about accessibility, applying a lens of disability justice to broader conceptions of accessibility. Cripping issues of accessibility changes the structural hierarchies of power inherent in exclusionary practices. The book thus deals with accessibility in the broadest sense of the word, and it explicitly explores access to creativity, pleasure, and sexuality as well as national discourse, land, and movement.

I discuss artists who rethink cultural and artistic accessibility through their disability, such as the vocal artist Victoria Hanna, the poet Shiri Oved, and the filmmaker Rona Soffer. Others mobilize the intersectionality of disability, sexuality, and ethnic identity: the theater actress and performer Limor Ashkenazi creates her own unique crip and Mizrahi sexuality in wrestling with the dominant Israeli discourse of denial and fear that rejects the sexuality of disabled women. In addition, dancers and filmmakers do not shy away from addressing accessibility to the political discourse, using their lived experiences of disabilities and representations thereof to challenge common perceptions of the Israeli-Palestinian conflict. Tamar Borer's dance will be the focal point of the gendered discussion I cultivate around disability dance in Israel as a form of political resistance, and films by directors Tamar Kay, Mohammad Bakri, and Ramzi Maqdisi will demonstrate not only the political agency of people with disabilities but also the connections between disability, global power dynamics, and geopolitical violence.

The geopolitical context is, of course, central to a book that deals with Israeli disability culture. More specifically, Jasbir K. Puar's concept of "debility"—bodily injury resulting from political forces—provides me with an essential framework for examining cinematic representations of how Israeli tactics create debility among Palestinians to enforce control.[7] To return to the case of the film *Please Stand Up*, the film indeed opposes the discourse of commemoration and offers challenges to the dominance of the military discourse in Israel . . . but it neglects its opportunity to push further. It is difficult to ignore the fact that, at the same time it offers critiques of this discourse, it also reinscribes it as normal and accepted. The viewer knows nothing about the circumstances of Gady's injury or about his time in his military service. Furthermore, the main affair of the IDF in the 2000s, namely—its involvement in the occupation—is not mentioned. The soldier in the film is a seemingly typical young adult whose injury marks him as different; his injury is seen as a sacrifice, as a price paid to the state, but his potential actions as a soldier and the very necessity of the Zionist project (and its implied righteousness) are never in doubt.[8] Gady is viewed as a victim of political tensions—as someone who became disabled through violence and war—but not as an active soldier himself, who, at least theoretically, might have disabled another person or persons, specifically Palestinians. In other words, while Rona Soffer's life experience as a disabled woman allows her to challenge certain basic national assumptions about disability in Israeli culture, her identification does not cross the boundaries of her Jewish Israeli nationality/identity. Put differently, the soldier's potential complicity in disabling a Palestinian person does not disrupt her conception of disability. So, paradoxically, the film exposes systematic injustices in relation to disability, nationalism, and the dangers of ableism, but pursues disability justice at the cost of covering up or glossing over other horrific injustices.[9]

Therefore, as in the example of Soffer's film, bringing up questions intrinsically linked to disability does not necessarily lead to disability justice—and furthermore, disability justice for one population does not necessarily imply or guarantee justice to other populations. To put it simply, identity consists not of a single axis but many (gender, sexuality, race, class, nationality, ability, and so on), and how they intersect can create a tangle of interests that sometimes overlap, conflict, or force deeply personal investigation. Due to the multiplicity of positions as well as the layered political and cultural structure of the disabled community in Israel, disability culture in the country makes it possible to examine questions of accessibility in a complex and multidimensional manner.

It is also important to note that while the director Soffer is a disabled woman, the wounded soldier in her film is a young and sturdy Jewish man, one who was assumedly able-bodied before his wound. This illustrates another key aspect in the discussion of disability justice in general, and in the intersectionality of gender and disability in Israeli disability culture in particular: the chosen body.

Scholar Meira Weiss uses this term—*the chosen body*—to indicate the ways Zionist culture celebrates visions of the masculine, the Jewish, the European, and the physically able.[10] This idealized image of the *chosen body* permeates almost every aspect of Israeli society, a society that treasures potency, heroism, and heterosexual masculinity, with the predictable result that disability is feminized and emasculated. At the same time, we live with the irony that Israel's many wars and armed conflicts have given us multitudes of wounded soldiers. Israeli men disabled in war and armed conflicts are regarded as national heroes—and are present in the public space. This dual view of disability within the Zionist context—as feminizing and exclusionary but also as elevating male heroism when the time calls for it—makes Israel a singularly unique case in its intersectionality of disability and gender.[11] Furthermore, disability culture in Israel is led mainly by women with disabilities. Women and girls with any form of disability are among the more vulnerable and marginalized in society. They find themselves constantly having to deal with multiple intersectional forms of discrimination due to both their gender and their disability. I address this multilayered experience throughout the book in my myriad attempts to explore the effects of the gendered experience of disability on Israeli dance, film, and literature.

In my analyses I draw on the important work of feminist disability scholars such as, but not limited to, Ann Cooper Albright, Rosemarie

Garland-Thomson, Margrit Shildrick, Alison Kafer, Eunjung Kim, and Julia Watts Belser. I extend my discussion on accessibility with a focused look at how the authors and artists discussed herein create new visions of disability justice. While disability is an intimate, daily, individual experience and identity, it is also inextricably interconnected to broader experiences of identity like gender, race, queerness, national affiliation, and geographical location. These intersecting layers of experience suggest that the aims of disability justice must address broader and insidious institutionalized and systemic ableism. With that in mind, I am able to question and then address how disability in Israel interacts with oppression in its various forms—ableism, male supremacy, enforced heteronormativity, settler colonialism, and state violence—in hopes of revealing how disability culture and the paradigms for progress that it invents might work against systemic oppression and violence in Israel/Palestine.

Translating Disability Culture

As part of the research for this book, I met with one of the artists I'm writing about on a visit to Israel. I borrowed my parents' car and arrived in an area in the center of the country that, like many other areas, is currently undergoing gentrification. I didn't know the place so I parked where the directions suggested. I got out of the car, looked around, and chose to walk toward a set of tall, newly constructed buildings with access features. The artist I was meeting is a wheelchair user, so I had assumed she'd be located in one of these. But after wandering around and asking directions from helpful passersby, it turned out her address was not one of the newer accessible buildings but one in a series of three-story railway residences that had been built in the 1950s, with neither elevators nor accessible parking lots.

When I arrived at her home, the artist welcomed me with joy and kindness and we had a wonderful conversation. She told me about the various projects she is involved in and shared many significant milestones in her life as an artist. At some point, we started talking about specific works of hers and I mentioned my feeling that her works correspond with or remind me of the paintings of the disabled Jewish American artist Riva Lehrer. She looked at me curiously and said she had never heard of Riva Lehrer. As we were wrapping up our conversation, she asked me what I might write about her work and I happily shared the aspects of her work that interest me, including various contexts of disability studies and crip theory that appeal to me as an academic. While she was both interested and enthusiastic, she told me that she was not at all familiar with these terms. As I was leaving, she asked if she might read what I had written about her work, clarifying that she doesn't read English, so I promised to translate the text for her when I finished and send it to her.

And since then, I have wondered about this promise.

From a technical point of view, it is of course not a problem to translate the text from English to Hebrew. However, I am more concerned with the broader question of translation in this particular project. Academic writing is often complex, and this book in particular has multiple layers that add complexity even before it's translated. Its interdisciplinary nature involves layers of cultural translation that build upon each other, such as converting visual language into written form, adapting academic contexts to artistic frameworks, and articulating experiences of disability for both disabled and nondisabled readers. Like Mel Y. Chen, Alison Kafer, Eunjung Kim, and Julie Avril Minich, I also wonder, "What imaginations would allow us to presume the presence of multilingual expressions?"[12]

The Un-Chosen Body is many things:

It is a book written in English about film and performance created in Hebrew and Arabic.

It is a study written in Boston about disability culture in Israel/ Palestine.

It is a compilation of research about art and poetry by disabled women, some of whom are very familiar with disability studies and crip theory and some of whom have never heard of or taken part in this theorization directly.

It is a book that deals with mediums of dance, performance, and cinema, but is written in an academic register of English.

This book, like most books on disability studies, is written from a privileged position. It evaluates and ruminates on art and literature that is often created by those who do not share the same privileges in terms of status, financial and occupational security, education, and the like.[13] This brings a new facet of translation and accessibility to bear: at what stage does translation take place and what is (or can be) lost in the process? What can be gained by it? What do words symbolic of entire disciplines and cornerstone works mean without the weight of theory behind them?

I do not intend or aspire to mediate, translate, or tell the story of the writers and artists in this book; my aim is not to "give" them a voice. They don't need me for that—they do it already without me, and their art plays a particular role in that. However, it would be patronizing and condescending to claim that my book offers only my personal interpretations and that it is meant to stay somewhat aloof from the art and the artists. Furthermore, I cannot (and would never want to) disavow the desire of the artists (or most artists, really) to be exposed to a wider audience. I acknowledge that my position, with the help of this book, allows me to help facilitate knowledge of their works and their significance to a larger demographic, both in Israel and the United States. Thus, I wonder how I can escape the potential for cultural and/or intellectual imperialism and perhaps even centering myself in a role akin to the "white savior" while, at the same time, I attempt to offer threads of a discussion dedicated to undercutting a more typical imperialism associated with the male/ heterosexual/white/Zionist chosen-body canon and its pervasive spread through mainstream Israeli media.

I've tried to think of ways to escape this trap—a method of neatly side-stepping the identity axis and its power dynamics, discussing it openly as I have, indeed, considered my positionality often in undertaking this project. Joint writing comes to mind as an option, but I am not an artist, and most of the artists I address in the book are not academics; I can imagine the potential for an amazing collaborative artist project at some point, but that is simply outside the scope of the current book and what it aims to achieve. I also considered combining texts, collecting responses from the artists themselves to feature in between the chapters of the book, but this also preserves an inherently hierarchical structure, leaving their words as curated tidbits like a highlight reel.

Certainly, every interpretation is a translation and vice versa, but the "translation crisis" that I describe here stems from my desire to expose the cracks and to acknowledge these affective ruptures between not just language but modalities of communication. "Languages" here, then, refers not only to a different alphabet and dialect but also to different mediums, different life experiences, different geographical spaces, and so much more, and I did not want to paper over those gulfs that define and outline our lived experiences. I do not try to minimize or eliminate the differences between me and the artists I address and discuss in the book, but rather, I would like to posit that my position as the author of this study is a complicated one: perhaps somewhat unethical, maybe even aggressive, but something that, by virtue of my biography, I simply have not found a way to escape.

All of this has circled back to the promise I made to the artist to make sure she could read a "translated" copy of my work. The chasms of what could be lost in translation when it comes to questions of references or colloquialisms, comparisons with artists she has never heard of, let alone language rather specific to experiences of academia and scholarship, are profound and intimidating. Since the "death of the author" in literary scholarship has highlighted the primacy of each individual reader's interpretation over any "definitive" meaning intended by the author, the artist's original intention is not necessarily as relevant as it once was.[14] Texts and media may communicate with each other without being referential; the creation of art may be indicative of a larger cultural milieu inspiring artists working as contemporaries, even when they don't necessarily know about each other. But there is something chilling to me about the fact that some of her motivation and her cultural influence is not part of my world and vice versa, so certainly some of my cultural interpretation may be unrelated to her life experience or cultural world. In other words, while the artist's request to read my scholarship about her art, translated from a language she is unable to read into one that she can, in order to get a better sense about a wider audience and potentially use this to help expand community and resources is perfectly reasonable, it did raise questions for me concerning the requirement to both historicize and geopoliticize disability.[15]

In the various discussions on disability in the Global South, scholars have revealed time and again that many studies and accounts are dominated by narratives from Global North experiences and perspectives—from interlopers and outside observers—and they often exclude the voices of disabled people in the Global South, especially those living in poverty. This concluding interaction with the artist zooms in on an interesting nuance in this context: while parts of the book that grapple with the hierarchical relations between Israel and Palestine, wherein Israel is positioned as a Global North entity and Palestine as a Global South one, are clear and immutable, other chapters and aspects of the book narrow in on the positionality of artists within Israeli society. Many of these artists are disenfranchised—some of them are Black, poor, or gender-marginalized women—and are therefore not categorized as privileged in the sense that they are benefiting from or maintaining a position of power associated with the Global North.

In this sense, the book *does* recognize the inert power relations in the relationship between the Global North and the Global South—both in general and in relation to disability in particular. It also shares an ethical and practical commitment to move beyond the restraints of hegemonic Global North epistemological foundations while presenting a case study that at times challenges a binary organization of power.[16] This raises questions about how intersections of power function at different locations, and how the axis might shift or bend in these spaces. In other words, while the field of disability studies has indeed developed in "glocal" ways, reflecting distinct regional contexts and acknowledging different specific colonial-settler histories, my book also examines the points of connection, as well as tensions, between Western/Northern disability studies and other unique "geodisability knowledges."[17]

Outlining *The Un-Chosen Body*

In her book *More Than Meets the Eye: What Blindness Brings to Art*, blind writer and scholar Georgina Kleege asks, "But what if I'm imagining a future for real blind people creating real art? What would that look like? . . . And how would these new, previously unstudied tactile aesthetics expand outwards from the realm of the fine arts to influence other aspects of the culture?"[18] *The Un-Chosen Body* takes up this question and explores how Israeli women poets, filmmakers, and performance artists with disability rethink artistic, cultural, and political accessibility through the lens of their disability and gender. The book consists of five chapters, each examining a different aspect of accessibility and its connection to questions of subjectivity and disability justice.

I begin with a chapter that centers on self-representations of women with disabilities and their resistance to symbolic representations of disability. By looking at the works of three Jewish Israeli authors and artists with physical disabilities—vocal artist Victoria Hanna, poet Shiri Oved, and filmmaker Rona Soffer—I examine how their experiences of living with disability, their *misfit* (that is, the manner in which the particularities of embodiment interact with the environment in its broadest sense), enables them to imagine and create their own accessible artistic futures.[19]

Since the concept of an accessible future is inextricably linked to the multitude of past disabled creators, chapter 2 deals with accessibility to the poetic history of disability, and it questions how disability can leave a legacy within poetry for others to claim and interact with. It centers on the poetry of Orit Marton, a wheelchair user living with cerebral palsy (CP), and Inbal Eshel Cahansky, who lives with a neurological syndrome called essential myoclonus, analyzing the intertextual dialogues that have inaugurated the establishment of an Israeli tradition of poetry written by disabled women. This chapter addresses the significance of the intersection of gender, illness, and disability within the self-explorations of contemporary disabled Israeli poets and their longing for a connection to their poetic ancestors.

While the first two chapters focus on the creative individualism of artists and poets and their interconnections, the third moves to incorporate yet another facet of identity: sexuality. Chapter 3 deals with questions of desirability and pleasure, fetishization and desexualization related to people with disabilities. In particular, it narrows in on the way that disabled women have used their lived experiences creatively to rebel against oppressive representations of disabled people's sexuality. It begins with an analysis of the critically acclaimed film *Sh'Chur* (1994), a story featuring an intellectually disabled woman, examining how it manifests a paradoxical and ableist characterization of women with disabilities being simultaneously asexual *and* sexually vulnerable. The chapter then moves on to more contemporary films, like *Next to Her* (*At li Layla*, 2014), which preserve such toxic tropes, continuing to uphold a mainstream cultural narrative about sexuality and disability. The chapter then shifts to a discussion of artists with disability, such as actress and playwright Limor Ashkenazi (born with the genetic syndrome Morquio), who present a powerful articulation of crip sexuality, taking pride in the sexual expression that evolves from disability itself, and who have been actively working to challenge negative representations, offering many different alternatives for viewing disabled women's sexuality, desirability, and autonomy.

The last two chapters of the book, chapters 4 and 5, deal with accessibility within the political space, mainly concerning discourse about the Israeli-Palestinian conflict and the Israeli occupation—the most charged and controversial topics in Israeli society.[20] The two chapters thus challenge the perception of disability as a political inferiority, addressing disability as a political force. (It should be noted that this book was completed prior to October 7, 2023, before the onset of the current war in Israel/Palestine.)

Chapter 4 focuses on the work of dancer and performance artist Tamar Borer (paralyzed in both legs as the result of a car accident). Adopting the insights of feminist disability studies that consider vulnerability and limitation as political devices and focusing on the political agency of people with disabilities, the chapter explores disability dance in Israel as a form of political resistance. The chapter depicts the ways in which disability challenges common perceptions of the Israeli-Palestinian conflict by examining how visual markers of "limited" mobility (walkers and wheelchairs, for instance) affect sociopolitical concepts such as control, agency, and authority.

Chapter 5 surveys Israeli and Palestinian documentaries that depict the experiences of people with disabilities living in the West Bank and the Gaza Strip. Focusing on the work of Jewish Israeli director Tamar Kay, Palestinian Israeli actor and filmmaker Mohammad Bakri, and Palestinian director Ramzi Maqdisi, this chapter considers the politics of debilitation and explores cinematic depictions of disability in the context of the Israeli-Palestinian conflict. By analyzing the connections—as well as the tensions—between Israeli and Palestinian documentaries, specifically regarding cinematic depictions of access to the land (the ability to own it as well as to travel through it), I explore the ways in which the maimed Palestinian body becomes a visible marker for the purposeful production of impairment and injury. Disability thus bears a claim for justice that embodies the injustices of geopolitical power.

The epilogue explores work of individuals with cognitive disabilities, considering how their creative expressions shape the contours of contemporary disability culture in Israel. By focusing on the poetry and art of the residents of Kfar Tikva—a lifelong inclusive community for adults with cognitive, developmental, and emotional disabilities—the epilogue questions the boundaries of what constitutes disability culture. It considers how cognitive ableism influences this category and who participates in the disability scene—exhibiting in galleries, publishing books, performing—and under what conditions. In this light, it reflects on whether disability culture in Israel is indeed cripping spaces within literature and the arts.

As a whole, then, *The Un-Chosen Body* unveils the power of the creativity-disability partnership and its ability to lead to social transformation. More specifically, the book explores the various ways in which Israeli disability culture can offer us a model for how creators with disability rethink, rework, and remake public the notions of artistic, sexual, and political accessibility. The exploration of the varied and powerful artistic contributions of women with disabilities is a critical and relevant window into the ways that disability culture defines new horizons—not only for these remarkable women but also for society at large, highlighting new kinds of debates over the agency of disability and the role of creativity for all of society.

I use here the metaphor of a window both to delineate the scope of my book and to signify its many limitations; one may glance inside and have a look at the room beyond, but many things remain obscured, not only by the larger wall and panes, but also by the inevitability of something like a billowing curtain or a smudge on the glass that obfuscates a perfectly clear look within. I think of my child, who now regularly meets with their speech therapist. Elisheva shares very little about their sessions, as might be both typical and predictable for a teenager. When they choose to share something, I am honored, as I admire their thoughtfulness in inviting me into their world, allowing me fleeting glimpses through the window, and I respect the times when they keep the window closed and draw the curtains. It is a small example, but an invaluable lesson nonetheless, one that informs my understanding of the nuances of disability culture and therefore encourages me to approach this book with a sense of humility. The poets and artists featured in this book, much like my child, have chosen to open windows into their worlds through their artistic creations. And, like my child, they retain full autonomy and control over these spaces—whether they open it more fully to let others see a more comprehensive view of the room or adjust the curtains to limit certain perspectives. They may even choose to close the window one day. My aspiration is that the observations and ruminations within this book align with their work in those moments when they have graciously opened it to the wider world. My hope is that the amplification of disability culture in Israel as I present it in *The Un-Chosen Body* will bring much-needed visibility to the work and lives of Israeli disabled artists and authors; my even more fervent hope, however, is that this work will provide ideas and strategies for comparative reflections for persons with disabilities and their allies all over the world.

1

"A NEW BEAT"

Misfit *and Accessible Futures in Israeli Disability Culture*

Training muscles of her soul in movements
they are not accustomed to,
to oversee, to anchor.

Teaching heartstrings
A new beat.

מְאַמֶּנֶת שְׁרִירֵי נַפְשָׁהּ בִּתְנוּעוֹת
שֶׁאֵינָם מֻרְגָּלִים לָהֶן
כְּמוֹ לְפַקֵּחַ, לְעַגֵּן.

מְלַמֶּדֶת נִימֵי לֵב
פְּעִימָה חֲדָשָׁה.

—Shiri Oved

Take a Seat

"Deaf, r—, normal, blind, dwarf, handicapped, all compete for their place in a game not designed for them. The rules of the game can invalidate them or bring about their success." This introduction by Ita Tal-Or and

Israeli artist, scholar, and disability activist nili Broyer sets the stage for their 2004 video art piece, *Take a Seat*, in which seven participants play "musical chairs."[1] Despite the provocative nature of the language used, the video art deliberately challenges societal norms and perceptions embedded in this violent language.

In the typical game of musical chairs, a set of chairs is arranged in a circle, with one fewer chair than the number of players. The players then move around the chairs as music plays. When the music stops, each player must quickly sit on a chair; whichever player does not reach a chair in time is eliminated. One chair is then removed and the process is repeated until the last player remains on the last remaining chair and he, she, or they is declared the winner. While in the typical game there is a definite advantage in being able-bodied, in *Take a Seat* wheelchairs are part of the game, so players in wheelchairs have the edge. The expectation in the typical game that victory will be awarded to the fastest player is transformed into a guaranteed win for the wheelchair user, who is already in their chair. This thought-provoking video art undermines the assumption in the original game that the players are children, that they are able-bodied, and that the chairs in the game are "regular" chairs. *Take a Seat* features adults with a range of disabilities, and some of the chairs are wheelchairs.

The video art begins with a row of empty chairs. The viewer only discovers that two of them are wheelchairs when the players join the frame. This movement from a visual of empty chairs to a visual of a variety of chairs alerts spectators that they will need to shift from an interpretation based on a normative or ableist world supposedly devoid of disability to a more diverse world of people with and without disabilities. The presence of wheelchairs prompts viewers to reread the scene of the empty chairs as incomplete and misleading. The seemingly automatically normative row of empty chairs in the typical game becomes a restrictive space that is literally not designed for the disabled. Thus, *Take a Seat* reveals the power relations that determine what is and what is not accessible.

This video art does not merely depict the experience of people with disabilities, or simply convey the notion that people with disabilities are excluded from a world physically and ideologically designed for the needs of the able-bodied. Rather, the very fact that the normative chairs are converted into wheelchairs and the able-bodied players are replaced by players with visible and nonvisible disabilities challenges the rules of the typical musical chairs game and transforms it into a "musical wheelchairs game." The wheelchairs (and the disabled participants) are an intrinsic part of the language of the game itself, not what David T. Mitchell and Sharon L. Snyder called a "narrative prosthesis," either a symbol intended to advance the video art plot or a symbolic figure that enables a culture to define and validate its norms.[2] In other words, the video art does not "make room" for the disabled, it does not call for the integration of people with disabilities into society—rather, it creates a new language and a new space that stem from and contain the lived experience of people with disabilities. Thus, the title *Take a Seat*—rather than "musical chairs"—is an invitation to the viewer not only to be part of the musical wheelchairs event, but also and primarily to engage in a serious, radical activity that upends the rules of the normative game.

The current chapter deals with authors and artists with physical disabilities who have accepted, so to speak, their own invitation to "take a seat," to be part of this cultural game. It centers on resistance to symbolic representations of disability and examines the ways in which the experience of disability as a lived reality constitutes art and literature. It focuses on the work of three Israeli Jewish authors and artists with physical disabilities who participate in a cultural space that is "not designed for them," and have reshaped it: the vocal artist Victoria Hanna, the poet Shiri Oved, and the filmmaker Rona Soffer. I discuss the ways in which they rethink cultural and artistic accessibility through their disability or, to use Rosemarie Garland-Thomson's term, through their *misfit*—the dynamic relationship between the body and its environment that shapes the experience of disability.[3] By exploring the embodied rhetoric of disability culture and the ways it defines new horizons, I thus also discuss how these three artists imagine their own futures and build what Alison Kafer termed "accessible futures."[4]

"A Choreography of the Mouth": Victoria Hanna

My stuttering was an incredible gift, because it allowed me to go deep into the roots of speech.

—Victoria Hanna

The Aleph-Bet Song (Hosha'ana): Misfitting Jewish Texts

The poet Sheila Black, co-editor of *Beauty Is a Verb: The New Poetry of Disability*, argued that "a strength of disability poetics is that it forces a questioning of many of the values that seem so much an uninterrogated part of our thinking today. . . . The badassery of the disability perspective is that it forces a destabilization of the status quo in ways that—while similar to those of other disenfranchised groups—are uniquely rooted in somatic experience, how the body is connected to our thinking and feeling in the world."[5] Disability culture focuses on and derives from the lived experience of people with disabilities; it is art created "because-of-rather-than-in-spite-of" the disability.[6] As in *Take a Seat*, it engages with political issues concerning people with and without disabilities, and challenges ableist stereotypes and expectations. At the same time, disability culture also develops "alternative aesthetics based on the particularities of the bodies and minds of people with disabilities."[7]

The Israeli vocal artist Victoria Hanna, who has stuttered from childhood, was born to an Egyptian rabbi father and a Persian mother, and grew up in a Haredi family in Jerusalem. In 2015 she released her first video single, *The Aleph-Bet Song (Hosha'ana)*, directed by Asaf Korman, followed by the song *Twenty-Two Letters*. Both were enormous successes, and she became "an instant internet sensation."[8] Her debut album was released in 2017 and was one of Israel's best-selling that year.

In the video clip *The Aleph-Bet Song (Hosha'ana)*, a schoolteacher—Victoria Hanna herself—is teaching the Hebrew alphabet to a classroom of Haredi girls (at times she multiplies her image to become one of the students herself). She repeatedly chants the entire cycle of the alphabet, each time vocalizing the consonants with a different vowel (*patach, holam, hirik*, and *kubutz*), while making the appropriate motions and gesticulations characterizing each sound. For example, when she pronounces the *patach* her arms are stretched out at her sides at shoulder height. She moves one hand up and around to trace a circle in the air for the *holam*, and the *hirik* is pronounced as though there were imaginary threads emerging from her ears that she pulls forward to represent the compressed dot of the letter. These movements are the externalization of what happens in the oral cavity when producing each sound. While teaching/performing the alphabet, she pats the different parts of

FIGURE 1. Victoria Hanna in *The Aleph-Bet Song* (*Hosha'ana*), 2015. (Courtesy of Victoria Hanna.)

her body that correspond to the relationship between each letter and the body in the ancient kabbalistic Sefer Yetzirah (The Book of Creation).

Victoria Hanna's use of language morphs phonetics, diction, and the sounds of words into physical entities. She has addressed the connection between her aesthetic choices and her experience as a person with a stutter in a number of interviews: "For most people, sound is highly accessible. I [as a person with a stutter] do not take the cavity in my mouth for granted and the projection of the sound extends beyond me."[9] Similarly, in a different interview she explained that "the person with a stutter, unlike those who speak fluently, has a more acute sensation of the word, the sound, the voice. I experience the tension created in my mouth in my whole body. The disability [*mugbalut*, can also be read as a 'limitation'] is what allows this awareness to emerge."[10] Without going into her choice of words or the fact that, implicitly or explicitly, she refers to stuttering as a limitation, her work deals with what is going on in the body, specifically in the oral cavity before and while a sound is produced. Thus, just like the wheelchair in nili Broyer and Ita Tal-Or's video art *Take a Seat*, Victoria Hanna's voice work is both physical and metaphysical. This transition between the physical and the metaphysical, between her disability and her art, creates her unique aesthetic, which she defines as a "choreography of the mouth."[11]

In her article "The Case for Conserving Disability," Garland-Thomson raises the bioethical question of "why we might want to conserve rather than eliminate disability from the human condition."[12] Exploring this important question and its ethical implications are beyond the scope of this chapter, but I would like to emphasize Garland-Thomson's counter-eugenic arguments for conserving disability: "the principle of honoring the 'is' rather than the 'ought.'" She argues that "the characteristics, the ways of being in the world, that we think of as disabilities would under such a definition be understood as benefits rather than deficits."[13] In other words, the benefit of stuttering is embodied in Victoria Hanna's art, in her "choreography of the mouth." The lived experience of stuttering permits unique involvement with Jewish texts, while at the same time this exploration of ancient scripts elicits an exploration of stuttering itself.

In *The Aleph-Bet Song* (*Hosha'ana*), Victoria Hanna recites the *hoshanah*, a Jewish prayer for rain, each line of which is in alphabetical order. This prayer is one of a series of seven liturgical poems traditionally recited by the congregation on the seventh day of the Jewish holiday of Sukkot. *Hoshanah* (literally, "please save [us]") calls upon God to rescue and redeem the Jewish people, primarily by sending rain. The sacred text—usually performed in the synagogue—is shifted in the clip to a girls' classroom. When the text is removed from its usual context, a new space is created. By pulling apart and reconstructing language, Victoria Hanna addresses the physical experience of the text, thus extending and radicalizing the world of scholarship. Her engagement with the sacred text does not involve studying traditional commentaries, but rather constitutes a physical, emotional, and spiritual probe of pronunciation. The Jewish ritual is experienced as a sensory one that can be studied through the body and the physical and concrete pronunciation of letters and words. This is done through breathing, dancing, eating honey, banging on the blackboard, touching the ground, and beating *aravot* (willow branches).

Jewish tradition attributes meaning to the physical manifestation of the shapes and sounds of each letter. However, the notion of a bodily connection to the letters and the holy scriptures is not foreign to Judaism. When Victoria Hanna hits the board with a willow branch she is actually performing the ancient Jewish custom of *waving the four species* (palm, willow, myrtle, and etrog) and then beating them on the ground during the Sukkot holiday when praying for rain. This ritual is thought to call on nature; it creates a movement that communicates with God. Similarly, when she licks honey spilled on the alphabet letters, she connects—in her own way—to the Jewish tradition of learning. In the shtetl, boys were sent to the cheder at the tender age of three to learn Hebrew letters and the Torah. Their teachers traditionally gave them honey to comfort them and to symbolize the sweetness of learning Torah.[14] Thus, the sacred language was acquired through the body, and became part of the body.

Victoria Hanna brings us back to the Jewish bond between the Hebrew letters and the human body.[15] When she stutters, she halts her speech to verify where each consonant is being placed in the mouth and how each vowel is produced in the oral cavity. Stuttering embodies the body's presence in language. Each stage of the vocal process becomes a significant aspect of the spiritual ritual. She thus suspends semantic meaning—of language, Jewish texts, and tradition—to view it from the perspective of her *misfit*; her disabled embodied place is transformed into a unique subject position, totally capable and significantly endowed with power to elicit new meanings. Garland-Thomson argued that the concepts of fitting and misfitting "speak directly to the issue of reshaping body and world."[16] Although misfitting can lead to sociocultural exclusion, in Victoria Hanna's case it fosters a new relationship with Jewish tradition.

Twenty-Two Letters: Stutter-Gain

While Victoria Hanna's "choreography of the mouth" rereads ancient texts, it also explores stuttering itself as an enabling rather than a restrictive space. Joshua St. Pierre noted that "stuttering is consistently framed as an individual, biological defect to be coped with, managed or cured. Little attention has been given to what can be learned from resisting the urge to 'fix' stuttering and instead reflecting upon what it can reveal about the ways we are accustomed to understanding speech, communication and disability."[17] Victoria Hanna's vocal exploration turns stuttering into a divine and human channel of creation. In the song *Twenty-Two Letters*, she further explores the letters of the Hebrew alphabet, which are showcased in calligraphy throughout the video.[18] In this song she combines excerpts from Sefer Yetzirah (The Book of Creation) that describe how God created the universe by breathing life into the Hebrew alphabet. This mystical work addresses not only the divine but also the Hebrew language itself and its meanings as an instrument for creating worlds. The Hebrew letters in Sefer Yetzirah control cosmic reality and direct its course.

When Victoria Hanna relates to the mystical and kabbalistic meanings of Sefer Yetzirah, its focus on the dynamics of the spiritual domain, and the central role played by letters and sounds in the creation of the world, her choice of passages also attributes new meaning to the ancient text. Her vocal selection and editing of Sefer Yetzirah become a description and an exploration of stuttering itself. The song begins with a quote from Sefer Yetzirah:

> Twenty-two foundation letters engraved in voice,
> hewn in wind, set in the mouth in five places:
> in the throat,
> in palate, the tongue, the teeth, the lips.
> Twenty-two letters he [God] fused to his tongue
> and revealed his secret.

FIGURE 2. Victoria Hanna in *Twenty-Two Letters*. (Courtesy of Victoria Hanna.)

עשרים ושתים אותיות יסוד
חקוקות בקול חצובות ברוח קבועות בפה בחמשה מקומות:
בגרון
בחיך בלשון בשניים בשפתיים.
עשרים ושתים אותיות שקשר בלשונו
וגילה את סודו.

The chorus continues with similar motifs:

He [God] created substance from chaos
Made no-thing into some-thing
Hewed great stones
From the air that cannot be conceived.

יצר מתוהו ממש
עשה אינו ישנו
חצב אבנים גדולות
מאוויר שאינו נתפס.

While these quotes refer to God and to the mystical connection between the creation of the world and the Hebrew letters, they also simultaneously describe the human process of producing letters and words. When Victoria Hanna performs the line "He created substance from chaos (*yatzar mitohu mamash*)," she captures her sensation of speaking while stuttering. The biblical/kabbalistic story of the creation of the world becomes her story as an artist who stutters. This allows her and her listeners to be suspended at the moment of passage from the spiritual to the material, and from the abstract to the concrete. Just as the world was created from chaos, there was chaos before words could come out of her mouth. Before they are uttered, the words are like abstract, inconceivable air. This experience is physical but also spiritual and existential. The transition between the metaphysical world and the physical world occurs by producing sound. Although sound is not material and cannot be touched, its frequencies are quintessentially physical and vibrational. The voice thus is mysterious, spiritual, and physical. Victoria Hanna commented that her teacher, the vocal artist Ruth Wieder-Magan, told her that every time she opened her mouth she must not expect to know what would come out of it.[19] The sound and the production process of the voice transmit hidden secrets, and the artistic act reveals and explores this wonder.

Just like other kinds of disability that are used as a "narrative prosthesis"—a characterization or metaphor that fails to further develop disability as a concrete and complex point of view—so stuttering has been viewed by various scholars as a symbol.[20] Gilles Deleuze's essay "He Stuttered," for instance, addresses "creative stuttering . . . [that] puts language in a state of perpetual disequilibrium."[21] Stuttering for Deleuze is thus a way of destabilizing language and disrupting its function in a creative way. The few scholars of Israeli culture and Hebrew literature who have addressed stuttering have mainly discussed it as a narrative device rather than as a life experience. Roni Henig, for example, shows how "stammering was a tool employed by Hebrew authors [during the first decades of the twentieth century] to present an ambivalent relationship to the transforming language," whereas Haviva Pedaya states that "stuttering must tear the social stupidity. Stuttering must resist the herd's laughter, the barren deafness."[22]

Unlike poetic stammering, Victoria Hanna's actual stutter does not disrupt or dislocate language. Rather, she returns to the concreteness of language, its pronunciation, and the raw materials—the letters, consonants, and syllables that go into forming language in the vocal apparatus. In so doing, she rejects the dominant view of disability as either a symbol that serves able-bodied narratives or as a deficit to be rejected, tolerated, patronized, or protected. Her art refuses "the ideology of ability" that refers to disability "as what we flee in the past and hope to defeat in the future."[23] Instead, she celebrates her disability because it produces valuable opportunities for knowledge and communication.

Inspired by the term *Deaf-gain*, which was coined by H-Dirksen L. Bauman and Joseph J. Murray, Victoria Hanna can be considered to produce a "stutter-gain." Bauman and Murray noted that "in this light, deafness is not so much defined by a fundamental lack, as in *hearing loss*, but as its opposite, as a means to understand the plenitude of human being, as *Deaf-gain*. Deaf-gain . . . is the notion that the unique sensory orientation of Deaf people leads to a sophisticated form of visual-spatial language that provides opportunities for exploration into the human character."[24] By the same token, stuttering in Victoria Hanna's work should not be defined by a lack (of coherent speech, for instance), but rather as a powerful sensory experience that enables her to explore her own voice and disability and to assert her claim to the Jewish tradition and its texts and languages on her own terms.

"Reviving Faded Yearnings with New Colors": Shiri Oved

In 2016, the poet Shiri Oved published her first book of poetry, *Chiseling My Own* (*Ehaye li haismel*). The book opens with a depiction of suffering: "Walking in an ancient desert, / My being fluctuates in furrows of pain."[25] The pain returns in other poems, such as this untitled one:

> Wallowing in bile absorbing echoes,
> Recurring pains.
> Welding scourging floggings,
> Like a shell about to fall off,
> Battling to survive.[26]

מִתְבּוֹסֶסֶת בְּמִיצֵי קֵבָה סוֹפֶגֶת הֵדִים,
כְּאֵבִים חוֹזְרִים וְנִשְׁנִים.
מַלְחִימָה הַלְקָאוֹת צוֹרְבוֹת,
כִּקְלִפָּה שֶׁעוֹמֶדֶת לִנְשׁר,
נִלְחֶמֶת לִשְׂרֹד.

A long-standing literary tradition leads educated readers to think of pain in poetry as representing emotional pain, mental distress, sadness, or agony. The reader's initial tendency is thus to consider pain in Oved's poetry in these terms. Since Oved is a wheelchair user living with cerebral palsy (CP), in a poetry tradition that is part of a larger "ideology of ability," most readers would probably understand the pain in Oved's poems as expressing emotional suffering related to her disability.[27] Because disability in an ableist tradition is seen as a negative and undesirable thing, not only is the suffering of the disabled speaker perceived as her natural state, the fact that her writing focuses on her unhappiness as a disabled woman is seen as the correct poetic move.[28] Therefore, the inclusion of the following untitled poem is hardly surprising:

Suffering from constipation,
Taking self-hatred laxative.
Disgust and misery excreting.
Respiration wipes

Small moments of pardon and again
It never ends. When will I cease, when will I desist.[29]

סוֹבֶלֶת מֵעֲצִירוֹת,
לוֹקַחַת מְשַׁלְשֵׁל שִׂנְאָה עַצְמִית.
תִּעוּב וַעֲלִיבוּת יוֹצְאָים.
מַגְּבוֹנֵי נְשִׁימוֹת

רְגָעִים קְטַנִּים בִּסְלִיחוֹת. וְשׁוּב
זֶה לֹא נִגְמַר. מָתַי אֶחְדַּל, מָתַי אַנִּיחַ.

While the poem expresses self-loathing, treats disability as a perpetual state of suffering, and reflects an ableist position that disability is comparable to if not worse than death, it is equally possible to reject this ableist reading and not "blame" Oved for internalizing an ableist approach to disability.[30] In other words, what would happen if the reader refused to interpret the pain in Oved's poetry as referring to emotional pain, and think of pain (also) in physical terms? What would emerge if, instead of thinking of the speaker as existing in the realm of sadness and sorrow, the reader interprets the descriptions as referring to concrete bodily pain and physical syndromes? What if we distance ourselves from the symbolic and orient ourselves toward the concrete, and consider Oved's descriptions of gastric juices, constipation, bone crushing, and "an enlarged finger inflamed from internal destruction" as referring to the speaker's concrete body and in particular to her fragile bones, abdominal pain, and inflammation?[31] What kind of poetic avenue will open up to us if we listen to what Oved shares about her experience of disability? Which real experiences of disability rather than "fantasies of disability"—that is, disability as society fantasizes and imagines it—would unfold before us?[32]

What would we discover if we believed Oved when she declares in one of her poems that she is "reviving faded yearnings / with new colors," that she rejects self-loathing and insists on creating a reality with new hues?[33] This interpretation would depict the experience of disability and would not deny the descriptions of physical disability in her poetry. Thus, the poetic moves in Shiri Oved's book can be read as a political act that presents her disability—her embodied *misfit*—and thrusts it into the socio-poetic space of Hebrew literature and Israeli culture. Her poetry does not eliminate or "overcome" disability. It fuses her poetic identity with her identity as a woman with disability. Thus, Oved's work establishes her identity as a poet who consciously creates a disability culture.

Accessible Futures

The title of Shiri Oved's book, *Chiseling My Own* (*Ehaye li haismel*), literally means "I will be my own scalpel," and the poem that starts with the same line alludes to the proactive position of the speaker. She does not wait for an external acknowledgment, but rather sculpts her identity, her story, and her future. To an Israeli reader, the title of the book is a nod to the title of David Grossman's well-known 1998 novel *Be My Knife* (*Shetihiyi li hasakin*). In contrast to Grossman's novel, in which a male writer tells the story of a female protagonist, Shiri Oved tells her own story of a female poet with a physical disability. Here, the knife from Grossman's novel, an aggressive and threatening instrument, becomes a chisel, a hand-held tool used to produce delicate sculptures. Above all, unlike a knife that can injure and destroy, Oved "wants to disassemble, reassemble, / while having the upper hand."[34] Her chisel deconstructs in order to construct something new.

Oved may also be aiming to dismantle a long tradition of ableism in general, and gender-based ableism in particular. However, what is more intriguing than the deconstruction is precisely what she wants to reconstruct: the very fact that her poetry primarily articulates her aspiration to think by herself about herself and her disability in the future tense, "I will be my own scalpel." To understand the radicalism inherent in this aspiration it is worth dwelling briefly on the connection between disability and futurity. Alison Kafer begins her book *Feminist, Queer, Crip* with an anecdote that captures this issue:

> I have never consulted a seer or psychic; I have never asked a fortune-teller for her crystal ball. No one has searched my tea leaves for answers or my stars for omens, and my palms remain unread. But people have been telling my future for years. Of fortune cookies and tarot cards they have no need: my wheelchair, burn scars, and gnarled hands apparently tell them all they need to know. My future is written on my body.
>
> In 1995, six months after the fire, my doctor suggested that my thoughts of graduate school were premature, if not misguided. He felt that I would need to spend the next three or four years living at home, under my parents' care, and only then would it be appropriate to think about starting school. His tone made it clear, however, that he thought graduate school would remain out of reach; it was simply not in my future. What my future did hold, according to my rehabilitation psychologist and my recreation therapist, was long-term psychological therapy. My friends were likely to abandon me, alcoholism and drug addiction loomed on my horizon, and I needed to prepare myself for the futures of pain and isolation brought on by disability. . . .
>
> My future prospects did not improve much after leaving the rehabilitation facility, at least not according to strangers I encountered, and continue to encounter, out in the world. . . . Their visions assume a future of relentless pain, isolation, and bitterness, a representation that leads them to bless me, pity me, or refuse to see me altogether. Although I may believe I am leading an engaging and satisfying life, they can see clearly the grim future that awaits me: with no hope of a cure in sight, my future cannot be anything but bleak.[35]

Alison Kafer describes what others saw as the fate of people with disabilities: a future of no future. She rejects the notion of disability as a predestined limitation and calls for an accessible futurity. Her approach challenges perceptions of the future that arise from and serve compulsory able-bodiedness and able-mindedness, and envisions new possibilities for crip futures. She does not (only) demand that what is built or learned in the future be accessible, but that the very possibility of imagining a future should become accessible to people with disabilities.

Shiri Oved seems to respond to Kafer's call by describing how the speaker creates her accessible future in terms of someone who sculpts and chisels raw material. The speaker "hoists a sharp stone to remedy, / Smashes her head," and "gathers her body parts."[36] She carves "corners in the dark" with the chisel and deconstructs and constructs herself anew.[37] A gust of wind blows through her, and at the end of this process she affirms:

I will come out smeared in mud
Wearily with slightly rough skin.
Curious to look at and smell a purified tomorrow.[38]

אָבוֹא מְכֻתֶּמֶת בֹּץ
בַּעֲיֵפוּת עִם עוֹר שֶׁהִתְקַלֵּף קְצָת.
סַקְרָנִית לְהַבִּיט לְהָרִיחַ—מָחָר טָרִי.

Like the fable of the Golem, or in the Assyrian creation story, a new entity with a beating heart is formed. The speaker creates herself out of the "raw woman" she was. She becomes a woman who looks toward the future, to "a purified tomorrow." After re-creating herself, after her sculptural work is complete, Oved shifts to the next section, entitled "Teaching Heartstrings a New Beat," which starts by addressing language and speech, wherein she "throws words into the whirlwind."[39] As part of this self-creation, in the poem that serves as the epigraph for this chapter, the speaker trains her soul and teaches her heartstrings a new beat. Her heartstrings (*nimey lev*), which were indoctrinated in the ableist tradition that views disability as a source of constant suffering, self-hatred, and difficulties, are transformed and re-created to vibrate and emanate the actual disability experiences of the speaker, binding together body, society, and mind.

This self-construction of meaning and physicality leads to the next section, "New Permanence," which opens with "a willingness to be constructed as a future memory."[40] One of the untitled poems in this section reads:

Toying with discarded shells of silence,
That shed off of me.
Curious, how they will be constellated tomorrow.[41]

מְשַׂחֶקֶת בְּקַלְפּוֹת שֶׁקֶט,
שֶׁהִתְפַּשְּׁטוּ מִתּוֹכִי הַחוּצָה.
סַקְרָנִית, אֵיךְ יְשֻׂרְטֵט אוֹתָן הַמָּחָר.

The speaker addresses her future, which is open and is an integral part of her disability experience. She establishes the possibility of containing and imagining her own future. The book produces a constant tidal motion of "spreading out and gathering, gathering and spreading out."[42] In numerous poems and in different ways, the book navigates a course of constant dismantling and assembling that becomes a poetic and ideological stance. The disabled body disentangles itself from its ableist meanings, distances itself from the social set of expectations that constitute it as bound, and reassembles it anew. This is a repetitive process of "soul-muscle flexing," during which nothing is self-evident or taken for granted.[43]

Defining an accessible future involves risk-taking and daring, as can be seen in the following untitled poem:

Unleashing my organs to the wind,
Exposed risks
crushing bones. . . .

Or perhaps, unawares,
I will feel a touch on my shoulder
meeting, groping.[44]

מְשַׁלַּחַת אֲבָרַי לָרוּחַ,
חֲשׂוּפָה מִסְתַּכֶּנֶת
בְּרִסּוּק עֲצָמוֹת . . . .

אוֹ אוּלַי, מִבְּלִי מֵשִׂים,
אַרְגִּישׁ נְגִיעָה בִּכְתֵפִי
פּוֹגֶשֶׁת מְגַשֶּׁשֶׁת.

Casting organs into the wind and the danger of their being crushed is reminiscent of Icarus in Greek mythology. Disobeying his father's warnings, he flew too close to the sun, which melted the wax in his wings and caused him to fall into the sea and die. The figure of Icarus is a symbol of human ambition, daring, and the uncompromising attempt to fly, touch the sun, and follow the dictates of the heart. Although aware of the myth of Icarus and the danger embodied in her act ("risk / crushing bones"), the speaker does not refrain from physically and metaphorically launching her organs into the wind.

This willingness to take risks is an important component of creating an accessible future. Numerous scholars and activists have addressed the importance of "the dignity of risk," to the disability rights movement and disability culture.[45] The dignity of risk is the right to take risks when engaging in life experiences, and the right to fail in those activities. Andrew Pulrang noted that people with disabilities "cherish this right to take risks all the more because most disabled people at some point in our lives have to contend with some kind of outside authority either informally or formally telling us what we can and cannot do, simply because of our disabilities."[46]

The danger of hurling one's organs into the wind in Oved's poem can refer to an actual physical experience of testing the body's abilities while risking injury, but it may also be interpreted as an ars-poetic claim. Writing autobiographical poetry about the experience of living with a disability, especially within the Hebrew cultural space—which, as I demonstrate in the next chapter, features few role models of women poets with physical disabilities—is in itself a risk that Oved takes, and that she fights for.

Along with the danger described in the poem, there is also the comforting possibility that the speaker may "feel a touch on my shoulder," that is, that there will be a fleeting touch (human or divine). This touch on the shoulder is a reference to Rachel Bluwstein Sela's untitled 1927 poem that opens with the line "Waking up in the hospital in the early morning." The poem describes the experience of a person who is hospitalized. It starts with her despair, a feeling a healthy person is not capable of understanding, and it ends with the comfort of being cared for, a grateful emotion that a healthy person likewise cannot understand:

The sound of the doctor's footsteps in the hallway,
A comforting hand
Gently touches your hand.
What can the healthy sense about this instant of decency?[47]

קוֹל צַעֲדֵי הָרוֹפֵא בַּפְּרוֹזְדּוֹר יִשָּׁמַע,
וְנָגְעָה בְּיָדֵךְ רַכּוֹת
יַד-נֶחָמָה.
מָה יֵדַע הַבָּרִיא מִשָּׁעָה הַטּוֹבָה הַזֹּאת?

Shiri Oved conducts a poetic dialogue with Bluwstein (1890–1931), who became the ultimate symbol of illness and suffering in Hebrew literature, to the extent that Sunny Yudkoff called her "the tubercular poet," claiming that "much of Raḥel's renown results from her public experience of tuberculosis."[48] It is worth recalling that within the tradition of Hebrew poetry, Shiri Oved does not have a literary genealogy of poets with physical disability whose shoulders she can stand on. Carla Rice and her co-authors have argued that in order to establish an accessible future, artists with disabilities should embrace their connection to the legacies "of those who came before us, carving out new possibilities for life with difference, new possibilities for disability futurities." They recognize that those legacies "stream from formative disability rights and justice activists, those who appear in our disability history as well as those who have been written out. . . . We receive these legacies as bequests from the past, are enlivened by them, and draw on them for power and strength as we battle to make the world a more livable place, forging new meanings of embodied difference and a world capable of embracing such legacies as we do."[49] This is why Rachel Bluwstein's poetry, which deals with her illness and dying becomes a 'bequest from the past,' a central model for Oved, despite the huge difference between Rachel Bluwstein's tuberculosis and Shiri Oved's cerebral palsy.

Rachel Bluwstein's poem differentiates between the sick and the healthy, stressing the inability of the healthy to understand the sick ("What can the healthy sense about this instant of decency?"). While Oved's poetry can be associated with Rachel Bluwstein's writing about illness/disability from the perspective of the sick/disabled subject, the touch of the hand in Oved's poem symbolizes the exact opposite. Rachel

Bluwstein addresses the tender and terrifying application of the medical touch. When she describes the comforting touch of the doctor, it is not clear whether this is a moment of comfort or whether it symbolizes the impending death of the sick speaker. The touch in Oved's poem, on the other hand, symbolizes salvation from crushed bones; it suggests the ability (physical or spiritual) to unleash organs to the wind without crashing. In addition, the touch in Oved's poem is a "meeting, groping" touch: not the precise touch of a doctor (a person of authority and knowledge) but rather a touch from an equal position. It is a touch that gropes and explores, just like the speaker.

Moreover, unlike Rachel Bluwstein's poem, which takes place in a hospital, Oved's poem implies a completely different location. While the verb *groping* is used biblically in Isaiah 59:10 to derisively describe the movements of a blind person, reflecting stigmatized perceptions of how blind individuals navigate, Oved's specific use of "groping" (*megasheshet*) at the end of the poem ("I will feel a touch on my shoulder / meeting, groping") alludes to the sayings of the Chazal, the acronym for the Jewish sages in the Jerusalem Talmud, about the Holy of Holies in the Temple: "Before the ark was taken away [in the days of the First Temple], he [the High Priest] would enter and depart [on Yom Kippur] by the light of the ark [in the Holy of Holies]. After the ark was taken away, he would enter groping and groped as he departed."[50] In other words, the touch on the speaker's shoulder refers to the touch of the High Priest on Yom Kippur, one of the most important days in Jewish tradition. According to tradition, when the Temple existed in Jerusalem, the main role of the High Priest was to enter the Holy of Holies to atone for the sins of the people. Since the High Priest was the only one allowed to enter the Holy of Holies, the speaker in Oved's poem actually situates herself in a place she is forbidden to enter. Just as at the beginning of the poem, when the speaker sends her organs to the wind and, like the mythological Icarus, tries to do what is perceived as impossible, so also at the end she enters a dangerous, sacred, and forbidden place. Imagining the future is a privilege restricted to nondisabled people; that is, it is part of a cultural space from which Shiri Oved, as a poet with a physical disability, is excluded. Thus, in insisting on her right to take risks and enter the Holy of Holies, she is establishing her right to an accessible future.

A Raw Woman

While there is a flourishing disability culture in the United States and the United Kingdom, Shiri Oved's poetry is part of a relatively new trend in Israel. It aspires to change the social and legal discourse on disability by representing the perspectives of writers and artists with various disabilities. Shaylee Atary's films *Neurim* (2020) and *Single Light* (2023), Itamar Beck's music, and Amalia Hatzir's children book *Broken Eyes* (2005) and art exhibitions *Transitional Object* (with Gil Wertheimer, 2017) and *A Woman at 5 Degrees* (2019) are only a few examples of works by artists with (in this case physical) disabilities who have contributed to developing disability culture in Israel in recent years.

Steven E. Brown's remarks in the 1990s describing the initial phases of disability culture in the United States resonate today with respect to Israeli culture: "The existence of a disability culture is a relatively new and contested idea. Not surprising, perhaps, for a group that has long been described with terms like 'in-valid,' 'impaired,' 'limited,' 'crippled,' and so forth. Scholars would be hard-pressed to discover terms of hope, endearment, or ability associated with people with disabilities. But as rights and social standing have become more available to disabled individuals so too has the need and belief in the integrity of group, community, and cultural identity."[51] Scholar and activist Vic Finkelstein has worked to create "our own distinctive culture"—a thriving alternative culture of people with disabilities.[52] He argued that integrating people with disabilities into the dominant culture actually preserves the hierarchy between able-bodied people and people with disabilities, and "encourages us to aim at able bodied standards and values rather than to create our own standards."[53] Nevertheless, as nili Broyer pointed out, the narrative of integration in Israel is still dominant.[54] Nissim Mizrachi argues that a critical discourse on disability, as is the case with other identity discourses in Israeli civil society, remains within the narrow confines of the secular and educated. It remains unclear why it has not gained wider public sympathy among religious or traditional audiences.[55]

Whereas various artists in the U.S. such as Yulia Arakelyan and Erik Ferguson (*Wobbly Dance*), Patricia Berne and Leroy Franklin Moore (Sins Invalid), Maysoon Zayid, and Nicola Griffith (and other writers at her hashtag #CripLit) celebrate the uniqueness of disability, Shiri Oved's poetry takes a more ambivalent stance with respect to her disability.[56] Her work reflects her affinities with the integration attitude embodied, for example, in her aversion to her disability and attempts to "overcome" it. At the same time, her work challenges this approach by creating cultural alternatives through, for instance, the way she fashions an accessible future. Her poetry thus ranges from descriptions of difficult and complex feelings about her own disability to radical conceptions of disability; from striving for integration into Israeli culture to preserving her cultural uniqueness and creating an alternative disability culture.

This multifaceted approach to her disability is patent from the beginning of the book, which starts with a section entitled "Raw Woman" (*Isha golmit*). The word *golmit* in Hebrew is suggestive of the unprocessed or raw, or alternatively can refer to a pupa, the stage between the larva and the adult insect. However, it can also evoke the Golem, the medieval creature created from matter but infused with a soul when Rabbi Judah Löw ben Bezalel of Prague uttered magical sacred names and incantations in the sixteenth century. Oved's poetry hints at all these associations. The book deals with pain, anger, and frustration and treats the disabled body as an intermediate raw, immature, and incomplete state ("I want to recover and stand up").[57] At the same time, it also describes the development of a woman who chisels and sculpts her self, a woman who will bloom and fly away like a butterfly emerging from the pupa.

These meanings of the raw woman recur in her untitled poem that opens with the lines "Burnt smell up my nose, a jolt. Raw woman / sets out to plow thin the body fields."[58] The plowing of the fields of the body can be understood in two ways. In one, the raw woman explores her body in depth; in the same poem she goes out in search of "a faint possibility of beauty, of compassion." The other is more closely related to self-harm. The raw woman rejects her body and injures it (in the same way as in a different poem she "[is] taking self-hatred laxative").[59] This contradiction can seemingly be resolved by seeing the speaker's self-hatred as a kind of internalization of an ableist conception, and her exploration of her body as a more "evolved" stage of metamorphosis into a positive disability identity. However, this interpretation may advance a judgmental and perhaps patronizing attitude toward the notion of identity Shiri Oved aims to convey in her poems.

Colin Barnes and Geoff Mercer noted that despite the rise of disability culture and disability pride, many people with disabilities still do not necessarily identify with the celebration of their disability, although they are convinced of the sociopolitical origins of many of the obstacles people with disability face. They suggest that "disabled people are more likely to develop an attitude of ambivalence toward impairment, insisting that people with perceived impairment should be allowed to lead valued lives while also refusing to glorify impairment."[60] Similarly, not only does Oved celebrate her disability, she also does not internalize repressive social perceptions of disability as a source of misery and pain. Instead, she shares the complex diapason of these perceptions. Oved's poetry does not shy away from physical and emotional extremes but also does not range from static nonacceptance to stolid acceptance. Her poetry creates a multifaceted spectrum of dynamic moves that change and take shape as functions of her actual experiences of living with cerebral palsy. Her poetry thus constitutes a poetic and political *misfitedness* that transitions between possibilities and does not opt for one narrative over the other.

"I Dream My Dreams and Then I Live Them": Rona Soffer

Where to begin? Should I start with my car accident while I was a turbulent teenager, which suddenly changed everything I thought about body and life? Or simply the fact I grew up as a rebellious young girl in Jerusalem at the end of the last century? After the catastrophic car accident, I lost my body while transforming myself to be solely a body. I went through a very lengthy rehabilitation process and had to re-learn everything as a teen: how to talk, walk, breathe, rage, love and appreciate. But more than anything, I discovered the strength of my embodied cognition, even though my body is totally different.

—Rona Soffer

"Being Me, Being Different": *A Redheaded Sheep*

The films by the Jewish Israeli filmmaker Rona Soffer explore her identity as a woman with disability. In her 2004 film *Until the Wall Breaks Down: A Film About Rona* she returns to Alyn Hospital a decade after she was hospitalized there with severe injuries after a car accident at the age of fifteen. In her documentary *Love Davka* (2010) she examines her life as a young woman with disability looking for an intimate relationship, raising difficult questions about disability and sexuality. Her 2010 short feature *Please Stand Up*, discussed in the introduction, delves into the unspoken connection between Israeli nationalism and disability, and in her 2014 short feature *A Redheaded Sheep* she examines the connection between creativity and disability, a theme she develops in her latest film, *Ms. VeRtigo* (2018).

The documentary *Love Davka* opens with Rona Soffer's statement: "When people meet me for the first time they always give me tips on how to drink my tea. One woman assured me that if I drank green tea with turmeric, I would get my voice back, just like that. They do not understand that it is permanent. That this is how I talk. That this is the only voice I have. And with it I became the person that I am. Because in order to hear me, you need to do more than hear. You need to listen." Soffer's whisper—one of the most obvious features of her disability, along with her limp—opens the film and is used to formulate what she demands of her viewers. She asks them to listen, not because of her whisper but through it. As is the case with Victoria Hanna's works and Oved's poetry, in order to understand Soffer's films the viewer must not overlook her disability but engage in the opposite: one has to listen, physically and symbolically, to her *misfit* voice telling her story.

Nuni is the main protagonist in Soffer's twelve-minute feature film, *A Redheaded Sheep* (*Kivsa ktuma*). Nuni used to paint sheep graffiti on the streets of Jerusalem until she contracts an infection and her leg has to be amputated. In the aftermath, she distances herself from everyone she knew. Some years later, by chance, she meets Matan, her former graffiti partner and possibly lover. Matan asks her to draw him a sheep as a token of those days, but since everything is different for her now, she refuses at first. The film is about her slow decision to relent.

The film starts with a close-up of Nuni's stump attached to her prosthesis followed by a sound of pain as the prosthesis is removed. This is how from the very beginning the film depicts its own space as a work that cycles from hiding the disability to externalizing and coming to terms with it through physical and emotional pain. Nuni relearns and reestablishes her artistic voice, thus making the film a statement about changes in her subjectivity. The protagonist examines who she was and if/how her disability fits into her present subjectivity. Matan wants Nuni to paint a sheep as she did before the amputation, claiming that her love of graffiti should not be affected by her disability, but Nuni believes that "not everything is possible." Throughout most of the film she refuses to walk without the prosthesis despite the inflammation and pain it causes her, yet after she removes the prosthesis she is able to paint the graffiti of the sheep. That is, she manages to express herself artistically only when her disability is seen, only when she comes out of the closet of disability, can reconcile herself to her disability, and is able to share it with others.

Nuni herself, with her curly reddish hair, looks like a redheaded sheep, thus making the sheep she painted a kind of self-portrait. That she is able to paint her self-portrait only after she has removed the prosthesis reflects acceptance of her disability. The film does not show us the sheep she used to paint before the amputation, only the sheep she paints in the present. The film thus lets the viewer decide whether or not it is the same sheep, whether or not the disability has fundamentally changed Nuni and her art.

The film depicts a disability that in a way cannot be seen as one, since her disability is neither fully visible nor fully invisible. If Nuni uses her prosthesis, despite her lameness, her disability is almost invisible (this is why in most scenes when she is with Matan she stands or sits with the prosthesis so Matan actually experiences her as nondisabled). Nuni can thus choose to pass as an able-bodied person, reflecting Cameron's revision of the Shakespearean "To be disabled, or not to be disabled, that was the question."[61]

The question raised in the film is not about the meaning or implications of the relationship between a disabled person and her environment, which usually revolves around the advantages of passing as a nondisabled person (in the workplace or when dating, for example), compared to the personal and social price of this choice, such as the burden of hiding who you are and the loss of connection to community. Rather, the reflexivity is turned inward. Nuni the protagonist and

Soffer the director ask *themselves* about the boundaries of their disability: how disabled they are and how it affects their lives; what has changed in them since the illness/injury and what has stayed the same. In other words, the inquiry is focused on how the protagonist is perceived by herself, what image she projects/passes as. Coming out tends to be applauded, whereas passing as something other than who you are is seen as assimilationist and self-degrading. However, Ellen Jean Samuels, who analyzed nonvisible disabilities, defines passing as a subversive and autonomous act: "The passing subject may be read not as an assimilationist victim but as a defiant figure who, by crossing the borders of identities, reveals their instability."[62] This liberating instability allows Nuni to come out of the closet of disability and create her own self-portrait.[63]

Cameron and Swain argue that coming out of the disability closet "is a process of redefinition of one's personal identity through rejecting the tyranny of the *normate*, positive recognition of impairment and embracing disability as a valid social identity. Having come out, the disabled person no longer regards disability as a reason for self-disgust, or as something to be denied or hidden, but rather as an imposed oppressive social category to be challenged and broken down. . . . Coming out, in our analysis, involves a political commitment."[64] While this interpretation may not take full account of other experiences, as Ellen Jean Samuels shows, it does reflect Nuni's experience.[65]

In the last scene of the film, Nuni crosses the street. A person in front of her is crossing holding a mirror. When she looks into it, for a moment we see the legs and the cane of the director Rona Soffer (who is also in reality a kind of redheaded sheep) peek out, and then we hear her voice saying: "The only thing I am afraid of is being me, being different. But from my pain, from this body, everything becomes more intense, even wanting you. I can't be afraid of being strong. And I can't be afraid of being weak." The acceptance of the disabled body allows her to come to terms with "being me, being different." In the closing sequence we see Nuni and hear Rona Soffer; the character in the film and the character of the director merge, thus converting the work into an autobiographical film. In other words, Rona Soffer, who initially hid behind Nuni's character, comes out of the autobiography closet and identifies herself as the main character of the film.

FIGURE 3. A woman (Viola Yamit Gotman) in a waiting room gazes at the prosthesis of her right leg in *A Redheaded Sheep*. (Courtesy of Rona Soffer.)

Crip Mirrors: *Until the Wall Breaks Down* and *Ms. VeRtigo*

I buy a full-length mirror . . . not to fix myself but to find myself.

—Harilyn Rousso

Until the Wall Breaks Down: A Film About Rona is an autobiographical documentary made in 2004 by Rona Soffer on the tenth anniversary of her car accident. Directed by Uri Harel, the film combines interviews with Soffer and footage from her rehabilitation at Alyn Hospital, a pediatric and adolescent rehabilitation facility in Jerusalem. Toward the end of the film we see Soffer standing in front of the mirror of the rehabilitation room where she was treated as a teen. She declares that she has overcome her injury, that she has learned to breathe on her own and walk. In this scene, the film shifts from the black-and-white footage of Soffer looking in the mirror of the physiotherapy room during her rehabilitation to contemporary color photography of her in the same location, scrutinizing the same mirror. During the quick transitions between images of Soffer in the past and in the present, she says in a voice-over: "It took me a while but the wall broke down at the end. Pshsh, Damn! It was me . . . and today I am Rona!" as she takes a few dance steps with a proud smile lighting up her face.

Garland-Thomson, in an analysis of the self-representations of people with disabilities, argued that "encountering ourselves face-to-face before the mirror, we become both subject and object of our stares. The work of self-scrutiny can be affirming or alienating, but always absorbing, often up against the edge of baroque staring."[66] nili Broyer, in remarking that the mirror is a visual medium that duplicates what is in front of it, states that it "offers the viewer another look at bodies and especially a different look at one's own body." She cites Garland-Thomson, who "notes that the mirror enables subjects to gaze at their own reflection as if it was another person's body. . . . This opportunity is especially significant to people with (visible) disabilities, who must negotiate their self-image due to society's negative perspective on disability."[67] Broyer states that as far as she is concerned, for her, as a woman with disability, the mirror "offered a means for re-examination and negotiation of my body and identity."[68]

Similarly, the mirror in *Until the Wall Breaks Down* lets Soffer examines herself and raises broader questions about identity, body, and disability. The mirror is multidimensional and dynamic since it shows Rona the teenager, the patient during her rehabilitation in Alyn, as well as Rona the adult director who returns to visit the hospital, but it is also the mirror that reflects her past image in the present. It is a deceptive and inaccurate mirror because it does not reflect what is expected of it and does not respond to the temporal order: it is a crip mirror. Hence, just like the public mirrors that Broyer describes in the context of public restrooms, so the mirrors in *Until the Wall Breaks Down* "show that within the medium of the mirror, intense encounters occur, ranging from alienation through negotiation to self-acceptance and even love. The autobiographical narratives of disabled people suggest that for them, the mirror is a transformative dialogue medium. They crip mirrors for their own needs of affirmation and resistance."[69] In *A Redheaded Sheep* Soffer asked questions about the relationship between identity and disability, and between her disability and her art. In *Until the Wall Breaks Down*, she mainly examines her body in front of the mirror and details the physical changes and developments she experienced. Her dance steps in front of the mirror in the closing scene of *Until the Wall Breaks Down* develop into resistance and a revolutionary dance in her 2018 film *Ms. VeRtigo*.

In *Ms. VeRtigo* Soffer is the director and the lead actress. Whereas *Until the Wall Breaks Down* is an autobiographical documentary and *A Redheaded Sheep* is a feature film with autobiographical dimensions, *Ms. VeRtigo* is a feature autobiographical film. The soundtrack for this virtual reality (VF) film was composed and is performed by Yair Even-Haim and Anton Turusov. Most of the film takes place in the building where her physiotherapist's office is located, a building she describes in the film as follows: "Everyone is engaged with the body in this building. On the second floor there is a Tai Chi clinic, and right next to it, a dance studio." The film shows Soffer entering the dance studio and attempting to dance there and ends with her exiting the studio and happily dancing on the street.

In this 360-degree film, when Soffer stands in front of the transparent wall of the studio and looks through it, a visual effect is created so that the wall looks like fun house distorting mirrors that deform the body in different ways. This distorting mirror, which warps any physical body reflected in it, presumably reflects an ableist projection of the disabled body. Broyer also discusses the complex relations between mirrors, reflections, and disability:

> The environment provides each and every one of us with a mirror through which we can define ourselves. This "mirror" that I get from the environment alienates me from myself. The responses make me see myself as strange, abnormal and maybe even monstrous. I want to move from the mirror that is reflected to me through other people's stares at me to a more materialistic mirror—the mirrors set in public spaces, such as the restroom at the mall. In each restroom there is a mirror that I [as a woman with dwarfism] can hardly ever see myself in. They are hardly suitable for me and begin somewhere around the top of my forehead. Lacking a mirror through which I can reveal myself, I am left with the distorted social mirror. In the public space, the only mirrors I have are the people around me and their stares. In order to build a positive self-image of myself I need a new mirror.[70]

Rona Soffer rejects the ableist gaze and she, like Broyer, feels the need to create "a new mirror." The distorting mirror created by Soffer through

VR as she stands outside the dance studio looking in constitutes a realization of the mirror/gaze that "makes me see myself as strange, abnormal and maybe even monstrous." Soffer is cognizant of the ableist gaze that treats her body as distorted and defines her as monstrous (when leaving the physiotherapist's office, for example, Soffer states that "what I hate most is to leave when the dancers arrive. They always stare at me"), but rather than simply reject it, she makes it the central setting of her film. She processes it and works through it and with it to create a new dance and a new cinematic language that makes her experience of disability the object of her cinematic inquiry and her artistic mode of creation. She owns this reflection and creates her own *misfitedness*.

Garland-Thomson proposed the term *misfit* to reframe dominant understandings of disability. Whereas disability is often seen as the opposite of able-bodiness, the alternative terms *fit* and *misfit* emphasize the interdependence between able-bodiness and disability: "*Fitting* and *misfitting* denote an encounter in which two things come together in either harmony or disjunction. . . . The problem with a misfit, then, inheres not in either of the two things but rather in their juxtaposition, the awkward attempt to fit them together. . . . Misfit emphasizes context over essence, relation over isolation, mediation over origination."[71] The construction of "the new mirror" suggests a renegotiation of the *fit* and the *misfit*, and the creation of a new space in which the *misfit*, the disabled body, determines its mode of encountering the world. As in Broyer and Tal-Or's video art *Take a Seat*, as well as in the vocal art of Victoria

FIGURE 4. Soffer stands before the window of a dance studio in *Ms. VeRtigo*. The photograph's angle distorts the view. (Courtesy of Rona Soffer.)

Hanna and the poetry of Shiri Oved, the disabled body is no longer (and in fact never was) a passive object that simply internalizes or responds to ableism, but a subject with agency that disrupts the existing order and defines the new rules of the game.

Hence, unlike the Soffer in her early film *Until the Wall Breaks Down* who stays in front of the mirror, and unlike the Soffer in *A Redheaded Sheep* who hides behind the mirror, in *Ms. VeRtigo*, as a kind of Alice in Wonderland, Soffer jumps into the looking-glass room of the dance studio (from which she is culturally excluded). Once there, she examines the social boundaries that limit her and define her "as strange, abnormal and maybe even monstrous," as well as her own wishes and aspirations.

Soffer's portrayal echoes Lewis Carroll: "I [Alice] will tell you all my ideas about Looking-glass House. First, there is the room you can see through the glass—that's just the same as our drawing-room, only the things go the other way. . . . Well then, the books are something like our books, only the words go the wrong way."[72] Likewise, the dance studio is similar to other spaces in Soffer's life, but things are different there: they "go the other way"; they "go the wrong way."

In Lewis Carroll's Wonderland and Looking-Glass land, Alice drinks a potion to grow or to shrink to fit and be able to wander freely. Thus, "Carroll's use of the human-made architecture as a means of confinement anticipates disability theory's focus on the idea of society as a space intentionally exclusive to or disabling for an impaired individual."[73] Just as Alice needs to process the ways in which the design of her surroundings disables or affects her ability to navigate her environment, so Soffer's entry into the dance studio illustrates the incompatibility and disparity between her (physical and creative) space and the able-bodied space.

When Soffer enters the dance studio, the dance instructor (actor Hagai Saharai) invites her to dance with everyone, explaining that "at my place here, everyone dances, not just looks." As he tries to persuade her to enter the studio and dance, he takes her cane away from her. This supposedly chivalrous gesture, which from his perspective signals her welcome, actually concretizes her exclusion from the studio. This chauvinist and ableist gesture acts out (probably not at all consciously) the fact that in this space, canes (and disabilities) are unacceptable. As he grabs Soffer and tries to get her to dance, he places the cane on the floor next to him and we hear him saying, "You've given up on yourself," and in the background we hear another empathetic female voice saying Soffer "is scared." In other words, the dancers provide ableist interpretations for Soffer's assumed lack of cooperation.

Soffer grasps the ableist nature of the situation: "What mostly drives me crazy, is people who think they understand my body better than I do," she says, and explodes into a juicy curse. When the instructor continues to proffer ableist explanations for her refusal to dance, she proclaims, "I have a rhythm, but mine is different." This is meant to rebuff the instructor's "compulsory able-bodiedness," the inherent bias in his pronouncement that "at my place here, everyone dances."[74]

Throughout the film, the two musicians (one with a disability) relay the imaginary voices in Soffer's head by producing a melody that guides her. When Soffer enters the dance studio this music falls silent; we no longer see or hear the musicians—only a different music playing in the studio. In other words, just as the cane had to disappear when she entered the studio, there is no place for Soffer's inner music or for the music of the disabled musician, and perhaps this is why she is unable (or unwilling) to dance there.

At the end of the film, however, Soffer exits onto the street and we again see and hear her two musicians. At this point she also dances (with her cane, of course) and invites the dance instructor to join her. Thus, although Soffer did not dance in the ableist studio, in that physically and culturally closed space, she does not give up dancing, but instead dances a dance, with her cane, that she created for herself to the sounds of music she generated.

The film thus ends in a kind of "third space," neither inside the dance studio nor outside it, but on the street. Instead of a space that maintains a polarized contrast between the able-bodied and the disabled, Soffer creates a common cultural space, akin to the third space that Homi Bhabha defined as "in-between-ness."[75] Bhabha challenged the notion of multiculturalism, claiming that while it attempts to create a consensus of cultural diversity, it in fact serves to blunt the subversive threat inherent in the cultural Other. Bhabha's third space is created by cultural difference in a given cultural space. The third space is a place of cultural diversity and hybridity that allows for new negotiations between identities, as well as new political initiatives that do not fit into accepted categories of knowledge. This third space permits a variety of experiences to coexist side by side. It is not a simplistic space of dialogue, acceptance, or understanding. Rather, by working through the asymmetry between disabled and nondisabled, this cultural space includes the recognition of oppression as well as resistance to it. Thus, the asymmetry between the disabled and nondisabled not only forms a third common space of dialogical communication, it also becomes a question and a problem in itself that repeatedly challenges this space. This alternative space created by Soffer relies on the nonlinear fluidity of the common space. Her third space allows for the expression of her resistance to oppression and exclusion while rejecting the discourse of integration that overlooks and represses experiences of disability and does not authorize the creation of disability culture.

Like Shiri Oved's raw woman, Rona Soffer's films also constitute an Israeli disability culture that does not detach itself from Israeli mainstream culture but at the same time calls for something more than integration into that culture. This disability culture proclaims its experience of disability, enacts its unique creativity, and refuses to be defined by others.

Summary: Dis-topia

> I speculate on the place of disability in the future, questioning whether "utopia," by definition, excludes disability and illness.
>
> —Alison Kafer

The movie *Ms. VeRtigo* enables its viewers to be fully immersed in a safe, controlled, 360-degree virtual environment. This medium allows Soffer to communicate some of her physical experiences as a woman whose disability is manifested, among other things, in franticness and difficulty in maintaining her equilibrium. In an interview when the film came out, she noted, "When I look at the horizon, that horizon is straight but I am tilting all the time from side to side and I lack stability. . . . People there [at the screening] experienced the VR film from my point of view, seeing the world as I see it."[76] Watching the film with VR glasses indeed sometimes creates a feeling of vertigo, to the point that in some instants the viewer becomes herself a kind of Ms. VeRtigo.

In addition to experiencing Soffer's franticness, the viewer is constantly active throughout the film. Because the viewer can choose what to look at and what to look away from, watching the film becomes an active gesture. Soffer's choice to create a film using a VR technique gives a great deal of freedom and agency to the viewer. Just as at the end of the film different people join Soffer's dance on the street (some dancing, some taking pictures, some watching), the film itself invites different types of interactions with what is happening on the screen, thus prompting new relationships between the movie and its viewers.

Similarly, just as Victoria Hanna's stutter prompts a rereading of Jewish texts, and Shiri Oved's CP engenders an innovative poetic space in Hebrew literature, Soffer's life experience with disability facilitates her unique cinematic language. Those new social, artistic, and political possibilities constitute what Carla Rice et al. called "dis-topia":

> The term dis-topia playfully stands in phonetic relation to utopia's antithesis dystopia—the dys acting as a negation of a preferred topos. Though disability is not typically figured into utopian landscapes, it finds a home in any dystopian genre fiction fixated on the grotesque or abject. Conceived as outside this binary, dis-topia finds itself more closely related to the roaring chaos of Mad Max's open desert and motley crew than to the uniformity, sterility, and rigidity of utopian paradise . . . for through dis-topia our futures may be built in response to disability, open to possibility rather than committed to perfectibility. What we theorize here is an alternative to the singular utopic ideal.[77]

The dystopian future that is expected of people with disabilities, the same future described by Kafer as the future of no future, becomes a dis-topia in the works of Victoria Hanna, Oved, and Soffer. It becomes a future constructed through their disability in the midst of their *misfitedness*.

The notions of *fit* and *misfit* depict the dynamic material relationship between the body and its environment that constructs disability: "The discrepancy between body and world, between that which is expected and that which is, produces fits and misfits."[78] Garland-Thomson's concept of misfitting theorizes disability as a way of existing in an environment, a material arrangement related to time and place because it occurs when the environment does not sustain the shape and function of the body within it. The use of the term *misfit* serves to focus on a variety of encounters between the disabled body and its environment. By locating the disabled body against and within its given spaces, this term makes it possible to move away from the dichotomy of ableism versus disability, and to emphasize the intersections between the two. As such, the idea of disability as a range of encounters between *fit* and *misfit* confers agency and value on disabled subjects: "Each meeting between subject and environment will be a *fit* or *misfit* depending on the choreography that plays out. Fitting and misfitting extend the concept that shape carries story."[79]

Owning and creating the story of the disabled body make it possible to escape the fate of a future with no future, and to imagine more accessible futures. Victoria Hanna, Shiri Oved, and Rona Soffer each experience their *misfitedness* differently, but each in her own way turns it into a creative space in which she is a subject with agency. Each of their embodiments—their particular shapes and their "rhetorical bodies"—conveys a unique story that creates crip futurity, a narrative that enables "seeing 'disability' as a potential site for collective reimagining."[80]

2

TOWARD A NEW GENEALOGY OF POETRY WRITTEN BY WOMEN WITH DISABILITY

It is so difficult to write both what sucks about disability—the pain, the oppression, the impairment—and the joy of this body at the same time. The joy of this body comes from crip community and interdependence, but most of all, of the hard beauty of this life, built around all the time I must spend resting. The bed is the nepantla ["torn between ways" in Nahuatl] place of opening.

—Leah Lakshmi Piepzna-Samarasinha

Disabled Ancestors

In the introduction to *Disabled and d/Deaf Poets Anthology*, writer and activist Leah Lakshmi Piepzna-Samarasinha explains, "We learn from each other and write to and with each other across generations. We claim and find disabled ancestors. We make our lineages."[1] The verbs employed in this opening statement—*learn, write, claim, find, make*—help to articulate the long, complex process of establishing a lineage that simultaneously exists and is repressed or deemed unworthy.

There has been noticeable growth in the number of anthologies emerging from English-speaking communities of disabled poets, though the movement itself has yet to fully garner the attention it assuredly deserves.[2] The artistic content being produced draws rich and vibrant connections between poets and their narratives. However, this type of connection and collaboration can be more difficult to locate in non-English literary communities—in Israel in particular. The life experiences of poets with physical disabilities are, at best, overlooked in Hebrew literature by readers and literary scholars alike and so the idea of establishing and discussing the poetic connection between these artists is nigh unimaginable.[3] Within the tradition of Hebrew poetry, there are few disabled poets who center their experiences in their work, let alone a recognized literary genealogy of physically disabled poets; this chapter, therefore, aims to draw attention to the intertextual dialogues of poets fighting to establish (and therefore celebrate) such connections. It foregrounds the poetry of Orit Marton, a wheelchair user living with cerebral palsy, and Inbal Eshel Cahansky, who lives with a neurological syndrome called essential myoclonus, and uses close analysis of their works to demarcate the intertextual dialogues that have inaugurated the establishment of an Israeli tradition of poetry written by women with disability; by highlighting the poetical touchstones present in both Marton and Eshel Cahansky's work, we learn not only about differences in lived experiences on the spectrum of disability, but also how relativity and crip culture can provide points of intersectionality across these chasms of personal experience.

Lived experiences of disability permeate Hebrew literature but seem to be reserved for the genre of memoir and autobiography (with the notable exception of Erez Biton, the 2015 recipient of the Israel Prize for Hebrew Literature and Poetry, whose poetry centers on his experiences as a blind person).[4] Additionally, the disability represented seems to be rather limited in scope, as most of these narratives feature the experiences of men whose bodies are broken either by illness or by war.[5] Avot Yeshurun, for example, wrote his cycle of poems *All Laws* (*Kol diney*) when he underwent surgery to remove his prostate in 1975, and Abba Kovner wrote his poetry book *Sloan Kettering* during and after his hospitalization at Sloan Kettering for throat cancer. There are quite a few stories of wounded male soldiers, such as Yoram Kaniuk's novel *Himmo, King of Jerusalem* (*Himmo, melech Yerushalayim*, 1966), Yaacov Haelyon's *A Doll's Leg: A Story of a War Injury* (*Regel shel bubah*, 1973), and Yoram Eshet-Alkalai's *A Man Walks Home* (*Adam holech habayta*, 2010). Similarly, many poets are remembered in Israeli culture almost exclusively in connection with illnesses that led to their untimely deaths, such as Rachel Bluwstein Sela (tuberculosis), Hezy Leskly (AIDS), and Yona Wallach and Tali Latowicki (cancer). To put it simply, mainstream cultural narratives about the sick and the disabled neglect to acknowledge many voices, while characterizing other artists almost exclusively by their illness or condition, reducing people to caricatures rather than engaging in some of the complexities inherent in disability studies, such as reconciling pain and pride, the interdependence of care, and how to grapple with texts steeped in frustration, sadness, or despair.

Additionally, Hebrew literature has not, to this point, concerned itself overmuch with recognizing disabled voices in intersection—the experiences of those born with physical disability, chronic conditions, and women, for example, are related to the existing canon under the umbrella of disability but remain definitively separate in reality. This makes claiming connection and lineage difficult (if not impossible) and therefore raises many questions about how to establish these links. This chapter addresses the significance of the intersection of gender, illness, and disability within the self-explorations of contemporary disabled Israeli poets and their longing for a connection to their poetic ancestors; it asks how disability can leave a legacy within poetry for others to claim and interact with. Poets with disability are engaging with a rich textual inheritance not only to claim a past, but to stake out the trajectories of future intertextual dialogues and map a coalition of intersectional experiences that could eventually carve out new prospects for disability futurities.

"In My Poetry I Am Not Disabled / and That's the Magic of It": Orit Marton

Orit Marton's first book of poetry, *To Be Trapped in My Body* (*Lihiyot kluah begufi*), was published in 2010. Its title reflects her view that her disability is a kind of prison, a limiting thing from which it is impossible to break free. Lines and imagery throughout the book testify to this position: "Sitting hat in hand, not belonging / Behind me and facing me the walls of disability are rising"; "I'm just disabled / Nowadays a disabled's daughter / Imprisoned in my life's oubliette"; "And all I want is to flee my prison"; and "A mature woman, an almost grown-up person, trapped in a body of a six-month-old."[6]

In an era that is constantly challenging the perception of disability as a limitation or a lack, how, then, does one address this position? Understanding and accepting negative representations of disability in autobiographical writing seems, on the surface, to struggle against the current of a larger cultural demand to view difference exclusively through the lens of positivity.[7]

While many problems associated with disability can be rightly attributed to ableism and social inaccessibility, Liz Crow stimulates a difficult yet important discussion about the relationship between this social model of disability and the reality of painful elements of disability. She reminds us that "impairment is not always irrelevant, neutral or positive. . . . How can it be when pain, fatigue, depression, chronic illness are a constant part of life for many of us?" She further wonders, "If we once 'admit' that impairment itself carries problems, will we undermine everything we have ever achieved?"[8] Margaret Price continues with this "heretical" reflection to ask, "How then do we confront the point that impairment is sometimes bad, especially impairment that involves pain?"[9] The current chapter utilizes these questions, alongside an acknowledgment of difficulty and pain, to discern the foundations of a poetic genealogy rather than attempting to force a more common celebration of disability that ignores these realities.

The complexity of this struggle can be found at the heart of many discourses on marginalized identities. In her book *Feeling Backward: Loss and the Politics of Queer History*, Heather Love points to the tension between the desire to establish a positive queer existence that leads to progress and "queer suffering," defined as the wide range of negative feelings and emotions that could be associated with a queer existence, and that "at times can simply mean living with injury—not fixing it."[10] She argues that only by acknowledging the negative aspects of queer history can we be more insightful about how this past continues to impact the present. By adopting this same position within disability studies, and understanding the very real struggles disability can entail outside of the social realm of access and ableism, Orit Marton's suffering can be better understood, removed from the social expectations of scholars and readers alike. Love explains that while queer readers try to rescue and save characters who express negative or complicated feelings in the texts, "it is hard to know what to do with texts that resist our advances. Texts or figures that refuse to be redeemed disrupt not only the progress narrative of queer history but also our sense of queer identity in the present."[11] Therefore, in spite of my temptation to interpret Marton's perception of disability as a limitation in a way that would expropriate her experience and expose the ableism internalized in this view, I want to dwell on her direct refusal to fall into the oft-forced cheerfulness of Disability Pride.[12]

Referring to her disability as a prison and a barrier is central to Orit Marton's poetry, but reviews of her work have picked up this theme and centralized it in demeaning, ableist ways. Referring to her writing style, Oren Ailam notes that "the poet's life is limited by her disability and she does not need additional limitations of rhyme and structure;" Balfour Hakak writes that "in her writing she rises above her disability and soars to the realms of poetry," and that "the poet's writing frees her from the deep pit she fell into when she was born into this destiny."[13] While Marton's poetry may give space to feelings of negativity and confinement, it does not justify ableism and condescension as a response; it is important to take seriously the negative feelings—the ugly feelings, the crip negativity—that Marton expresses in her poetry and subsequently acknowledge her lived experiences as a disabled woman.[14]

Orit Marton has published three books of poetry so far: *To Be Trapped in My Body* (*Lihiyot kluah begufi*, 2010), *A Camera View from Sitting Height* (*Matslema migova yeshiva*, 2013), and *A Woman, After All* (*Ishah lamrot hakol*, 2018). In the essay that opens her first book, Marton reveals she suffered from respiratory distress during her birth that caused her severe physical disability. She lives with cerebral palsy, uses a wheelchair, and has minimal mobility in her hand. She dictates her poems to her aide, who types them for her, and she reads audiobooks from the Library for the Blind.

In honor of the publication of her first poetry book, her editor Shoshana Vig interviewed Marton and asked her the following questions: "Have you written in the past? Where did your rich vocabulary come from? Do you read? What do you like to read? Or what do people read to you? Who are your mediators to the world? Would you like to read more materials, and would you like to expand your field of knowledge?"[15] This line of questioning regarding influences, a typical question in writers' interviews, indicates an implicit assumption that writers are also avid readers and their writing, consciously or unconsciously, is influenced by other writers. Marton's answer challenged this premise: "I have never written on my own (except for a few years when I tried to type with my nose, which did not go well). I dictate most of my life. I learned to make the most of it. It's hard for me to say where the language I use comes from, since I can't read with my eyes. For decades I listened to various audiobooks from the Library for the Blind, without my choosing [that is, she listened to random books based on availability]. I miss reading and studying a lot and I would like to read more—at the moment mainly on the topic of creativity and writing—in order to progress in this field."[16]

Marton's answer refers to the concrete and literal dimensions of her past writing, not her history of creative writing, as is implied in the interviewer's question ("I have never written on my own [except for a few years when I tried to type with my nose, which did not go well]"). Similarly, her answer to the question regarding her literary preferences and past reading underscores the physical inaccessibility of books ("For decades I listened to various audiobooks from the Library for the Blind, without my choosing"). In other words, significant aspects of what we usually attribute to writers (written drafts, books, libraries) do not exist in Marton's world because they are not accessible to her. This dimension raises questions not only about the physical aspect of writing but also about writing as a physically and culturally dependent process. Orit Marton's writing process challenges the myth of the reclusive artist; she is a poet who physically needs the support of someone else to write and to read. Her creative process, therefore, like that of many other artists with disabilities, inherently challenges the concept of Western autonomy and individualism. Among activists, artists, and scholars of disability studies, dependence is perceived not as an obstacle or a weakness but as an inherent part of personhood, and this involves the conversion of the ideal of singular autonomy into an interdependence that allows people to grow and flourish.[17]

Marton's emphasis on her physical dependence on others and various other interdependencies also inevitably includes artistic connections and poetic links with poets who preceded her. In other words, the poetics of disabled poets involves an establishment of disability lineage—the intimate knowledge of a rich, deep history of disability. Jennifer Natalya Fink, explaining that disability is hidden, repressed, and covered over in cultural and family histories, uses the term *de-lineate* to refer to the separation of disabled people from their lineage and the ways in which those connections and the historical work and legacy of disabled people can be both destroyed . . . but then potentially repaired. She goes on to note that the word *delineate* also means to describe or portray, "so within the word itself lies the potential to re-lineate: to sew a [disabled] family member back into the fold. To describe, portray, and, thus, connect."[18] Marton's frank emphasis on the negative and painful dimensions of her disability enables her both to connect to and repair the de-lineation of disabled poets in Hebrew literature.

While establishing this genealogy is an essential component of Marton's poetic self-discovery, it is also a way of creating a care web, which Leah Lakshmi Piepzna-Samarasinha theorizes as "crip-made access," access made by and for disabled people.[19] For Piepzna-Samarasinha, for example, recording the narratives of sick and disabled Queer, Trans, Black, Indigenous, and People of Color and using those stories to build ways to create and access care are a core part of disability justice work.[20] While Piepzna-Samarasinha addresses physical and emotional care, I argue here that creating a poetic lineage of disabled poetry is also part of this care web—a form of self care with poetic, cultural, and didactic implications.[21]

However, poetic genealogy, by definition, assumes a literary repertoire and familiarity with the writings of previous poets, even narrowly defined as reading through the work associated with certain artistic movements, historical periods, or cultural parameters. This assumption of necessary background is undermined in cases such as that of Orit Marton, to whom those bodies of texts were not often accessible. Therefore, the genealogy of the poetry of disabled poets is inherently a fragmented lineage. It is a history with no center and no predictable order, flying in the face of the way a normative literary canon is established. Disabled poets often experience a lack of access and/or a lack of desire to interact with a textual history that is often exclusionary or discriminatory.

While I do not propose to compare the lived experiences of disabled poets with the experiences of trans people, it is often helpful in critical theory to draw connections among marginalized peoples in order to better understand how reclamation of genealogy can be achieved, and serves both political and social purposes. For example, Hil Malatino's discussion of trans, intersex, and queer archives and the motivation behind reconstructing connections with notable figures from the past is extremely insightful, showing how historical links of commonality can impact people's lives profoundly (especially in spite of cultural energies invested in attempting to deny or subvert knowledge of such history). Malatino explains that to care for these archival traces of trans, intersex, and gender nonconforming lives means "admitting that there are unknowable dimensions to our entanglements. This necessitates a historical witnessing in excess of a logic of succession, clear precedent and antecedent" and acknowledging that historical figures are "deeply implicated in our current conditions of possibility."[22] Turning to the past is not, therefore, an attempt to reconstruct a continually denied or repressed history or to create an unquestionable and unbreakable canon, but instead is mainly intended to allow individuals and communities to imagine a different future. Studies of disability in the archives (or lack thereof) highlight the ways discovery and knowledge of one's own history can be not only empowering but also a catalyst for social change.[23] Stacey Milbern, who wrote beautifully about crip ancestorship, explained that "not considering our ancestors is electing only to see a glimpse of who we are."[24] Queered or cripped understanding of ancestorship holds that "we grow knowledge and movements with them. We crip futurism with them. We demand and entice the world to change the way things have always been done, with them. We change ourselves with them. They learn through us."[25]

To return to the specific genealogy Orit Marton establishes in her poetry, the essay at the beginning of her book *To Be Trapped in My Body* addresses the story of her birth, demarcating a sort of division between her disabled body and her "thought, emotion, and the desire and ability to experience and create."[26] The story of her own birth and then her reflection on the birth of her book merge into an autobiographical book of poems that deals with what she perceives as a split between her disabled body and her creative soul. In one interview published in honor of the publication of her book, Marton declared, "For me, the importance of exposure in the assisted living facility [where I live] and especially outside of it is the possibility that other people will read and hear the cry (*zeaka*) of my soul that is torn between my very limited body and my intact (*takin*) head."[27]

In the following poem, written in October 2004 and published in *To Be Trapped in My Body*, Marton refers explicitly to the connection between her disability and her writing:

To Write About Disability

They said I'm good at wording
Putting the mundane into words and lines:
Joy and grief, love and fate.
So why when I set out to write
About the heart of my life—the disability,
It is as if the pen's ink dries out?
Maybe it's because in my poetry I am not disabled,
And that's the magic of it.[28]

לכתוב על נכות

אָמְרוּ שֶׁטּוֹבָה אֲנִי בְּנִסּוּחַ
הַכְנָסַת הַחֻלִּין לְמִלִּים וְשׁוּרוֹת:
שִׂמְחָה וְעֶצֶב, אַהֲבָה וְגוֹרָל.
אָז לָמָּה כַּאֲשֶׁר בָּאתִי לִכְתֹּב
עַל לִבַּת חַיַּי—הַנָּכוּת,
כְּאִלּוּ יָבַשׁ הַדְּיוֹ בְּעֵטִי?
אוּלַי כִּי בְּשִׁירָתִי אֵינֶנִּי נָכָה,
וְזֶה הַקֶּסֶם שֶׁבָּה.

The speaker becomes a poet by "putting the mundane (*hulin*) into words and lines," which suggests that the role of poetry is not to deal with the transcendental; rather, poetry should be committed to the mundane. The word *hulin*, which is not common in contemporary Hebrew, seems to be a nod to Leah Goldberg as a major source of influence in Marton's poetics.[29] The 1970 Israel Prize Laureate Leah Goldberg (1911–70) published poetry, children's literature, translations, plays, and reviews; simply put, Goldberg is one of the most prominent and influential poets in modern Hebrew literature. In 1938, she published her well-known essay "The Courage for the Mundane" ("Haometz lehulin") in the *Turim* periodical.[30] In this essay, Goldberg stated that the function of literature is not to produce "shining ideals and colorful lights of ideas that capture the heart" but exactly the opposite.[31] Literature has an arduous and noncelebratory role that requires courage and patience: a slow and in-depth examination of mundane life. Focusing on people and on seemingly small actions in day-to-day life obviously had a definite value in 1938, and Goldberg's position on the mundane expressed opposition to ideas about strong leadership and comprehensive national solutions that were gaining strength in Europe at that time. Goldberg spoke about literature becoming timeless precisely by dealing with the personal and political reality of the time, rather than employing fascist movements in big mythological stories. In this poem, Marton identifies with this position; writing for her is the attempt to capture life experiences by, as she writes, "putting the mundane into words and lines."

But precisely in the midst of the mundane, in the midst of writing about what is most personal and most familiar—"About the heart of my life—the disability"—Marton disconnects from Goldberg's writing philosophy. For Orit Marton, the poetic act is not a description of the experience of disability but an erasure of it ("in my poetry I am not disabled, / And that's the magic of it"). Thus, according to this poem, writing in general, and writing about disability more specifically, means performing a kind of magic in making the disability disappear. The disabled poet is not a magician simply because she managed to overcome an ableist tradition that excludes disabled women from the poetic tradition—as discussed in the previous chapter in relation to Shiri Oved's poetry. Rather, it is the opposite: the "magic" is her ability to write as though she is a nondisabled woman, to step outside the bounds of her own experience. Thus, paradoxically, moving away from Goldberg's call to focus on the mundane positions Marton closer to Goldberg, the abled-bodymind poet who received widespread national recognition. Hence, in order to join the tradition of women's poetry, Orit Marton breaks free from what she sees as the prison of disability. However, this supposed transition from the imprisonment of disability into the "freedom" of a tradition of women's poetry, as I will soon show, is exactly what later brings Marton back to address her disability wholeheartedly.

A Woman, After All

Orit Marton's third poetry book, *A Woman, After All* (*Ishah lamrot hakol*) was published in 2018. It opens with the poem "Woman":

Woman

A man is walking down the street
He doesn't see me
Coming towards him in a wheelchair
Undressing him with my eyes
He doesn't think of going to bed with me
And I want to scream:
"I am a woman"
But I don't[32]

אישה

גֶּבֶר עוֹבֵר בָּרְחוֹב
הוּא לֹא מַבְחִין בִּי
הַבָּאָה מוּלוֹ בְּכִסֵּא גַּלְגַּלִּים
וּמַפְשִׁיטָה אוֹתוֹ בְּעֵינַי
הֵן הוּא לֹא חוֹשֵׁב
לְהִכָּנֵס אִתִּי לַמִּטָּה
וַאֲנִי מְבַקֶּשֶׁת לִזְעֹק
אֲנִי אִשָּׁה
וְלֹא זוֹעֶקֶת

The poem opens with the speaker looking at a man and immediately moves to the man's oblivious gaze—a gaze that does not recognize the speaker. Carol J. Gill differentiates between the objectifying patriarchal gaze experienced by women and the negating, dismissive, and disaffirming gaze that is often directed specifically toward disabled women. She claims that the disabled female body is invalidated and overlooked; it is situated as an illegitimate object of desire. In other words, disabled women are not recognized as sexual beings by the abled gaze.[33]

The oblivious (and therefore dismissive) gaze of the man in the poem is answered with a female gaze that objectifies the man (the speaker undresses him with her eyes), serving to highlight the speaker's lack of visibility. This conflict of gazes, which is inherently a struggle for visibility and recognition, is at the root of the desire to cry out—a desire that, like the sexual potential present in the poem, is not realized. The text, therefore, becomes a poetic embodiment of blatant disregard and lack of fulfillment (the man does not notice the speaker or think to go to bed with her, and the speaker does not scream).

The only thing that materializes in the poem is the poem itself and the poetry book it opens. The speaker does not scream, but the book itself becomes an unvoiced cry. That unfulfilled howl instead becomes "a charming chain of words on a white page" ("Sefer shiray halavan"), to allude to the 1930 poem "My Book of Poems" ("Sefer shiray") written by Rachel Bluwstein, considered one of the "founding mothers" of modern Hebrew poetry. Bluwstein's poem opens with the following stanza:

> My desperate cries of loss and pain,
> of misery and rage,
> have turned into a charming chain
> of words on a white page.[34]

Although this poem describes a process different from Marton's, a process of "excessive screaming" that is sublimated into poetry, the channeling of difficult emotions into a book of poetry is common to both poets.[35] But while the reason for Bluwstein's howls and the nature of her distress remain vague, Orit Marton provides a concrete reason for her cry. It stems from her feeling that her femininity and sexuality are not perceptible due to her disability. In the poem "The Scream" ("Hazeaka") from the same book, she explicitly defines her scream that is not cried out: "Sometimes even the closest ones / Cannot grasp this desire / At nights the yearning for a man's touch / Turns into pain / an unspoken scream."[36]

The intimate poetic connection with Rachel Bluwstein is also evident in the fact that Marton's poem "Woman" alludes to Bluwstein's 1929 poem of the same title:

Woman

From bottom to top . . .
[It's] like this:
With a devoted forlorn stare
Of a slave, of a clever dog.
The moment is replete and pure.
Silence
And a frustrated longing
To kiss the master's hand—.[37]

אשה

מִלְּמַטָּה לְמַעְלָה . . .
כָּךְ:
בְּמַבָּט מָסוּר וְעָגוּם
שֶׁל עֶבֶד, שֶׁל כֶּלֶב נָבוֹן.
הָרֶגַע גָּדוֹשׁ וְזַךְ.
דּוּמִיָּה
וְכֹסֶף סָתוּם
לְנַשֵּׁק אֶת יַד הָאָדוֹן—.

The woman in Marton's poem and the woman in Bluwstein's share a perception of inferiority in relation to the man they desire, and both construct this desire by looking at the men. But while in Bluwstein's poem the female gaze observes the man "from bottom to top . . . / With a devoted forlorn stare / Of a slave, of a clever dog," the speaker in Marton's poem undresses him with her eyes—fully objectifying the passing man as nothing but a body, therefore sexualizing his presence in an almost lecherous manner.

When writing about her experience as a disabled woman, Marton turns to Bluwstein as a model for writing about sick/disabled femininity. Rachel Bluwstein Sela, known by the pen name Rahel, is one of the most prominent poets in modern Hebrew poetry. She is seen as a quintessential representative of the Second Aliyah (the immigration of Jews to the Land of Israel, 1904–14), and someone who, in her poetry, preserves the values and ideas of Labor Zionism, such as the conquest of the land by building agricultural settlements. However, she actually wrote most of her poems in the last six years of her life while living alone in different apartments in Safed, Jerusalem, and Tel Aviv after being expelled from the Degania group (the first Zionist settlement based on communal living) when she was diagnosed with tuberculosis. Most of her poems were published in the Labor Zionist newspaper *Davar*. In 1927, her first book of poetry, *Aftergrowth* (*Safiah*), was published, followed three years later by her second, *Across From* (*Mineged*). A year after her death in 1932, another book, titled *Nevo*, was released. Her poetry is hugely popular to this day, to the extent that in 2011, Bluwstein was chosen as one of four great Israeli poets whose portraits would feature on Israeli currency (the other three being Leah Goldberg, Shaul Tchernichovsky, and Nathan Alterman).

Perhaps more than any other Hebrew poet, Rachel Bluwstein Sela is identified with illness in general (tuberculosis in particular). Since in the Israeli collective memory she represents the legacy of Israel's vivid early pioneers, her illness is perceived as a tragedy. Contrary to popular narratives viewing her illness as a hindrance, Dana Olmert reads Bluwstein's poetry as a substitute for an active pioneering existence, claiming that because of her illness, Bluwstein could not employ ready-made ideological and collective definitions of identity within the pioneering narrative. Therefore, Olmert argues, her illness actually forced her to consolidate both her identity and her subjective poetic voice. Olmert points out that while Zionism indeed conferred upon her a privileged social status derived from the concept of the national victim, the source of Bluwstein's suffering was a "private" illness, devoid of a national aura.[38]

Olmert understands Bluwstein's "Woman" as a work that expresses masochistic erotic pleasure, a dynamic based on humiliation and gender drama that invokes men as masters and women as subjugated (but also as deriving pleasure from such enslavement)—thus, the speaker of the poem experiences a complicated series of emotions when in the presence of the "master."[39] Marton's poem, then, stands in direct contrast to this representation of femininity rooted in gendered inheritance; the submissive gaze transforms into an objectifying one in its own right. Thus Marton invites the reader to understand Bluwstein's "Woman" as a poem that expresses the unfulfilled sexual desire of a sick and disabled woman, rather than a narrative of submissive desire that aligns with traditional femininity. The lack of sexual fulfillment does not express a drama of masochistic pleasure but rather a frustration that is rooted in the erasure of the sexuality of sick and disabled women.

Thus, through the poetic connection to Bluwstein's femininity and illness, Marton reveals the erasure of disabled sexuality in society more broadly, as well as "the disability phobia we find in the women's movement" (that is, the fact that traditionally scholars of women and gender studies have paid almost no attention to the existence and experiences of women with disability).[40] Moreover, Marton seems to call for recognition of intersectionality in this case, as disabled women are subjected to double discrimination: both sexism and disability bias. By creating intertextual connections with Rachel Bluwstein and reinterpreting her poem based on the two poets' common biographical experiences, Marton reveals the intersections of gender and disability that result in many aggravated forms of discrimination and human rights violations against women and girls with disabilities, which often remain invisible and unaddressed.

"There's Talk About a Different Kind of Sex"

Orit Marton's focus on the experience of disability (or lack thereof) in the work of her disabled poetic lineage is also reflected in her deep connection to Yona Wallach's poetry. Yona Wallach (1944–85) published four books of poetry during her lifetime, and three more were published after her untimely death. A huge and mesmerizing presence in Israeli culture from the beginning of her career in the mid-1960s, and to this day, Wallach is regarded as a major cultural and artistic influence. Extroverted and openly bisexual, she was also mentally ill; at certain points in her life, she was institutionalized. While mental illness still carries negative stigma, Yona Wallach is perceived as "a poet who turned madness into verse"—her "madness" is seen as a creative drive that enabled her to compose unconventional and powerful poetry previously unseen in Israeli literature.[41]

One of the sections in Marton's book *A Woman, After All* is titled "There's Talk About" ("Omrim lanu shyesh"). This title alludes to Yona Wallach's well-known poem, "Presomnolent Poem" ("Shir kdamshnati"), from her second book *Two Gardens* (*Shenei gamin*):

Presomnolent Poem

a propos Godard

There's talk about a different kind of sex.
Good to have someone in the know.
If there is different sex bring it hi
ther and let us know it let's s
peak plainly, yes or no.
Cause we are all sotired of
our virgin friends and wives and they
keep showing us in pictures that there's
really sumthin else and w
e feel too it must be true.
And if there is different sex in a different
world women new and knowing w
hy not bring over a few to i
nstruct our weary wives and m
aybe even stretch the bounds w
hen we're spent and sosuffocating.[42]

In a move typical of Yona Wallach's artistic style, the use of the phrase "a different sex" (*sex aher*) in the poem implies a double meaning. It might refer to a different gender identity or to a different way of having sex—or both.[43] Her works' preoccupation with gender identities and sexuality is understood among scholars and the general public alike as a feminist protest against a patriarchal society that exploits and restricts women.[44] Wallach's poetry treated sexuality and gender in a way that changed the landscape of Hebrew poetry. Ahead of her time, she dealt with the fluidity of gender and the gendered aspect of the Hebrew language, and her poetry presented possibilities of writing about liberated and powerful sexuality that challenged gender power relations and offered a nonbinary exploration of language, gender, and sexuality.

The "different kind of sex" in Wallach's poem challenged perceptions of heterosexual sexuality, paving the way for her poetic articulation of female sexuality in other poems. In the section "There's Talk About" Orit Marton adopts Wallach's concept of "There's talk about a different kind of sex" and uses it to make her own references to sexuality. While Wallach's original work was concerned with the possibilities in women's sexuality, Marton's poems deal specifically with the sexuality of disabled women, addressing her perceived lack of sexuality as a disabled woman and its accompanying frustrations.

What's more, while Wallach's "different kind of sex" refers to various options of sexual and gender fluidity, Marton's "different kind of sex" actually refers to normative heterosexual sexuality that is denied to her due to social perceptions that establish women with disability as undesirable and unattractive. Thus, while Wallach, despite being a disabled woman, revealed the mechanism of patriarchal oppression in relation to women and female sexual subjectivity in particular, Marton explicitly addresses the intersectional oppression embodied in being not only a woman but also disabled. Unlike Limor Ashkenazi, an artist who celebrates her crip kinky disabled sexuality (described in the next chapter), Orit Marton reveals her exclusion from typical heterosexuality. In her intertextual dialogues with Rachel Bluwstein and Yona Wallach, Marton reveals the fact that both writers have overlooked issues of disability in their works, which have subsequently been used in mainstream Israeli feminism to perpetuate ableism by leaving issues of disability out of the broader conversation on feminism and gender.[45]

In addition, Marton reveals the tension between different portrayals of female disabilities. She exposes the gap between the portrayal of female mental illness as the unhinged and oversexualized "madwoman" (noticeable in Wallach's character, who is depicted by the broader public as an exceptionally sexual, mad, and creative woman) compared to the invisibility and supposed lack of sexuality of physically disabled women (documented in her own works). Thus, while one layer of Marton's criticism refers to the lack of disability recognition in Wallach's writing and reception, another dimension criticizes the fetishization of disabled women's sexuality.[46] In other words, by revealing her own life experience as a woman whose sexuality is socially denied due to her disability, Marton challenges Wallach's participation in a stereotypical depiction of disability. More specifically, she takes issue with Wallach's exploitative portrayal of the "madwoman," which she believes is harmful on multiple levels. This is because it lumps all symptoms of mental illness into one ambiguous female "madness." It both stigmatizes and simplifies

female mental illness, portraying mentally ill women as sexually pro-
miscuous and suggesting that "unfeminine" activities that defy gender
roles are a byproduct of that illness. In the genealogy that Marton produces and references within her own work, therefore, she connects to
Wallach as a touchstone while acknowledging that different cultural
perceptions of their disabilities informed their life experiences in radically different ways; it also permits Marton to criticize these troubling
portrayals of female mental illness, and instead to evaluate these "mad-
women" narratives for their reflections of gender bias and the stigmatization of mental illness.[47]

That Marton's poetical role model transitions from Rachel Bluwstein
to Yona Wallach, then, is not accidental. It is part and parcel of the constant tension existing for physically disabled poets writing in a space
devoid of literary models that reflect their life experiences. Although
Wallach developed breast cancer in 1981, dying four years later at the
age of forty-one, she is seen by Israeli society as a mad poet, not a sick
one. Both Rachel Bluwstein and Yona Wallach died young as a result of
their illnesses, but while mainstream culture viewed Bluwstein's sickness as a form of weakness that confirmed normative attitudes toward
women's vulnerability, it responded to Wallach's illness differently. While
her cancer received almost no public or scholarly attention, her mania
was regarded with appreciation as a disorder that enabled Wallach to
express her powerful and feminist voice.[48] These conflicting representations raise questions about the intersection of gender, illness, and
disability, and thus it is not surprising that in generating her poetic genealogy, Marton alludes to a relatively early poem by Yona Wallach (and
therefore to her emotional disability) rather than to later works written
while she was sick with cancer. Since, as mentioned, in Hebrew literature
physically disabled poets do not have physically disabled role models, Orit
Marton adopts Rachel Bluwstein, the sick poet, and Wallach, the mentally disabled. While neither of these models represent Marton's experience per se, the different social coding of Bluwstein's illness (feminine
weakness) compared to the supposed vigor of Wallach's disability allows
Marton to emphasize contradictions that reflect her attitude toward her
gender and disability within her genealogy; it enables her to express a
set of frustrations related to being "trapped in my body" while simultaneously celebrating her poetry, her womanhood, and her sexuality.

"Paradise Lost": Cripsex

While Hebrew literature has no recognized poetic tradition featuring female poets with physical disabilities, there is a wide corpus of female poets with emotional disabilities. Apart from Yona Wallach, Dahlia Ravikovitch is probably the Israeli poet most publicly identified with mental illness. It is, then, not surprising that Orit Marton turns also to Ravikovitch when navigating the experience and stigmatization of disability, as is evident in the poem "The Temptation" ("Hapituy") from Marton's *A Woman, After All*:

The Temptation

Come here my love and know my body
Nothing is left to come between us
Paradise lost, no apple tree on the horizon
Serpents aren't lurking at our feet in the grass
And even God who hides in the blue of the sky
Will close his eyes for a mere second
When you come my love and know my body[49]

הפיתוי

בּוֹא אֲהוּבִי וְדַע אֶת גּוּפִי
אֵין עוֹד דָּבָר שֶׁיַּפְרִיד בֵּינֵינוּ
גַּן הָעֵדֶן אָבַד, אֵין עֵץ תַּפּוּחַ עַד אֹפֶק
נְחָשִׁים אֵינָם שׁוֹרְצִים לְרַגְלֵינוּ בַּדֶּשֶׁא
וְגַם הָאֵל שֶׁמִּסְתַּתֵּר בִּתְכוֹל שָׁמַיִם
יַעֲצֹם אֶת עֵינָיו לְרֶגַע
כְּשֶׁתָּבוֹא אֲהוּבִי וְתֵדַע אֶת גּוּפִי

This erotic poem alludes to Dahlia Ravikovitch's poem "Like the Rolling Dust Before the Whirlwind" ("Kegalgal lifnai sufah"). Ravikovitch (1936–2005), the 1998 Israel Prize Laureate, published eight books of poetry and three collections of short stories that garnered not only the adoration of the Israeli public but also high praise from scholars of modern Hebrew literature. In the public consciousness, Ravikovitch's work articulates vulnerability and victimhood. Like Wallach's, Ravikovitch's mental illness is seen as enabling the hypersensitivity of her writing, but while Wallach is perceived as a sexual and intense poet, Ravikovitch is considered restrained and almost devoid of sexuality.

Ravikovitch's poem "Like the Rolling Dust Before the Whirlwind" describes a strong wind blowing in the month of Tammuz. The wind is portrayed as "roaring," and the speaker points out "how bitter it is when the wind roars (*Hruach shoeg*)."[50] While the work may be a nature poem in that it describes the changing of the seasons, it could also be descriptive of the speaker's state of mind: the word for wind in Hebrew, *ruach*, means both wind and spirit. In my book on Ravikovitch's oeuvre, I read the poem in the context of her autobiographical experience as a woman living with bipolar disorder, a mental illness characterized by extreme mood swings between low depressive states and manic or hypomanic episodes, which are often marked by high energy, feelings of euphoria and self-importance, rapid thought, and impulsivity. While the poem expresses a manic state, it also challenges the dichotomy between mania and depression that stands at the center of the standard conception of bipolar disorder. Without ignoring the differences between the manic and depressive states, Ravikovitch's poem emphasizes the oscillation into, out of, and within these diverse states.[51]

At the peak of the poem's mania, the line "There's a god hiding behind the rain" repeats twice.[52] While the manic experience is concrete and real, it also contains an awareness of something mysterious, of something that cannot be known. It is not clear whether this information is given as a neutral fact, if it is a consolation, or if it is "the face of the omnipresent and omnipotent violence."[53] Orit Marton references that same "hidden" god in her poem "The Temptation," associating him with the erotic rather than the spiritual, although he remains in hiding. In contrast to the mystery in Ravikovitch's poem, in Marton's paradise is "lost" because there is no myth and no idealization; even the god hidden beyond the rain in Ravikovitch's work is humanized, opting to hide to give the lovers privacy: "And even God who hides in the blue of the sky / Will close his eyes for a mere second / When you come my love and know my body."

The temptations of knowledge and access to that which is forbidden, then, are the enticements of flesh and blood, of sex and intimacy, written by a disabled poet who has explicitly referenced such desires across her work. Marton adapts Ravikovitch's autobiographical experience of emotional disability to her own life, centering in her case on physical experiences. While Ravikovitch invites her readers to know something about her manic experience, Marton invites her loved one to know her body: "Come here my love and know my body." The Hebrew verb *da*, translated here as "know," has many meanings—on the surface, it references the biblical sense as a euphemism for sex, but to know also means to acknowledge. In other words, the speaker in Marton's poem invites her loved one to know her *and* to acknowledge her. Thus, the temptation refers not only to the sexual act itself but also to the acknowledgment and mindfulness—on the part of the lover, as well as of the speaker and the readers—of the disabled female body. The combination of sexual knowledge with recognition of the disabled bodymind becomes a call for cripsex; an expression of the subversive potential of the intersection between disability and sexuality.

The term *cripsex* utilizes the power of the reclaimed word *crip* (shortened from "cripple") to express the political nature of the sexuality of disabled people. Cripsex is a call for a significant alteration to social norms that suggest a conflation between conventional attractiveness and perceived normality and also a demand to acknowledge the spectrum of sexuality in disability and difference. Cripsex is a crip intervention, a radical alternative that subverts the conventional definitions of beauty, attractiveness, and normative pleasure and sexuality.[54]

While Marton's poem "Woman" grapples with the lack of visibility of disabled women in spaces of pleasure and sexuality, "The Temptation" goes on to address the desire for recognition, the cultural denial of the sexuality of disabled women, and the need to acknowledge disabled sexuality. Not only does the myth of the Garden of Eden, a significant cultural touchstone for Western narratives about mainstream sexuality, have to be lost in order for her to reclaim her sexuality ("Paradise lost"), but above all, the gaze of God, which represents an overseeing, possibly oppressive masculine presence, has to disappear in order to allow the encounter between the speaker and her lover. Thus, while "Woman" marked the absence of a male gaze in relation to the sexuality of disabled women, in "The Temptation," Marton rubs out the same negating and oppressive male gaze to offer a new cultural and sexual perspective.

Orit Marton confronts the oblivious male gaze, and from this imposed invisibility arises the question of who else is present in this unseen space. "Who are we and where are we?" asks Carol Gill in the conclusion of her article "Becoming Visible: Personal Health—Experiences of Women with Disabilities."[55] Marton, throughout her work, poses a similar question, and her connection to Rachel Bluwstein Sela, Yona Wallach, and Dahlia Ravikovitch—that is, her establishment of a poetic genealogy of sick and disabled female poets—begins to reveal her answer to this question.

Though Orit Marton has a very different lived experience of disability than Ravikovitch, and wrestles with entirely different subject matter, she connects to Ravikovitch as a partial but significant role model for writing about disability; the two share a perspective rooted in creating from the experience of disability itself. Ravikovitch's autobiographical writing about her own depression, which enabled her to challenge myths regarding mental illness, becomes a model for Marton as she challenges stigmas regarding the sexuality of disabled women in her poetry. Similarly, even though Marton is a poet with a physical disability and not a sick woman, she connects with the pain, loneliness, melancholy, and despair she finds in the poetry of Rachel Bluwstein. In contrast to a poet such as Shiri Oved who, as I showed in the previous chapter, challenges negative narratives of disability, Orit Marton turns to Rachel Bluwstein and Dahlia Ravikovitch in order to highlight their shared link in the stigmatization of disability and weakness. Bluwstein's suffering and Ravikovitch's vulnerability form the point of connection between her and them. Marton turns to Ravikovitch, who does not shy away from the pain inherent in her condition, and also reads into Bluwstein's poetry concrete content from her experiences of living with illness and disability.

Marton thus actually establishes a genealogy of disabled women that is not based on success, resistance, or high points of pride, but rather on the interdependence of pain—where individual struggles resonate collectively—on common struggles, and on suffering. To once more invoke Heather Love's postulations (which, as mentioned earlier, originally referred to queer history), Marton succeeds in creating an affective genealogy and a "backward future," an acceptance and embracing of past failures and other painful experiences while—or for the purpose of—orienting oneself toward the future.[56] Marton recognizes her continuity with Rachel Bluwstein Sela, Yona Wallach, and Dahlia

Ravikovitch—the three "founding mothers" of Hebrew poetry, and it is through such an act of identification that she not only reclaims her poetic history and determines how she wants to define herself and her struggles, but also presents us with the opportunity to use the foundation of the history of disability culture within Hebrew literature in order to glimpse its continuing legacy—into the present and possibly the future.

In the House of Illness: Inbal Eshel Cahansky

In honest, neutral terms, without tragic drama or empowering vindication, I understand that no matter where I sit or sleep in this life, I will be doing it in the house of illness.

—Johanna Hedva

"In the Beginning She Created the Ceiling and the Bed": The Sickbed as a Political Space

The Jewish Israeli poet Inbal Eshel Cahansky (b. 1977) is an active participant in the Israeli literary scene. She takes part in poetry readings and festivals, edits poetry books, and leads writing workshops. Her first book, *Wilds of Day (Prai hayom)*, was published in 2009, and since then she has published four more poetry books. She lives, as mentioned, with a neurological condition called essential myoclonus, which is characterized by involuntary body movements, sometimes accompanied by tremors and convulsions that trigger shortness of breath and stammering. The following poem is taken from her second book, *Samael My Beloved (Samael ahuvi)*, and the subject matter deals with the aggravation of her condition and depicts her disability experience. The book was written over the course of three and a half years, during which the syndrome worsened, her physical and mental condition deteriorated, the convulsions became more and more intense, and her ability to speak was impaired.[57]

On Bed Linen, on a Sofa, on Dusty Floors

Inbal Eshel Cahansky commits a lot of involuntary actions,
Slams herself into things and people close to her
Causes pain for no reason
Incapable of asking for forgiveness.
Dragged by her own saliva strings
Onto bedsheets linen
Onto a greenish sofa in the living room,
Onto a floor covered by her dog's hairs,
Inbal Eshel Cahansky is very much sunk into her dog's hairs
Wallowing like an animal, that has long forgotten
To moan the word.[58]

עַל מַצָּעִים, עַל סַפָּה, עַל רִצְפָּה מְאֻבֶּקֶת

עִנְבָּל אֵשֶׁל כַּהֲנְסְקִי מַרְבָּה בִּפְעֻלּוֹת לֹא רְצוֹנִיּוֹת,
מְטִיחָה עַצְמָהּ בָּעֲצָמִים וּבָאֲנָשִׁים הַקְּרוֹבִים לָהּ
מַכְאִיבָה לְלֹא סִבָּה
לֹא מְסֻגֶּלֶת לְבַקֵּשׁ סְלִיחָה.
בְּחוּטֵי הָרֹק שֶׁל עַצְמָהּ נִמְשֶׁכֶת
עַל מַצָּעִים
עַל סָפָּה יְרַקְרַקָה בַּסָּלוֹן,
עַל רִצְפָּה מְאֻבֶּקֶת שַׂעֲרוֹת כַּלְבָּתָהּ,
עִנְבָּל אֵשֶׁל כַּהֲנְסְקִי שְׁקוּעָה מְאֹד בְּשַׂעֲרוֹת כַּלְבָּתָהּ
מִתְפַּלֶּשֶׁת כְּחַיָּה, שֶׁכְּבָר מִזְּמַן שָׁכְחָה
לִנְהֹם אֶת הַמִּלָּה.

The poem describes both some symptoms of Eshel Cahansky's condition and the external or internalized reception of them. Although the relationship between the two is fascinating, I am actually more interested in the poem's lingering over Eshel Cahansky's location; the poem dedicates three lines to her placement: "Onto bedsheets linen / Onto a greenish sofa in the living room, / Onto a floor." This location is referenced in other poems by Inbal Eshel Cahansky. Thus, for example, in the poem "Days and Years" from the same book, she writes: "[You, the mother] parachute me on the sofa, green and pale, / In your spring living room like a heavy sack, / there I spend days and weeks and months / can hardly move, I can hardly look, my eyes are watery."[59] The sofa, or in other poems the bed, is featured as a dramatic space in Eshel Cahansky's works. The sofa and bed turn from pieces of everyday furniture into spaces that enable her "bedlife" fully—she creates spaces in which "the work of sickening" occurs and thus establishes "a politics and poetics of illness that is antithetical to coloniality's hold on the body as only of value while productive and profiting for itself and for another."[60]

This bedlife is simultaneously a safe space and a space of eruption, lack of control, and debilitating pain; it is a space of stammering and inability to speak, and a space (in other poems) of blatant sexuality. The sofa and the bed become locations that enable creativity and comfort when there is no physical relief to be found. This is a sickbed that disengages the speaker from "the compulsion of cure" and sends us, the readers, to Virginia Woolf's renowned essay, "On Being Ill."[61] Written from Woolf's sickbed in 1925, "On Being Ill" is considered the first published essay in English literature devoted to the representation of illness.[62] Woolf wonders how illness "has not taken its place with love and battle and jealousy among the prime themes of literature" despite how common the experience is.[63] She also speculates about the poetics emerging from the experience of sickness and, more specifically, about the perspective made possible by a prolonged presence in bed. She points out that during illness, "the bed is called for, or, sunk deep among pillows in one chair, we raise our feet even an inch above the ground on another, we cease to be soldiers in the army of the upright; we become deserters. They [the healthy] march to battle. We float with the sticks on the stream; helter-skelter with the dead leaves on the lawn, irresponsible and disinterested and able, perhaps for the first time for years, to look round, to look up—to look, for example, at the sky."[64] Woolf sought a literature that allowed sick people to write truthfully about their experiences. She proposed that illness has a distinctive ability to renew our awareness of worlds both inside and outside of us. Because of their recumbent position, those who are ill (and therefore must be at rest) have access to different experiences than those who are upright. Sickness for Woolf becomes a great defamiliarizer, causing us to experience the world—mundane things, poetry, or the sky—with the awe of a first-timer.

From a very different positionality, steeped in disability theory and care webs relying on transparency and mutual support, Leah Lakshmi Piepzna-Samarasinha relates to the subversive dimension of the sickbed. She explains that crip emotional intelligence is "understanding that beds are worlds," and stresses the political significance of the sickbed.[65] They say they grew to understand: "that me writing from my sickbed wasn't me being weak or uncool or not a real writer but a time-honored crip creative practice. And that understanding allowed me to finally write from a disabled space, for and about sick and disabled people, including myself."[66] Writing or creating both about and from the sickbed is therefore a way to connect with other disabled artists, and this shared common ground, while often intrinsically physically isolating, helps to establish a community of sick and disabled people. In the following untitled poem Inbal Eshel Cahansky investigates the power of this recumbent political position discussed by Woolf, Piepzna-Samarasinha, and so many other sick and disabled authors.

*

In the beginning she created the ceiling and the bed.
And the bed was without form and void, men are coming
in and out. And her spirit was hovering without reason.
And she said let there be light, and she turned on the switch
And she saw letters and words and sentences written in honey
On the ceiling. And she opened her mouth because they were good.
And she separated the ceiling hours from the bed hours.
And she called the bed Night and the ceiling she called Day. And
    there was evening
And there was morning, her entire being until now.[67]

*

בְּרֵאשִׁית בָּרְאָה אֶת הַתִּקְרָה וְאֶת הַמִּטָּה.
וְהַמִּטָּה הָיְתָה תֹּהוּ וָבֹהוּ, גְּבָרִים נִכְנָסִים
בָּהּ וְיוֹצְאִים. וְרוּחָה מְרַחֶפֶת לְלֹא טַעַם.
וַתֹּאמֶר וַיְהִי אוֹר, וַתָּסֶט אֶת הַמֶּתֶג וַתִּרְאֶה
אוֹתִיּוֹת וּמִלִּים וּמִשְׁפָּטִים כְּתוּבִים בִּדְבַשׁ
עַל הַתִּקְרָה. וַתִּפְתַּח אֶת פִּיהָ כִּי טוֹבִים הֵם.
וַתַּבְדִּיל בֵּין שְׁעוֹת הַמִּטָּה לִשְׁעוֹת הַתִּקְרָה.

וַתִּקְרָא לַמִּטָּה לַיְלָה וְלַתִּקְרָה יוֹם. וַיְהִי עֶרֶב
וַיְהִי בֹּקֶר, כָּל חַיֶּיהָ עַד כֹּה.

The poem alludes, of course, to the story of creation in Genesis, but instead of God in the biblical story creating the heavens and the earth, seeing that which was good, the woman in the poem creates the ceiling and the bed. At first reading, it seems that the poem paints the experience of illness in a negative and confining light. The infinite space between the heavens and the earth in biblical creation is converted into a limited space between the bed and the ceiling—a depressing loop, endless and without a future. But the artistic genealogical connections woven into the words—touchstones referenced through the imagery of the sickbed and sickroom—turn the poem into an act of political agency that claims the history of the creative sickbed and then takes an active part in it.

The creation of the ceiling and the bed is actually the creation of a sickroom; it is both a private and a literary space. The sickroom, in Victorian literature and beyond, argues scholar Miriam Bailin, becomes a gendered space but also exists "as a realm of freedom fashioned from the materials of restriction."[68] The description "And the bed was without form, and void [*tohu vavohu*], men are coming / in and out" marks the bed as a potentially sexual space as well, rather than one solely consecrated to artistic creation. But at the same time, in order to understand Eshel Cahansky's role in establishing a genealogy of disabled poets, I think we should understand the presence of the men in the poem as an important reference to Rachel Bluwstein's sickroom.

In modern Hebrew literature, the sickroom is often associated with Bluwstein's writings. Referring to the sickroom "as a heterotopic space in which women could redirect their experience of illness from one of restricted movement to one of expansive opportunities," Sunny Yudkoff postulates how Rachel Bluwstein's sickroom (both real and poetic) became a space in which she "would craft a poetic agenda over and against the willfully masculine, antidiasporic, and insistently healthy vision."[69]

In fact, Yudkoff explains that Bluwstein hosted a sort of "sickroom salon" that allowed the poet to entertain visitors and to conduct business in the privacy of her own room, as "it was a gathering where the formerly off-limits space of a woman's bedroom became the site of social engagement."[70] Here Bluwstein hosted friends and met with literary figures, such as *Davar* editors Zalman Shazar and Moshe Beilin-son, and with admirers, aspiring writers, and prominent writers, includ-ing Uri Nissan Gnessin and Hayim Nahman Bialik. Yudkoff describes this space as one that challenged gender conventions of the time and allowed the sick poet to establish her unique poetic identity precisely from her supine position.

The reference to the men who come in and out of the speaker's sick-room in Eshel Cahansky's poem might allude to Bluwstein's visitors and other such "sickbed salons." The ambiguity of the reference leaves room for arguments about whether it is meant to be exclusively autobiographi-cal or if it also describes part of Bluwstein's life. (It might even suggest the broader shared experience of many creative women working from a sick-bed, with Devorah Baron [1887–1956] a prominent example in modern Hebrew literature. In the last decades of her life, Baron confined herself to her home, where she continued writing, translating, and receiving distinguished guests like Asher Barash and Nachum Gutman while in her bed.) Does "her entire being until now" in the last line refer to the life of the subject of Eshel Cahansky's poem in her sickroom (or even to Eshel Cahansky herself, if we consider the poem autobiographical) or to Rachel Bluwstein, who "experienced the sickroom as the space in which she could dominate and determine her posthumous legacy"?[71] Or does it refer to genealogy and lineage once more, grounding both artists in the same space, despite the differences in time and lived experiences of disability and illness?

One way or another, the act of poetry occurs in the sickroom. The bed and the ceiling mark the perspective of the sick poet's gaze as it moves from the ground up: "And she said let there be light, and she turned on the switch / And she saw letters and words and sentences writ-ten in honey / On the ceiling. And she opened her mouth because they were good." The image of letters, words, and sentences written in honey alludes to the traditional Jewish custom wherein children are given honey-coated Hebrew letters in the cheder (a traditional primary school) as part of the process of learning to read the Torah. In the first chapter I addressed the way the vocal artist Victoria Hanna links this tradition to her stammer and uses it as an artistic attempt to reinscribe tangibility in the pronunciation of spoken words. In a similar manner, for Inbal Eshel Cahansky, the letters, words, and sentences become a poem relying on a fully sensory experience through her bodymind experience of being ill. The sickroom or sickbed is, therefore, not just a physical space in which the poet creates, but also an emotional and cultural space that creates roots for the poems themselves.

In her "Sick Woman Theory," Johanna Hedva raises the question of what modes of protest are afforded or available to sick and disabled people: "How do you throw a brick through the window of a bank if you can't get out of bed?"[72] To that end, Leah Lakshmi Piepzna-Samarasinha explains that writing from bed "is a time-honored disabled way of being an activist and cultural worker. It's one the mainstream doesn't often acknowledge but whose lineage stretches from Frida Kahlo painting in bed to Grace Lee Boggs writing in her wheelchair at ninety-eight."[73] The sickbed is thus a historical-political space that Inbal Eshel Cahansky marks in her poetry not as a new and unique occurrence, but as a space that has existed since the beginning of creation: "In the beginning [*bereshit*] she created the ceiling and the bed."

A Politics of Care

My discussion thus far may be guilty of idealizing the space of the sickbed or sickroom; therefore, it is also crucial for me to highlight the difficult and painful dimensions of being disabled or ill in that space. Inbal Eshel Cahansky tackles this in her work, but so do other sick and disabled writers and poets, which makes the intertextuality inherent in these poems a significant part of the politics of establishing a lineage of "a life lived with the certainty that one's fragile body is the *only* certainty."[74]

The following poem from Eshel Cahansky's third book of poetry, *Roaring in an Infinite Loop* (*Shoeget belulaat einsof*), depicts a difficult moment of pain:

**

Naked on a hard bed, dripping pain, and Verdi's requiem beating
    inside her skull.
Watching the treetop flailing wildly from the window, stretching
    pale-brownish arms,
Her fingers shaking like pale leaflets,
Knocking on transparent glass gone cloudy.[75]

**

מְעַרְטֶלֶת עַל מִטָּה קָשָׁה, נוֹטֶפֶת כְּאֵב וְהָרֶקְוִיאָם שֶׁל וֶרְדִי הוֹלֵם בְּגֻלְגָּלְתָּה.
רוֹאָה מֵהַחַלּוֹן אֶת הִשְׁתּוֹלְלוּת הַצַּמֶּרֶת, הַמְשֻׁלַּחַת זְרוֹעוֹת חוּמוֹת-חִוְרִינִיּוֹת.
אֶצְבְּעוֹתֶיהָ רוֹעֲדוֹת כְּעַלְעַלִּים בְּהִירִים,
דּוֹפְקוֹת עַל זְכוּכִית צְלוּלָה כְּשֶׁאֲטוּמָה.

The poem describes the harrowing experience of a woman confined to bed during a flare-up of an illness or chronic condition. The woman is "dripping pain" and the bed feels hard; she is exposed, with nothing to protect her or soften the contact of the body on the bed. The physical pain is not separated from the emotional pain, and the anxieties associated with pain, suffering, and death (or the fear of death) are intensely present in the poem. Eshel Cahansky uses the term "her skull"—*gulgalta* in Hebrew—which sounds like Golgotha, the site where Jesus is said to have been tormented and crucified.[76] The mention of the requiem is also connected to the presence of death in the poem, referring to the music that Giuseppe Verdi wrote for the Latin text of the Catholic funeral mass.

While it seems that the poem describes a difficult personal experience of pain, I would posit that it also cleverly hides yet another intertextual connection, joining once more to a genealogy that aims to make pain (inherently personal and unique) a more shared narrative, a fluid and relational experience.[77] This poem, like her others, is written in the third person; the speaker observes herself from the outside. This positionality of text and perspective, which supposedly separates the woman from her body, might allude to Yona Wallach's poem "Outside the Body":

Outside the Body

The hypnotist was here
she spoke of the body tired from all the years
serving and doing things for us
and I went out from the body
and sat on the edge of the bed
looked at it
and climbed up to lick it
stroke it
take care of it.[78]

מחוץ לגוף

הַמְהַפְּנֶטֶת הָיְתָה אֶצְלִי
דִּבְּרָה עַל הַגּוּף הֶעָיֵף מִכָּל הַשָּׁנִים
מְשָׁרֵת וְעוֹשֶׂה בִּשְׁבִילֵנוּ
וַאֲנִי יָצָאתִי מִתּוֹךְ הַגּוּף
וְיָשַׁבְתִּי עַל קְצֵה הַמִּטָּה
הִסְתַּכַּלְתִּי בּוֹ
וְעָלִיתִי לְלַקֵּק אוֹתוֹ
לְלַטֵּף אוֹתוֹ
לְטַפֵּל בּוֹ.[79]

"Outside the Body" was written while Wallach was hospitalized because
of her cancer in Tel Hashomer; it was not published until after her death,
when it first appeared in 1984 in the periodical *Hadarim* and subsequently
in another book, *The Unconscious Unfolds like a Fan* (*Tat hakara niftahat
kemo menifa*) in 1992.[80] The poem describes the speaker taking care of
her sick and tired body as though it were a separate entity; it is situated
in a multidimensional position of sickness and care. Yona Wallach writes
from her sickbed about sitting on the edge of the bed, perhaps dwelling
between life and death, in and outside of her self, looking at her body
and returning to lick, stroke, and care for it.[81] Licking the body evokes an
image of an animal taking care of itself and may be a reference to Rachel
Bluwstein's 1927 untitled poem:

In my great loneliness
of a wounded animal,
I lie for hours and hours. Lie silent.
Fate has harvested my vineyard, not even sparing
the young grapes.
But the humble heart has forgiven.

If these days are my last days,
I shall be quiet
lest my defiance sully
the peaceful blue of the sky,
My longtime friend.[82]

בִּבְדִידוּתִי הַגְּדוֹלָה, בִּדְידוּת חַיָּה פְּצוּעָה
שָׁעוֹת עַל שָׁעוֹת אֶשְׁכַּב. אַחֲרִישׁ.
הַגּוֹרָל בָּצַר בְּכַרְמִי אַף עוֹלֵלוֹת לֹא הוֹתִיר.
אַף הַלֵּב הַנִּכְנָע סָלַח.
אִם הַיָּמִים הָאֵלֶּה אַחֲרוֹנֵי יָמַי הֵם–
אֱהִי-נָא שְׁקֵטָה,
לְבַל יַדְלִיחַ מִרְיִי אֶת כְּחָלוֹ הַשָּׁקֵט
שֶׁל שַׁחַק–רֵעִי מֵאָז.

Bluwstein's poem describes a feeling of great loneliness in the sickbed, the
isolation and sadness "of a wounded animal" that seems removed from
humanity. Yona Wallach relates to this image, but instead of ruminating
on her loneliness, she adopts a self-care technique of the wounded animal. In addition, Bluwstein describes a surrender that allows her to reconcile herself to her condition and the future, although it is a temporary
appeasement that does not eliminate her rebellion against fate. When
Wallach comes out of her body to take care of it, she joins Bluwstein in
forgiveness of the sick and disabled body and acceptance of her pain.

Inbal Eshel Cahansky, then, reaches across words to establish a
connection both biographical and poetic between Rachel Bluwstein and
Yona Wallach. In her poem "Compassion Without End" she interweaves
references to *both* Wallach's "Outside the Body" and Bluwstein's "In My
Great Loneliness":

Compassion Without End

When I got up and walked away from my body
Tormenting itself in terrible spasms,
Part of my soul came out and rested with it.
Maybe now we could sit in the kitchen,
And hear wordless solitude.[83]

חֶמְלָה לְלֹא תּוֹעֶלֶת

כְּשֶׁקַּמְתִּי וְהָלַכְתִּי מִגּוּפִי
הַמְיַסֵּר עַצְמוֹ בַּעֲוִיתוֹת נוֹרָאוֹת,
יָצָא חֵלֶק מִנִּשְׁמָתִי וְנִשְׁאַר אִתּוֹ.

אוּלַי כָּעֵת נוּכַל לָשֶׁבֶת בַּמִּטְבָּח,
וְלִשְׁמֹעַ בְּדִידוּת לְלֹא מִלִּים.

While Wallach emerges from her tired body to care for it, Eshel Cahansky leaves her tormenting (and tormented) body, perhaps even abandoning it to seek peace, but a part of her soul remains. Whether that part of her soul is meant to take care of the body or to suffer with it is unclear. What is obvious is the connection to Wallach, which in turn allows Eshel Cahansky to also link to Bluwstein's silent loneliness "and hear wordless solitude." Unlike Orit Marton, who associates with Wallach's emotional disability, Inbal Eshel Cahansky chooses to reference one of Wallach's later poems, written in a hospital during difficult and painful stages of cancer and which, in turn, reaches back to reference Bluwstein's work written in the throes of her own illness. In that manner, Eshel Cahansky connects to her physically sick poetical ancestor, creating a genealogy of sick poets who write on—and from—their sickbed about their lives as sick and disabled women, underscoring gentle themes of self-care and self-compassion. As Johanna Hedva reminds us, "The most anti-capitalist protest is to care for another and to care for yourself. . . . A radical kinship, an interdependent sociality, a politics of care."[84]

Thus, while self-care is a poetic theme recurring in the work of each of these poets in ways specifically related to her individual bodymind and illness, the genealogy that the poets create through their connections to one another's sickrooms establishes a care web—a network of poetic care by and for sick and disabled poets working within Hebrew literature.

Summary: "Pain Is a Useless Thing"

The establishment of the care web stands in both contradiction and support of the title of Inbal Eshel Cahansky's poem "Compassion Without End" ("Hemla lelo toelet"). While the title may be a bitter allusion to the fact that compassion is fundamentally unable to help when the body is "tormenting itself in terrible spasms," the genealogy referenced within the work places compassion and self-compassion at the center. Here it is not so much the use of compassion that strikes me as the words *lelo toelet*—literally, "without end," without benefit or use; the poem raises questions about the links between illness, poetics, and questions of benefit or usefulness.

Inbal Eshel Cahansky's choice of the words *lelo toelet* sends us once more to the words of Dahlia Ravikovitch; her poem "A Private Opinion," published in 1969, opens with the well-known line "Pain is a useless thing" ("Keev hu daver sheain lo toelet").[85] Ravikovitch refuses to attribute collective or heroic meaning to pain, and she opposes the idea that any profit can be derived from it.[86] Later in the poem she writes, "Pain is an inhuman thing, / I would argue, / for me there are no extenuating circumstances. / look, isn't it ugliness incarnate."[87] Ravikovitch rejects the idealization of pain and the notion that pain is the source of creativity. Contrary to Orit Marton, who subscribes to Rachel Bluwstein's famous position regarding the sublimation of pain into aesthetic poetry, Eshel Cahansky joins Ravikovitch's discourse on the futility of pain. She highlights pain as a hindrance, something to cope with (and inevitably ultimately fail to cope with) rather than a source of creativity, and she draws attention to the way in which disabled and ill poets preserve this knowledge through intertextual dialogues.

While so many discourses of pain frame it as an individual and isolated bodily or mental experience, Eshel Cahansky's genealogy recognizes "pain as an experience that exceeds the boundaries of individual bodies."[88] She situates her own pain and that of other sick poets within frameworks of relationality, underscoring a major convention within disability studies that values interdependence over independence.[89]

Inbal Eshel Cahansky's writing, like Orit Marton's, therefore, does not constitute an aestheticization of pain but functions as a kind of archive. It preserves traces of writing by sick and disabled women in a social and literary space that previously held no room for recognition of disability culture, the commonalities between disabled identities, or discussions of the complex disabled histories of difficulties, joys, creativity, and human connection.[90] Wandering through this dispersed archive—and in many ways establishing it—is related to care: we turn to the archive for the purposes of support and self-care. But since the tradition of Hebrew poetry fails to acknowledge a literary genealogy of poets with physical disability, these poets are also confronted with the problems of partial information, with difficult to discern voices, and with a literary tradition that possesses traces but no firm discourse regarding these issues. "How do we care for these ghosts that take such care of us?" asks Hil Malatino (in regard to archival traces of trans, intersex, and gender nonconforming lives).[91] For Inbal Eshel Cahansky and Orit Marton, collecting traces of poetry written by sick and disabled poets and weaving them into their own work is a way of caring for those disabled pasts and surviving poetics that haunt Hebrew literature. Creating their own genealogy of poetry written by women with disability "sparks a sense of connection that resonates even as it remains opaque."[92]

This position offers a different orientation compared to Rosemarie Garland-Thomson's concept of the *misfit* and "The Case for Conserving Disability" as well as H-Dirksen L. Bauman and Joseph J. Murray's view of Deaf-gain, which I discussed in the previous chapter. Contrary to those concepts, which attribute to disability a value and an advantage, Inbal Eshel Cahansky's poetic genealogy conceptualizes a "system of connectivity" and builds ways of creating care.[93] Tobin Siebers reminds us that "the dominant social representation of pain in the West is the individual alone in pain, and it is difficult to find alternative representations," connecting his argument to the social origins of pain related to illness or disability.[94] Inbal Eshel Cahansky's poetic genealogy does not deny this structural oppression dictating our understanding of pain and it does not ignore the "cripistemology of pain," that is, the "process of knowledge production that situates pain within discursive systems of power and privilege," but it mainly considers living with pain an experience enabling connection in closeness, which is more in line with a feminist ethics of care.[95]

The poetic genealogy created by both Inbal Eshel Cahansky and Orit Marton addresses pain and negative experiences of disability and illness directly, without any attempt to reconceptualize them or reframe them as positive and desirable moments; it does not offer comfort to the reader or attempt to make disability simple or digestible. This is not a discourse that takes us back to the medical model of disability or even one that disconnects disability from its geopolitical context; rather, it creates a poetic support network of women who live with a wide variety of illnesses and disabilities. Care, argues Margaret Price so beautifully, "does not mean knowing exactly what another's pain feels like, but it does mean respecting each person's pain as real and important."[96] Inbal Eshel Cahansky and Orit Marton are not always fully aware of their poetic ancestors' exact life experiences as poets with disabilities, but they long for connection to them and they generate it through a recognition—often fragmented or imagined—of shared pains and other experiences of disability. Through their engagement with the textual inheritance of this mostly unknown tradition, they carve out new prospects for poetic care and interdependency.

3

CALLING THE ROLL

The Awakening of Sexuality and Disability in Israeli Art

This chapter deals with narratives of disabled women's sexuality and how they are addressed, dissected, and analyzed in Israeli media. Through critiques of the presence of disability and its multifaceted intersections with ethnicity and gender in classic films such as *Sh'Chur* and *Next to Her* (*At li Layla*), I will underscore recurring themes about, and stereotypes of, women with disability as they relate to their own sexuality. These representations can and should be viewed as microcosms of broader discourses pertaining to disability and sexual agency in Israeli culture. While these films, inextricably linked as they are, serve to open conversations about intersectional identity and sexuality—and, in fact, at times hold a mirror to the audience to call for self-reflection and prompt the contemplation of biases and assumptions—they are insufficient to my discussion, as they do not sustain or significantly advance the conversation. Nor do they begin to challenge or dismantle problematic aspects of how disabled women are viewed as sexual (or asexual) in broader Israeli culture. Therefore, I discuss the artistic trajectories of several disabled artists, such as Limor Ashkenazi, who center their femininity and sexual desire in their works in order to bring insight to the discourse of how we think about sexuality as difference and/or as a path to justice and inclusion.

Picture's Up: *Sh'Chur* as Urtext

While mainstream Israeli cinema rarely represents disability, let alone delves into the nuances of the sexuality of disabled women, the film *Sh'Chur* (1994) has become one of the most influential and formative representations of the sexuality of disabled women in Israeli culture. In this chapter, I will follow the film's far-reaching influence, both past and present.

Sh'Chur, directed by Shmuel Hasfari and written by Hanna Azoulay-Hasfari, released in 1994, quickly became an influential and foundational film in Israeli cinema and culture. In the year of its release, it was awarded six Israeli Oscars, and since then it has been showcased in various festivals worldwide. *Sh'Chur* follows the main character Cheli (Hanna Azoulay-Hasfari), a successful television presenter, as she is notified of her father's death and her subsequent journey to attend his funeral, accompanied by her daughter Ruth (Eti Adar), a child on the autistic spectrum, and her older sister Pnina (Ronit Alkabetz), a woman with a developmental disability who was involuntarily placed in institutional care. The movie unfolds as a road-trip narrative that blends scenes from the present with flashbacks, glimpses into the childhood of the sisters in the 1970s, telling the story of a Jewish family that has immigrated from Morocco to Israel. *Sh'Chur*, according to Hanna Azoulay-Hasfari, is autobiographical; she depicts herself in the figure of Cheli and represents her family dynamics and the neighborhood she grew up in. The mother of the family practices *sh'chur*, traditional magical rituals, which gives the film its name.[1]

Take 1: Gender and Ethnicity in *Sh'Chur*

Sh'Chur uses this very personal narrative to construct a story that grapples with the tension between ethnic and gender identities in the context of a broader hegemonic Israeli culture. Scholar Yael Munk argues that the film creates a compelling postcolonial, feminist, and critical narrative by struggling with ethnic and feminine identity, working through patterns of oppression within oppression. The film centralizes the oft-silenced voices of Mizrahi women (Mizrahi, Hebrew for "Eastern" or "Oriental," refers to Jews of Middle Eastern and North African origin, who are sometimes known as Arab Jews). This stands in contrast to a

larger colonial meta-narrative that focuses on white men and masculinity. Instead, the film centers the position of the native—the Mizrahi
"Other"—and her relationships, making them the central focus rather
than serving merely to advance the plot or characterization of a white
man. In doing so, Sh'Chur offers a nonstereotypical Mizrahi experience
that serves to challenge notions of a homogeneous, monolithic Israeli
culture and further works to fight against the myth of the integration
of Mizrahim into an unequivocal and fixed Israeli essentialism. By telling the story of women outside of the cultural hegemony of the West,
the film depicts the dual oppression Mizrahi women so often face—an
oppression in which both colonial and patriarchal rules come to bear.[2]

Yosefa Loshitzky reads the movie as part of an ongoing public discourse surrounding second-generation Mizrahim (the children of people
who immigrated to Israel from Arab and Muslim countries in the 1950s).
Sh'Chur illuminates a quintessential search for identity; Loshitsky claims
that "as a second-generation Israeli writer epitomizing the difficulties
experienced by immigrants in the transitional phase, Azoulay-Hasfari
created a diasporic film that challenges the repression of ethnicity in
official Israeli discourse."[3] Loshitsky also argues that even the genre of
the film—a road-trip narrative—becomes a feminist statement, as the
journey to the father's funeral is simultaneously a trip into the past and
into the trappings of patriarchal culture, which the main character Cheli
has worked to escape. This journey ultimately liberates her from this
suppressive past.[4]

Orly Lubin joins these interpretations by offering a feminist/ethnic
analysis of the film; she claims that Cheli's journey back to her former
town and her past leads her to deal with the rift that has separated her
from an inherently feminine tradition rooted in the practice of sh'chur.
Sh'chur, an Arabic term, is rooted in a mystical Moroccan tradition that
Moroccan Jews adopted and reworked. However, within the ethnic
dynamics of Israeli society, unlike Ashkenazi Jewish mysticism, which is
respected in certain contexts, Mizrahi sh'chur is often regarded as "popular" in a judgmental sense, seen as crude, unsophisticated, and "primi-
tive."[5] The practice itself, performed in the film by Cheli's mother and
sister, seems an essential link to Cheli's ethnic background in Moroccan
culture and to her own femininity—Lubin argues that the absence of
oedipal men and authoritarian father figures is a liberation from not only

patriarchy at large but also specifically from Western Ashkenazi oppression. In fact, the film is a representation of Cheli severing herself from the need to adapt or conform to the hegemonic ideals of an Ashkenazi-Israeli woman. At the end of the film—at the very conclusion of this introspective journey—Cheli acknowledges her lineage by asking her sister and daughter a question in Moroccan: "Do you want to go to Mommy?" Her smile as she speaks represents both her understanding and her embrace of the special power within her multifaceted identity, thereby supporting the power of a Jewish-Arab, Israeli-Mizrahi-Moroccan female dynasty.[6]

Take 2: Disability as Narrative Prosthesis in *Sh'Chur*

Whereas *Sh'Chur* does indeed tell the often untold story of Mizrahi women, centralizing and lifting up marginalized identities, it does so at the expense of other marginalized voices; *Sh'Chur* represses and silences the voices of people with disabilities. Pnina, one of the main protagonists, is portrayed as having no voice, subjectivity, or agency.[7] Her story as a woman with an unnamed intellectual or emotional disability is told by her nondisabled sister Cheli. Thus Cheli, in effect, ends up adopting the position of power in the wider dynamic of the gendered and colonial narratives that she struggles against and attempts to change. In fact, Pnina's character functions almost entirely as "narrative prosthesis," as she is represented less as an independent character and more as a crutch upon which the film's plot leans.[8] Moreover, Pnina's story seems to be used primarily as a vehicle for Cheli's own feelings of guilt for causing Pnina to be institutionalized (against Pnina's will); this furthers her characterization as prothesis in Cheli's narrative and once more sets Cheli's feelings about Pnina above the experiences of Pnina herself, robbing her of her own agency.

This is particularly unsettling as it is Pnina who helps Cheli restore her relationship with her daughter Ruth and also because she is the one who is most active in practicing *sh'chur* with her mother. Throughout the film, Pnina is portrayed as having powers that stand in opposition to and overcome Western ideas of progress, for example, being able to switch channels on a television without touching it or using a remote. Lubin explains that the television symbolizes both progress and the Israeli and Ashkenazi world on multiple fronts. The television is public and represents male privilege (such as the male gaze, control, money), while *sh'chur* resides in a private home as a symbol of women's power of resistance and survival in the face of oppression. As a practice that preserves both Moroccan ethnicity and feminine identity, *sh'chur* overcomes technology—Pnina (and later Ruth) control the television. Lubin claims that the language of *sh'chur* is entirely different from that of the television; rather than a language of rational masculinity and dominance, it is an inherently feminine knowledge, passed down from woman to woman through each generation. However, investigating this issue through the lens of gender alone is inadequate; the language characterizing *sh'chur* is one of Otherness and, in the context of this narrative, it hinges upon a framework of understanding that is neither able-bodied nor neurotypical.

Pnina's use of the *sh'chur* forces can be understood as the creation of an alternative discourse in the context of histories of oppression and oppressed peoples—perhaps a means of engaging in a conversation with broader Mizrahi disability culture—but it also relies upon an ableist trope to come to fruition. It becomes impossible to ignore that Pnina's "superpowers" play into an ableist stereotype of compensatory abilities, in which her disability becomes somehow more "acceptable" because of a supernatural and skilled ability to interact with the world in a way that others cannot. This tactic attempts to shape intellectual or emotional disability by adapting the disabled person to normative hierarchies centered on control, power, and capital; in other words, by gaining this unusual power, Pnina's character becomes a tool of capitalist neoliberal compensation. As an otherwise "limited" or "nonproductive" disabled person who becomes especially "productive" and has a unique capability, Pnina remains "worthy" of subjectivity.

The ableist representation of Pnina becomes even more problematic, considering the autobiographical nature of the film. Hanna Azoulay-Hasfri included Pnina in *Sh'Chur* as the only outside addition to her real-life family, basing the character on someone who lived in her childhood neighborhood. Azoulay-Hastri discusses this decision: "Choosing [to add the character of] Pnina and defining her as intellectually disabled (*mefageret*) or mentally ill (*meshugaat*) with mystical powers allowed me to project all my fears on her. Everything I felt about the culture from which I came—disgust and fear alongside an archaic understanding that this ancient culture continues to influence me even today."[9] Pnina's character serves as a vessel, then, for Cheli the protagonist (and Azoulay-Hasfri the screenwriter) to channel the entirety of her negative emotions.[10] Pnina's disability is not perceived in any way that would be considered a challenge or critique: as a mental illness in need of support, as a product of gender oppression (Phyllis Chesler), as a feminist alternative (Sandra M. Gilbert and Susan Gubar), or as a repository of lost histories. Instead, it stands, as Michel Foucault would suggest, as contrary to reason, dangerous, and threatening.[11] This representation embodies so many of the biases about madness that scholars and activists of mad studies are trying to change; rather than referring to Pnina as a woman who may identify as mad, mentally ill, a psychiatric survivor, or psychosocially disabled, or having her claim any of those labels for herself, her disability is depicted as something vague but inherently negative in nature—a challenge that needs to be overcome—and in that sense the portrayal serves the interest of abled-bodied society.[12] Pnina's disability, to use Rosemarie Garland-Thomson words, "constructed as the embodiment of corporeal insufficiency and deviance, becomes a repository for social anxieties about such troubling concerns as vulnerability, control, and identity."[13] In other words, Pnina's representation holds myriad anxieties: the disabled bodymind becomes a sort of container into which the anxieties of able bodymind are channeled, and as such, it is imbued with fear and imagined to be vulnerable and subject to danger and degradation.

Take 3: Vulnerability and the Body at Risk in *Sh'Chur*

Sh'Chur, as a representation of able bodymind anxieties about such vulnerability, includes many moments depicting Pnina as being threatened and vulnerable to attack—particularly to sexual violence. The camera focuses on Pnina during a scene showing the Jewish celebration of Shavuot, in which she happily participates in a tradition in which the neighborhood people spray water on one another. The camera then pans away to focus on an older man from the neighborhood, Yusuf, who is also depicted as having some kind of mental or intellectual disability, as he leans on a car and aggressively sprays water at Pnina. The spraying becomes more and more aggressive and the camera narrows in on the terrified Pnina and her failed attempts to extricate herself from the water pipe's stream. After Pnina's brother stops Yusuf, the camera focuses in on Pnina again, and in a slow (not to say erotic) shot, pans in upon Pnina's bare legs before slowly rising and centering on how her body is exposed through her wet dress. The viewer clearly sees her underwear, pubic hair, belly and, at last, her astonished face. At this point, Yusuf approaches Pnina and touches her in a sexual manner, while she tries to push him away.

For an Israeli audience, this scene does not operate in a vacuum; in fact, it alludes to Uri Zohar's cult movie *Peeping Toms* (*Metzitzim*, 1972). In one of the film's iconic scenes, the protagonist Gutte (Uri Zohar) is seen sitting on a lawn chair, holding a cup of coffee in one hand and in the other a hose, roughly at the height of his groin, which he uses to spray water on Dina's (Mona Zilberstein) exposed body. This scene is one of many sexist and derogatory events, images, and statements within the film, and although the moment is one of blatant sexual harassment, it is seen by Gutte and his friends—and subsequently by many viewers through the years—as nothing more than an amusing, "cheeky" incident. The movie depicts sexual harassment from the perspective of the perpetrator, and the viewer is thus positioned as voyeur who may derive visual pleasure from witnessing such exploitation and abuse.[14]

In *Sh'Chur*, Pnina's brother does intervene to stop the spraying and harassment, but fails to see the violence underpinning Yusuf's actions—in a way preserving the positionality of the male gaze that we see in *Peeping Toms*.

While the camera does take obvious pleasure in lingering over the image of Pnina's nearly naked body, the scene is a departure from *Peeping Toms* in that it leaves no doubt as to the threat inherent in this situation. The characterization of the figures central to these scenes likewise leaves little room for doubt—whereas Gutte in *Peeping Toms* is a young, playful boy with a bit of a vulgar streak, Yusuf in *Sh'Chur* is portrayed as an overtly aggressive man. Furthermore, Dina in *Peeping Toms* is a sort of "every woman," while Pnina is a disabled Mizrahi woman, adding layers of intersectional vulnerability that expose her even more obviously to the threat of sexual violence.

Indeed, this threat is fully realized later in the film when Pnina is raped. As part of an attempt to tell an untold story of Mizrahi femininity, the film also touches upon a massively silenced reality—the prevalence of the rape and abuse of women with disabilities. In general, disabled people—and in particular disabled women—experience domestic or sexual violence at a higher rate than people without disabilities. Despite the many indications showing both the prevalence and the particularly disturbing nature of abuse perpetrated against women with disabilities, such violence is rarely acknowledged or widely discussed. Negative social perceptions and the subsequent ostracism of disabled women condemn them to a lack of status and influence that inevitably results in increased exposure to violence . . . and far fewer opportunities for recourse or justice. Moreover, people with intellectual disabilities are consistently and constantly at higher risk for assault on a daily basis, as they are more likely than others to be assaulted by someone they know.[15] These assaults—often repeated—happen to women in places where they are supposed to be protected and safe, often perpetrated by a person they have been taught to trust and rely upon.[16]

When it was released, Sh'Chur was considered ahead of its time, debuting in a period when Israeli cinema was characterized by sexism and was rife with normalized sexual harassment and assault. That the film not only deals with the question of sexual violence but addresses the theme in relation to disabled Mizrahi woman would have been a powerful moment of representation—if not for the ableism inherent in Pnina's story. Pnina's family is unaware of her exposure to sexual violence; her brother, who witnessed her harassment, treats it as merely an act of mischief and subsequently disappears from the scene as the tension builds and Yusuf assaults Pnina. Pnina's rape later in the film occurs in the presence of two other family members—her younger sister Cheli, who is too young to understand what is happening, and her father, unable to bear witness because of his blindness. Thus, not only are Pnina's experiences of sexual violence rendered unseen and invisible by her family, but the family also regards her as an asexual being and therefore not subject to sexual danger.[17]

This contrasts with the way the family treats her sisters, who receive sh'chur, a spell or warding off, to protect them from sexual temptation when they leave home to work or study—something that Pnina is never given. Her perceived lack of sexuality stands out starkly in light of the hypersexualized and seductive sexuality so often imposed upon Black and Mizrahi women in society.[18] The film preserves an all too common stereotype of the assumed asexuality of the disabled female bodymind, but simultaneously reveals that this same bodymind is overly exposed to sexual danger.[19]

The impact the portrayal of the disabled woman as simultaneously asexual and sexually vulnerable had and continues to have on Israeli cinema and culture cannot be underestimated.[20] Just as *Peeping Toms* is a cult classic rooted in Israeli masculinity and has become an icon for the normalization of violence against women in Israeli culture, *Sh'Chur* is a cult film centering on Mizrahi femininity. In an Israeli cinematic environment that does not usually grapple with disabilities, it has become, unwittingly, a kind of urtext for this specific representation of disabled women as lacking sexuality and sexual agency while being constantly exposed to sexual dangers and abuses. It would not be an exaggeration to claim that the cultural representations of the sexuality (or lack thereof) of disabled women that appear in Israeli cinema from the 1990s onwards correspond, consciously or not, with this stereotype that was established in *Sh'Chur*. As I will show in the rest of the chapter, while hugely successful films in Israel such as *Next to Her* (*At li Layla*, 2014)—created by directors who do not identify as disabled—preserve and uphold this paradoxical and ableist representation, there are also artists with disabilities who are actively working toward more varied depictions of women's sexualities, aiming to challenge these problematic narratives and tropes.

Roll Camera, Roll Sound: Unveiling Ableism in *Next to Her*

Two decades after *Sh'Chur* was released and this problematic link between disabled women's assumed asexuality and their inherent vulnerability to sexual abuse was established within Israeli cinema, Israeli audiences met Gabby, a twenty-four-year-old woman with an intellectual or neurological disability in the 2014 film *Next to Her* (*At li Layla*), directed by Asaf Korman. The script for this feature was written by Liron Ben-Shlush, and it is saturated with autobiographical elements from her life—specifically drawing upon elements of her relationship with her younger sister Nati (Nathanala), who had an intellectual disability. The film depicts the relationship between the main protagonist Cheli (Liron Ben-Shlush) and her developmentally disabled sister Gabby (Dana Ivgy). During the film, which is mostly set within the confines of a small apartment in a poor neighborhood in Haifa, a romance develops between Cheli and Zohar, a gym teacher at the school where she works. It is the dynamic between these three characters that gives the film its strength and complexity.

Cheli and Gabby are two young Mizrahi women who live in an environment of hard-working people and in this aspect, *Next to Her*, like *Sh'Chur*, examines aspects of Mizrahi female resilience and interconnection. It is not a coincidence, then, that Cheli in *Next to Her* bears the same name as the protagonist of *Sh'Chur*—both films grapple with the complexity of identity in the lives of Mizrahi women living in Israel, both rely on scripts with autobiographical elements, and both examine the symbiotic relationship between two sisters, one of whom has an intellectual or emotional disability.[21] However, despite the surface resemblances between these two films and the manner in which they have positioned themselves to explore issues related to Mizrahi identity and the sexuality of disabled women, *Next to Her* actually ends up highlighting the problematic nature of *Sh'Chur* and seems to beg its viewers for self-reflection on their own ableist views, the fact that they may have internalized the standard set by *Sh'Chur*, and thus accuses them of inability to imagine a disabled woman as a sexual being.

Gabby's sexuality is present on the screen, but once more we see how a disabled woman's sexuality is repeatedly negated and erased by both Cheli and the camera. In one scene Cheli and Gabby are both in the living room, Cheli watching television with Gabby lying on the couch next to her. Gabby starts to masturbate and Cheli stops her, telling her that it is forbidden.

Another scene thirty minutes or so into the film hearkens back to this moment as the camera focuses on Cheli and Zohar playing backgammon in the living room, with Gabby sleeping in the background. When Gabby wakes up and begins masturbating, the camera shifts to Cheli, who is panicking and about to stop her. While the audience is aware of Gabby's masturbation in the background, the focus on-screen remains on the conversation between Cheli and Zohar. Zohar says to Cheli, "It's only natural, isn't it?" before they leave the room, and the camera follows them out. Thus, even when Gabby's sexual impulses are acknowledged, they are not only excluded from a place of prominence on the screen (unlike Cheli and Zohar's sex scenes), but the language that is used—"It's only natural"—codes Gabby's behaviors as instinctive rather than led by conscious desires.

However, a far more prominent erasure of Gabby's sexuality is reflected in the film's plot and direction. Toward the end of the film, Cheli is astonished to discover that Gabby is pregnant; she immediately concludes that Zohar has sexually exploited her sister. She throws his belongings out of the apartment and cuts off contact with him before taking Gabby to have an abortion. The direction of the film prompts the audience to share this suspicion of Zohar and viewers, like Cheli, assume that the pregnancy (as in *Sh'Chur*) is the product of rape. The entire premise of *Next to Her*, then, is rooted in the assumptions of both Cheli and the audience that, in spite of having seen evidence of Gabby's desire through two different scenes featuring self-pleasure through masturbation, Gabby is devoid of sexuality and lacks the agency to choose her own sexual partners. The film's direction plays up this assumption, combining, as the director himself testifies, elements of mystery, horror, and psychological thriller genres to guide the audience's suspicions, leading the viewer to think that Zohar is a predator and Gabby is the victim of repeated physical violence and emotional abuse.[22]

Although the filmmakers mislead the audience and the entire premise of the film's plot drives forward upon the assumptions that a disabled woman's nonexistent sexual agency *must* mean her pregnancy is the result of exploitation and forced sexual contact, *Next to Her* pivots to challenge these assumptions in the film's last scene. The plot twist here reveals "the wrong accused, and there is a crime that was not committed"; as it turns out that Gabby enthusiastically engaged in a consensual relationship with another disabled person in her adult day care center, which led to her pregnancy.[23]

This final scene, the only one in *Next to Her* to show disabled actors on-screen, can be understood as ableist in its creation and direction, however.[24] Dana Ivgy, an able-bodied actor, plays the role of Gabby; only at the end is there a moment when the camera shows actual people with disabilities, and then they are muted, meaningless to the plot, almost used as props in the background. This scene can be read also as a moment of self-reflection, however: at the moment when the disabled actors come on-screen, the film (the actors, director, screenwriter, camera crew, and production team) and its viewers are exposed to their own ableism. Just as the audience, encouraged to believe in the blatant stereotypes and assumptions about disability and sexual agency throughout the course of the film, learns of Gabby's acting upon her own desires, viewers are then confronted with a moment in which disabled actors "take over" the screen. In other words, in contrast to the unchallenged ableism present in *Sh'Chur, Next to Her*—made two decades later—uses ableism as a cinematic/political device to reveal the problematic bias regarding the sexuality of women with disabilities and forces a moment of reflection about the ableism of the viewers and of the Israeli film industry. The conclusion of *Next to Her* only underscores the fact that audiences and Israeli directors alike are unable to recognize and/or acknowledge the possibility of the independent sexuality of women with (intellectual) disability.

Action: The Artistic "Awakening" of Limor Ashkenazi

While I discussed *Sh'Chur* and *Next to Her* in order to explore how the sexuality of women with disabilities is imagined in Israeli culture, it is crucial to move forward with this analysis by presenting a rebuttal of sorts to this repressive, anxious cultural mindset, a refutation that comes from the perspective of an artist who is also a disabled woman. Although it was important to establish how the role of the "fantasy of disability" (that is, the cultural uses of disability in narrative rather than the lived experience of people with disabilities) functions within Israeli culture, it is now crucial to examine how these perceptions and stereotypes impinge upon the reality of the wide spectrum of sexual preferences and activities in the disability community in Israel, and in particular, to highlight the diverse artistic expressions that engage with and challenge these perceptions.[25]

Limor Ashkenazi is a multidisciplinary artist—performer, actress, playwright, photographer, and model—who lectures on accessibility, disability, and sexuality. She was born in 1973 with Morquio syndrome, a genetic condition that can affect growth and development. Her height is eighty centimeters (around thirty-two inches) and, to use her words, "despite all the vegetables I ate, I did not grow, and apparently dwarves exist not only in fairytales."[26] Since experiencing a brain aneurysm when she was sixteen years old, Ashkenazi uses a wheelchair. Her lived experiences have informed her artistic work, which is front and center in my discussion of disabled women's access to pleasure and sexuality in Israeli culture.

Take 1: A Reclamation of Crip Sexuality

In 2008, the Bat Yam Community Theater staged the play *Other Person* (*Zulat*), which, at its heart, dealt with the relationships and sexualities of disabled people. The play, directed by Nira Moser and written by Limor Ashkenazi and Nira Moser, is based on the lives of the actors, all people with disabilities. *Other Person* centers on the story of a tiny, sexually alluring female rabbit (played by Limor Ashkenazi) who seeks "true love," specifically desiring a giraffe as her partner. This story, according to Ashkenazi's testimony, is autobiographical, based on her own experience as a young woman falling in love with a tall, able-bodied man.[27] The bunny's insistence upon finding a giraffe as her partner raises questions regarding the complicated connections between normative sexuality (embodied in her object of desire, the nondisabled giraffe) and the crip sexuality of people with disabilities.[28]

Although the play preserves a heteronormative sexuality experienced within the heterosexual notion of "true love," the refusal to limit a disabled woman to intimate relationships only with someone else disabled marks an important step in the Israeli context. It tests the boundaries of sexuality and expands the social possibilities available for a woman with disabilities. This challenge to restrictive cultural norms stands out as it functions within a broader Israeli cultural conversation, as seen in other media released around the same time, such as Dan Wasserman's documentary *Do You Believe in Love?* (*Hashadhanit*, 2013), which follows the life of Tova Shamsian, who lives with ALS (amyotrophic lateral sclerosis) and runs a matchmaking office from her home. The explicit discourse of the film is that women with disabilities should "aim for" a match only with disabled men.

A disabled woman's search for an able-bodied partner in Ashkenazi's play may appear to be an erasure of disabled sexuality, holding up normative sexuality and able-bodied normativity as the standard. However, this portrayal is in fact unusual in the context of Israeli culture in the 2000s, a period when any awareness or discussion of the sexuality of women with disabilities was minimal and, when present, was filled with rhetoric that aligned with the *Sh'Chur* model of denying disabled women sexual autonomy and agency.

The mere representation of a disabled woman who sees herself as a sexual and attractive woman entitled to love and sexuality and who proactively works to find someone she considers attractive and right for her, challenges the stereotype of asexual disability that was established in the cultural conversations emerging from films such as *Sh'Chur, Next to Her*, and *Do You Believe in Love?* Thus, Ashkenazi's artistic representation, stemming from her own lived experience, flies in the face of the inherent ableism marking the mere existence of her sexual desire as "other" and problematic. She creates a "countercultural approach," resisting and confronting dominant ableist culture.[29]

Other aspects of Ashkenazi's art similarly both reference and call out ableism. A photo of her was featured in the 2016 *Selfie in a Limited Edition* exhibition, curated by Miri Krymolowski, which showcased selfies and selfie-inspired images of disabled individuals. Ashkenazi's piece, photographed by Omer Shaul, depicts her posed as a bride (figure 5).[30] Against a background of pink flowers, she sits in her wheelchair (not visible in the photo). She is wearing a white wedding dress, complete with bridal veil, and her face, adorned with makeup, is posed as if blowing a kiss to the viewer. The set-up and styling of this photograph simultaneously adopt and mock the cliché of a glamorous traditional wedding, with the trappings of flowers, a white dress, and posed femininity sanctioned by mainstream society. The excessive kitschiness of the selfie suggests a critique of the institution of marriage and the exclusion of so many women, especially disabled women, inherent within that system.

In September 2012, the State of Israel ratified the UN Convention on the Rights of Persons with Disabilities, which aims to ensure equal rights for persons with disabilities worldwide. While the convention also concerns itself with the right to found a family (section 23), the reality

FIGURE 5. Ashkenazi dressed as a bride in a photograph from *Selfie in a Limited Edition*. (Photographed by Omer Shaul. Courtesy of Limor Ashkenazi.)

is that people with disabilities wishing to marry encounter all manner of difficulties and obstacles, including finding partners, enduring negative social stigma, and facing challenges in receiving approval from the religious establishment.[31] In her photo at the *Selfie in a Limited Edition* exhibition, Ashkenazi plants herself firmly in the center of the space from which she is excluded, thereby claiming her right to be included within the parameters of the institution of marriage.

Take 2: BDSM and Consensual Power Play as Empowerment

The 2021 exhibition *Breaking Walls* (*Shovrim homot*), curated by Naomi Gordon-Chen and Michal Teomi Sela, presented art by people with physical and mental disabilities.[32] Among the works featured was Limor Ashkenazi's photograph *Awakening*, taken by photographer Gustavo Hochman, in which she distanced herself from the normative discourse surrounding relations and marriage (figure 6). In this black-and-white photograph, Ashkenazi lies on a mattress, covered by a loose sheet, on the floor. She wears only a short black negligee, her upraised arm holding a cat-o'-nine-tails, her wheelchair directly behind her as if she is about to strike it with the whip.

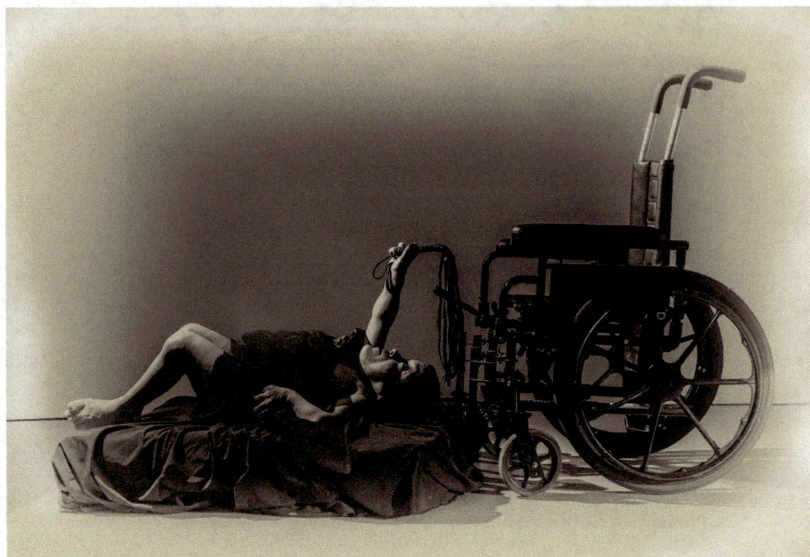

FIGURE 6. *Awakening*, a photograph from *Breaking Walls*. (Photographed by Gustavo Hochman. Courtesy of Limor Ashkenazi.)

Ashkenazi states that following the popularization of BDSM (bondage and discipline, domination and submission, sadism and masochism) in public discourse after the release of Erika Mitchell's novel *Fifty Shades of Grey* (translated into Hebrew in 2012), she embarked upon her own journey to learn more, eventually joining the BDSM scene: "It fascinated me and turned me on, especially as a woman in my situation, who all day depends on the kindness of others, starting with the Filipina who bathes me and ending with the one who drives me. It was especially important for me, who has experienced a lifetime of loss of control and surrender, to play [the role of a] 'queen' in those games of bondage."[33] In *Awakening*—and in additional photographs from the same series, which have not yet been shown publicly—Ashkenazi's wheelchair becomes her partner, and the imagery of BDSM stands in as a metaphor for her relationship to her disability and her mobility aid. To quote Ashkenazi again, "[I have] relations of control-surrender with my physical limitation (*migbala*) and my wheelchair. I once felt that my wheelchair was binding me. Over time, I realized that it actually gives me independence. . . . And in 'Awakening,' I am calling the others, let's wake up and depart from the norms and stigmas and everything that limits us. In the photo you can see that I am holding a whip. I took the whip into my hands—that is, I take responsibility [over my life] and I make the choices in my life."[34]

Within BDSM communities, there is often a greater emphasis on situating power play and consensual power exchange rather than a focus on the use of violence and pain, which is more often represented as the key dynamic in BDSM in normative media.[35] As part of this power play Ashkenazi gains physical and psychological control over her bodymind, which she frequently experienced as out of her control. The photograph and the process of posing allowed her to reclaim her disability in her own terms, and to feel control over her disability rather than being the one controlled. "Suddenly I felt feminine, sexy, in control," she said with a smile in an interview; "I fell in love with myself with every shooting."[36] BDSM became a space that enables Ashkenazi to engage positively with her disability in ways that make her feel both strong and sexual.[37]

While Ashkenazi explains her choice of the aesthetics of BDSM in this photograph as a metaphorical means of artfully presenting the reality of grappling with her disability, her choice to participate in BDSM as a way of life can also be understood as a response to the dominant discourse in Israeli society which, once more, tends to regard disabled women as asexual and yet at risk of sexual violence or abuse. Ashkenazi's artistic work preserves these questions of power dynamics within sexuality and disability, but also reaches past those limited conversations into a more general discussion of the politics of control, submission, and disability. She takes instances like the violence portrayed in *Sh'Chur* and the presumed abuse in *Next to Her* to a different level by intersecting disability with the dynamics of BDSM, turning potential vulnerability into strength that revolves around the fantasies played out by invoking the dominant-submissive power paradigm. For Ashkenazi, BDSM becomes a powerful tool for managing the emotional and psychological load of her disability and inverting social dynamics.[38] By adopting the visuals of BDSM, *Awakening* creates new discourses and aesthetics of difference, marginality, and sexuality. Not only does it present an image of female sexuality that is not inherently tied to either reproduction or erotic display as a passive participant, it also displays crip sexuality in a way that rejects and discards the stereotypical perceptions of disabled women seen in media such as *Sh'Chur* and *Next to Her*.

Almost two decades before Ashkenazi's *Awakening*, in 2004, a social initiative was established in Israel by a number of disabled people, headed by Iddo Gruengard, Roni Viner, and Talia Gal-Ed, to stimulate discourse about disabled people as sexual and attractive.[39] The initiative included the Disabled and Sexy fashion show, and one of the women who modeled was the artist, activist, and disability scholar nili Broyer. In a talk held to mark International Women's Day in 2011, Boyer spoke about her participation in the fashion show, addressing the tradition of the freak shows that still haunts performances of people with disability. She talked about her fear of becoming a grotesque figure, her self-representation as both a little person and as a woman, and how her participation in the Disabled and Sexy fashion show helped to allay some of those concerns:

> But in this fashion show, that danger has passed. And I said—I dare now to break the boundaries that society has put on me, that I have put on myself, and I go out in the most grotesque, freakiest way. I put on boots with 15-centimeter platforms and went out in an outfit that echoes BDSM—everything in black and red, wearing a corset and short pants, I have a kind of spiked fan above my head,

FIGURE 7. Photograph from the series *Awakening*, taken by Gustavo Hochman. (Courtesy of Limor Ashkenazi.)

a long trail behind me. The clothes were designed by Yuval Ravid, and you can see in the photos that the result is very sexual, and even connects to sexual deviance. The look that is received in the show is not the "acceptable" and refined look that I try to strive for on a daily basis. At the fashion show I had the opportunity to break through beyond the accepted and reach a place that threatens the social order. This experience was very liberating and fun.[40]

nili Broyer links her performance in the Disabled and Sexy fashion show to the aesthetics of BDSM. It is not necessarily a sexual or lifestyle practice that she applies personally, but rather a visual representation of sexuality that is not mainstream. It is an attempt to mark her socially othered femininity and sexuality as a disabled woman in a way that celebrates those deviances from bodily norms and socially imposed standards of sexuality. She links her choice of BDSM aesthetics to the long tradition of objectification and fetishization of disabled representations in freak shows, suggesting that instead of fearing this representation and excluding it altogether (as though it is something not to be seen or desired at all), she embraces the freak identity, adopting it as another means for experimentation and performance. Freak thus becomes a performative identity that allows her not only to reflect upon her own gender and sexuality as a little woman and a performer, but also to take pleasure in the process of reclamation ("This experience was very liberating and fun").[41] Rachel Adams suggests, "Freaks cannot be neatly aligned with any particular identity or ideological position. Rather, *freak* is typically used to connote the absence of any known category of identity."[42] Thus purposefully selecting the role of the freak and staging BDSM aesthetics made it possible for nili Broyer to explore myriad possibilities and enjoy the experience. Limor Ashkenazi has stated that for her, "freak" is not an unshakeable essence but an identity adopted for the purpose of performance and exploration.[43] By depicting herself as practicing BDSM, Ashkenazi embraces and celebrates her sexual subjectivity, posing questions about agency in the controlling of selves, bodies, and sexualities. She demands outside reflection upon the boundaries of the bodymind and the potential for performative and political power rooted within the sexuality of a disabled female bodymind.

In a different exhibition, *Standard Mark* (*Tav Teken*), curated by Nira Moser in 2016, Limor Ashkenazi presented her photo *The Woman in Red*, photographed by Shimon Bukstein (figure 8).[44] The photo was inspired by the animated character Jessica Rabbit in the 1988 film *Who Framed Roger Rabbit?*[45] Ashkenazi, wearing a red dress and feather boa, reclines seductively upon a chair draped in silky red fabric. Both her posture and the look on her face invite the viewer to observe and be tempted by her sexuality. "I give myself the standard mark (*tav teken*) for what it means to be a sexy woman," she claims, "even if I'm short, I'm still beautiful and feminine."[46] While, as an icon, the figure of Jessica Rabbit references "erotic" photography that objectifies women, Limor Ashkenazi reclaims this power of observation through this image and uses it as a means of affirmative self-expression. As a disabled woman and a little person, she does not conform to the pornographic ideal of beauty à la *Playboy* models or the figure of Jessica Rabbit. She displays her disabled body openly in the heart of a culture that excludes her.

Limor Ashkenazi's choice of a suggestive bunny is also associated with her intersectional identity, as elements of ethnic and racial

FIGURE 8. Limor Ashkenazi, *The Woman in Red* from *Standard Mark*. (Photographed by Shimon Bukstein. Courtesy of Limor Ashkenazi.)

background influenced her artistic representation in her play *Other Person*. As a Mizrahi woman (the daughter of an Iraqi mother and a Bulgarian father), her work reacts to the ethnic politics of the hyper-sexualization of Black women, but as a little person, she is viewed as asexual or lacking sexual agency. Flying in the face of oppositional and contradictory social biases that might otherwise limit her, she chooses instead to powerfully present her crip sexuality, in the process dismantling the sexual coding of both disability and ethnicity, freeing them from ableist and racist stereotypes. Her reclamation of a character such as Jessica Rabbit sheds the expectations of an ableist, sexist, anti-Black world, enabling her to instead center her own crip sexuality, subjectivity, and aesthetics to upend traditional and restrictive power dynamics.

Ashkenazi's artistic journey of reclaiming her sexuality while breaking the boundaries of performance reached even bolder territory after she met theater creator and fringe artist Ariel Bronze. The two created a performance and a subsequent video clip titled *32 Inches of Queen* (*Shmonim santimeter shel malka*, 2019), which enabled her to confront and break through additional barriers of self-acceptance she had been grappling with. Ashkenazi says, "I performed in underwear and a bra, with the catheter that I had difficulty accepting until then and was very ashamed of in the past. Then I said to myself, why are you ashamed? It is part of your reality today."[47]

In *32 Inches of Queen*, Ariel Bronze plays a dog and Limor Ashkenazi, seated in her wheelchair dressed only in underwear, bra, and garter, is its owner. The performance incorporates sex scenes onstage, including BDSM scenes in which Ashkenazi is dominant, featured as the queen and in control. This piece creates a breathtakingly new aspect to the politics of intimacy, in which the naked disabled body, which does not hide its unconventionality or its catheter, takes an active part in a self-reflective narrative about bodily appearance and function as well as both the limitations and possibilities of the disabled body.

The sex scenes onstage combine aspects of reality and fiction, revealing the duality of possible and impossible in a culture that widely erases the sexuality of disabled women by distancing them from their own sexual desires. Running contrary to the social demand to hide and/or overcome disabilities, Ashkenazi chooses to display her disability onstage; she creates an exploratory space to engage with a full spectrum of possibilities for pleasure, playfulness, fantasy, humor, reality, and sexuality.

The setting provides no barrier between the stage/performers and the audience, which transforms the performance into an invitation not only to gaze upon the disabled body but to do so while taking part in the exploration and subsequent celebration of Ashkenazi's sexuality.

Scholar Rosemarie Garland-Thomson writes about the stare-and-tell dynamic, explaining that in the social context of an ableist society, "the disabled body summons the stare, and the stare mandates the story. The stare, in other words, evokes the question, 'What happened to you?'"[48] She argues that disabled performance artists manipulate this stare-and-tell dynamic. The gaze that accompanies the demand for an explanation to justify the unexpected body is severed in these performances from its power. In the space of alternative performance, the constant questions demanded of the disabled body fade away; instead, it is the audience that has to deal with new and unexpected questions asked of it. In this way, both *32 Inches of Queen* and Ashkenazi's photographic art enable the artist to take hold of the gaze and subjugate it, regaining control over loaded messages about her disabled body.[49] She seizes control of her own representation and hypervisible body, which has been laden with an excess of stigmatized meaning. The stage becomes an experimental space where she examines the boundaries of her daring as well as of the audience's tolerance, since, as Margrit Shildrick puts it, "Both sex and disability threaten to breach certain bodily

FIGURE 9. Excerpt from *32 Inches of Queen*. (Photographed by Sharon Ovadia. Courtesy of Limor Ashkenazi.)

boundaries that are essential to categorical certainty and, as such, they provoke widespread anxiety."[50]

But more than anything, this performance blurs the boundaries between the imaginable and what Judith Butler deems the status of unthinkability. The blurring between real sexuality and the representation of sexuality onstage, between the symbolism of the artistic act and the concreteness of Ashkenazi's almost naked body, exposed catheter and all, creates a space that is neither recognizable nor excluded. Rather, this alternative form constitutes "sexual possibilities that will never be eligible for a translation into legitimacy. . . . It is not only not yet legitimate, but it is, we might say, the irrecoverable and irreversible past of legitimacy: the never will be, the never was."[51] For Butler—in her discussion of gay marriage that I adapt here to my discussion of crip sexuality—this status of unthinkability is critical, radical, and valuable: "As the sexually unrepresentable, such sexual possibilities can figure the sublime within the contemporary field of sexuality, a site of pure resistance, a site uncoopted by normativity. But how does one think politics from such a site of unrepresentability? And in case I am misunderstood here, let me state an equally pressing question: how can one think politics without considering these sites of unrepresentability?"[52]

The photograph of the bride in the exhibition *Selfie in a Limited Edition* and the character of the bunny in the play *Other Person* both express attempts to integrate into heterosexual normative discourses of sexuality and marriage—a process that, despite its importance in creating confrontation, inevitably inserts disability into the homogenous narrative of normalization. However, *32 Inches of Queen* outlines the crisis inherent within this attempt of integration, instead carrying a political call for radical change. While Limor Ashkenazi's earlier works cover and hide her body (through the wedding dress and the bunny costume), her later photographs and *32 Inches of Queen* expose her body, foreclosing the possibility of allowing her bodymind and her sexuality to be catalogued or molded into familiar, pre-prepared patterns.

End Board: Paradox and Progress in Postmodern Sexual Discourse

Scholar Tom Shakespeare asks, "Are we trying to win access for disabled people to the mainstream of sexuality, or are we trying to challenge the

ways in which sex and sexuality are conceived and expressed and limited in modern societies?"[53] This important question makes it possible to
challenge repressive concepts of sexuality and gender, but it also inherently sets up a dichotomous system that cannot aptly be applied to Limor
Ashkenazi's creative world. While her work remains within heterosexual
boundaries, within them she establishes a unique sexuality, idiosyncratic
to her as a woman living with disability. Thus, although on the surface it
seems that Ashkenazi's art is moving from a discourse of integration at
the beginning of her artistic journey—in her story of falling in love with
a giraffe or posing as a traditional bride, for example—to a much more
radical celebration of difference, this is not an unequivocal or linear transition. The title of the photograph *Awakening*, for example, indicates a
much less dichotomous position. In the interview I quoted earlier, in
talking about the title *Awakening*, Ashkenazi explains that she calls on
people to wake up from their bias and stigmas. In other words, it is a
call and a request both to the audience to confront their own prejudices
and preconceived notions, accepting instead a discourse of integration
through diversity, and to Ashkenazi herself as the artist to step away
from established patterns to celebrate her own sexuality.[54]

Jeffrey Weeks argues for the existence of two movements in post-
modern sexual discourse: one that highlights difference and sexual
uniqueness, and another that aims for inclusion, acceptance of diversity,
and broadening the definition of belonging. He explains that although it
seems that these are two separate trajectories in the discourse of sexual
politics or perhaps even contradictory trends, they are in fact comple-
mentary. Their potential for coexistence makes it possible to maintain
difference while also sustaining equality, equity, and safety for those
who manifest difference.[55] Similarly, despite the temptation to present
Limor Ashkenazi as an artist who celebrates her difference and works to
create a disability culture that does not aspire to integration within the
framework of Israeli mainstream society, her works stand as tribute to
a celebration of diversity that does not distance itself from the need
to integrate. It is, by all accounts, an artistic project of self-acceptance
that dares to hope for social acceptance and boldly claims rights to sexual
autonomy and justice.[56]

4

CHOREOGRAPHING
THE DISABLED BODY

*Performing Vulnerability and Political
Change in the Work of Tamar Borer*

With the most powerful tool we have as human beings—the
imagination—we produce change, healing and transformation of
both our mind and physical condition.

—Tamar Borer

The Israeli Jewish performance artist Tamar Borer, born in 1965, was
trained in many different forms of dance in institutions worldwide. She
studied classical ballet at the American Ballet Theatre in New York, modern dance at the Rina Sheinfeld Dance Theatre (where she performed for
seven years), authentic Balinese dance in Indonesia, and trance dance in
Mexico. In 1992, she traveled to Japan to study with Kazuo Ohno, the
well-known and skilled founder of Butoh soul dance. More than three
decades after this formative encounter, Borer remains one of the most
innovative and influential Butoh performers and teachers, not just in
Israel but worldwide.[1] She has been invited as an esteemed guest to a
variety of dance festivals across the globe and has won many awards and
prizes, including first prize at the Gvanim beMahol (Shades in Dance)
Competition for First Independent Work (1988), the Distinguished Artist

FIGURE 10. Borer lies atop a grand piano in the performance *Piano Forte* (2013). (Photographed by Tamar Lem. Courtesy of Tamar Borer.)

Award from ballet master Albert Gaubier's Foundation (1996), and the Buchman Hyman Fund's Promising Artist Award (1997).[2] While Tamar Borer has a worldwide presence, choreographing and performing solo, duets, and ensemble productions, the vast majority of her noteworthy performances and collaborations take place in Israel, where her studio is located in Tel Aviv. Her performances raise questions and concerns about Israeli subjectivity—particularly in relation to the Israeli-Palestinian conflict. In this context, while creating a home-grown as well as transnational artistic venue for addressing the political situation in which Israel is embroiled, Borer's work functions not just as a productive point of departure for social critique and change, but most pointedly as an invitation to a kind of social self-reflection for contemporary Israelis.

In 1990, Borer was involved in a car accident that left her paralyzed in both legs. This life-changing experience prompted a continued exploration of her body and sense of embodiment, alongside her physical training, creative expression, teaching, and professional performances. Her remarkable talent and dedication won her the Willie and Celia Trump's Virtue Award (Ot Hachesed) in 2002, "for serving as a role-model for growth and empowerment in the face of disability."[3]

Experiencing dance in a new way enabled—and forced—Borer to critically examine both her capabilities and her limitations, and it prompted her to encounter dance and performance through her unique body and self. This process is shared by many professional artists, but as Western dance traditionally idealizes and privileges the able and "capable" body—the Apollonian robust and stable body—the integration of a disabled body into contemporary Israeli dance resulted in radical redefinitions of physical expression and grace by disrupting and challenging the cultures that have evolved around dance.[4]

In understanding Tamar Borer's work as a physically disabled dancer, I examine the implications of disability and embodiment, focusing on the artistic and aesthetic in Israeli society. Thus, I am interested in questions such as: What does it mean to address the political arena from the position of the disabled occupier? In what ways do the visual markers of "limited" mobility, such as walkers, wheelchairs, or canes, affect sociopolitical concepts such as control, agency, and authority? And, in a broader sense, how can the physical, emotional, social, and existential perspectives of the non-Apollonian frame challenge Israeli perceptions of the Israeli-Palestinian conflict?[5] This book as a whole examines the nexus of disability and performance, introducing us to new perceptions of bodies, agency, and space, and inviting us to rethink our personal, collective, and national stability. In the current chapter, I am interested in the ways in which this rethinking of what constitutes stability challenges our conceptualization of the Zionist movement in general and of the Israeli occupation in particular.

Politicizing the Disabled Body

From its inception, the Zionist movement has created a conceptual connection between the revival of the nation and the well-being and prosperity of its people. National liberation is political but also distinctly physical, with the movement working to "embody" the experience of the New Jew. The vision of the New Jew, developed in opposition to the diasporic experience, was set with a sense of self-reliance—both physically and otherwise—informed by geographical and political circumstances, such as the escalation of antisemitism and the blooming of nationalist movements, as well as socialist ideology in Europe. Therefore, as national autonomy for the Jewish community came to fruition in the mid-nineteenth century, it was inextricably intertwined with an admiration for a strong and healthy body.

FIGURE 11. Borer dances hanging from a harness in *ANA*. (Photographed by Tamara Erde. Courtesy of Tamar Borer.)

Much has been written about the juxtaposition of nation-building and the body in a Zionist context, as well as about the gendered aspect of this "muscular Judaism."[6] Yet, as Meira Weiss claims, most of the critical discourse about the formative years of the Zionist movement (and subsequently early Israeli society) ignores a "no less important physical characteristic: the idealization of health, power, and perfection." Weiss coined the term "the chosen body" for this trope, as culture lauded visions of the masculine, the Jewish, the Ashkenazic, the wholesome and, of course, the physically able.[7] Bodily "perfection"—as defined by physical fitness and abledness—might seem obvious and understandable in the context of a society built around the (imagined or real) shared experiences of living under constant military threat.[8] This idealized image of the "chosen body," however, permeates almost every aspect of Israeli society, from Israel's inception as a nation-state to the present day.[9] It is in this space—the space in which the healthy, abled body is glorified—that Tamar Borer creates. The presence of her culturally unwelcomed disabled body, therefore, interrupts and disrupts the sociocultural processes of molding and regulating the faultless Zionist body.

Three decades have passed since Elizabeth Grosz's innovative book *Volatile Bodies: Toward a Corporeal Feminism*, which aimed to move the body from the periphery to the center of analysis, "so it can now be understood as the very 'stuff' of subjectivity."[10] Her project, as well as many other feminist approaches to the body, had an enormous effect on scholarly work about Israeli culture (mainly represented in Hebrew literature and Israeli cinema).[11] Nevertheless, most of these eminent efforts ignore the disabled body.[12] Israeli negation of the disabled body, and especially women's disabled bodies, becomes even more noticeable in the absence of visible bodily difference and disability in Israeli culture, especially in Israeli dance and performance. There are indeed some exceptions, such as the dance companies Kol Demama (The Sound of Silence), established by Moshe Efrati, active between 1971 and 2001, Galgalbamagal (Wheel Circuit), founded in 2000, and Orly Baor's Hora Galgalim (Hora Wheels), founded in 1986 within the Disabled Veterans Organization of the Israeli Defense Forces, featuring disabled IDF male dancers in wheelchairs accompanied by nondisabled female dance partners.[13] There are specific programs and performances as well, such as Vertigo Dance Company's *The Power of Balance* (2001), which integrates abled and disabled dancers, and Nataly Zukerman's *35 Steps but Who Counts?* (2010) and *The Other Body* (2013), which addresses her limp and explores her "damaged" or "lacking" body. The Nalaga'at (Please Do Touch) Deaf-Blind Acting Ensemble was established in 2002. Additionally, in 2005, the 100% Art Festival was created by Michael Kirshenbaum, a professional dancer who uses a wheelchair. This festival includes original productions from a range of arts, such as fringe theater, music, dance, literature, poetry, visual arts, and more, presented by disabled and nondisabled artists. In 2006, Festival Tsamid (The Special Needs Festival), a creative arts festival featuring those with special needs, was established in Jerusalem and now takes place there annually.[14] Although these wonderful and important exceptions indicate a growing involvement and inclusion of disabled artists in Israeli culture, they still underscore the extent of exclusion, both because they constitute a tiny percentage of the productions in Israel and because they continue to be on the fringe of Israeli culture.[15]

The juxtaposition between Tamar Borer's dance and her disability, then, is more than a personal matter; it becomes the crux of a new cultural position that challenges the most fundamental notions of Israeli culture. In the work of Alison Kafer, the political framing of the body and its situational ability play a central role. As disability (and all of its social trappings) cannot occur in isolation, Kafer offers a relational model of disability. This model is inherently political, as it "makes room for more activist responses, seeing 'disability' as a potential site for collective reimagining."[16] Even though she focuses on the implications of this concept for disabled individuals, in practice, it actually comes to include various identities in the sequence of disabled and nondisabled. In other words, establishing disability as a category of political, social, and historical analysis not only serves to underscore the oppression of disabled peoples or even to pluralize the ways we think about bodily instability, it might also affect society's premises on a broader scale and inspire political transformation in spaces allegedly not related to disability, as is the case in Borer's juxtaposition between dance and the Israeli-Palestinian conflict.

If we add to that the notion that "disability itself has agency, intention, and power," we might look into ways in which disability is not a condition to overcome or adjust to, but rather a starting point for radical social change.[17] In that same vein, Judith Butler encourages the exploration of the relation between vulnerability and political agency.[18] In her discussion of vulnerability and resistance, she proposes that "once we see how vulnerability enters into agency, then our understanding of both terms can change."[19] Vulnerability and agency are not terms of a distinctive binary; rather, they serve as two aspects of "an embodied critique of violence."[20] Vulnerability becomes a political effect that "acts on and through bodies."[21] Hence, the association of vulnerability and victimization does not always ring true, and in fact, it might also constitute (or act out) a form of agency that overcomes injurability.[22]

For the disability scholar, activist, and filmmaker Simi Linton, the voices of artists with disabilities "will need to be admitted into the canon" in order to create significant social change.[23] In a consideration of the political potential of disability to challenge society on numerous levels, Tamar Borer's art becomes a fascinating case study; she not only seeks entry into the canon as a performer, but does so by challenging and working to redefine our understanding of canonization in the first place. In the following pages I explore the ways in which Borer's personal and social vulnerability creates political resistance, and how her disabled (and at times vulnerable) experiences come to act out political agency. In particular, the implications of (a lack of) agency associated with the disabled body become important in both an artistic dancerly context and an Israeli political one. By inviting us to release the reins of power and rethink our sense of stability, Borer's work constructs an existential and choreographic stance that becomes an innovative political suggestion.

"Wounding the Wall"

In 2010 Tamar Borer and the Jewish Israeli photographer Tamara Erde produced *ANA*, a performance piece that depicts the personal, geographical, and political journey of an Israeli woman who cannot avoid confronting and exploring the brutal reality of the Israeli-Palestinian conflict and the Israeli occupation. For Borer and Erde, the artistic and emotional journey required for the production of *ANA* also required an actual journey: to various Palestinian areas occupied by Israel. They construct their performance by coalescing dance, performance, and video art. In the show, Borer performed on the stage while Erde's documentaries, filmed during their roaming, were also presented.

In *ANA* one cannot separate the human body from the land itself. Borer's body, wrapped in wool fabric sheets, is transformed into a vigorous primeval landscape. This vibrant topography of spirit and nature stands at the center of *ANA*. Throughout the show the land trembles, exploring its own texture, studying its own movement, and contemplating itself.

The viewer is almost drawn into this spiritual exploration of the land when a quiet murmur begins to sound. While rediscovering its existence, Tamar Borer—that is, the land—repeatedly recites lines from a poem by Mahmoud Darwish (1941–2008), an acclaimed Palestinian poet and peace activist.

> The longer you gaze at the rose wounding the wall,
>   and you shall say there is hope to be redeemed of the sand,
>   then your heart will turn greener.[24]

These somewhat enigmatic lines capture the complexity of Borer and Erde's project. "In our minds," they testify, "one should linger while gazing at the rose's beauty, at the deep wounds of the wall, and at the belief in the possibility of being reborn."[25] The political context of the land is added to its existential dimension. This spiritual exploration is thus entwined with the concrete political condition in Israel and the Palestinian occupied territories. Political reality merges with the essence of nature (and vice versa), compelling the audience and the performers to confront their own position in the world in general, and in the Israeli-Palestinian conflict in particular. Borer and Erde explained: "With the work *ANA*, we try to relate to the political condition in Israel, from within the personal, subjective point of view. . . . We took a resolute decision and chose to talk straight and directly about the situation. We, as artists who have adopted the goal of looking at reality in a clear, unflinching way, feel it is our duty to express our view of the occupation, discrimination, and the plunder taking place in this land, with a profound hope for change."[26]

They thus ascribe political power to their artistic project. The creative act enables them to actively observe the conflicted political reality. Paradoxically, it is thus the fiction of art that allows them to confront reality and overcome the walls of political rhetoric that allow and shape national injustices.

Tamar Borer's political voice is striking, considering the fact that Israeli dance tends to overlook the Israeli-Palestinian conflict.[27] In order to observe reality in "a clear, unflinching way," Borer and Erde did not seek history books but rather went on a psycho-political journey to disputed borders, walls, and abandoned villages and towns, as well as to populated, living zones. They filmed in places such as Abu Dis, an East

Jerusalem suburb, Hebron, a Palestinian city located in the southern West Bank, and the Gaza Strip, a self-governing Palestinian territory on the eastern coast of the Mediterranean Sea that is blockaded by Israel. In this way, Borer and Erde became both the active set of the performance and the essence of its exploration. These towns embody the Israeli occupation and its disastrous impact on the Palestinian people. Although as Jewish Israelis Borer and Erde do not voice a Palestinian perspective, they document and look directly into the suffering of the Palestinian population caused by the Israeli occupation, the military checkpoints, and illegal Israeli settlements.

Furthermore, and of no less importance, those zones of contention, which are largely invisible to most Israelis, are placed at the center of the performance. When they are projected on huge, wall-length-sized screens, it becomes impossible to ignore the existence of this political catastrophe. Those documentary images, thus, impel the audience to confront the political reality of the occupation. One of the many ways in which violence is normalized is by distancing it from public view, so by bringing to the fore images of those Palestinians villages, Borer and Erde subvert the mechanism that enables harsh political acts. In other words, by presenting the concrete reality—and not the vague history—of these places, they unveil the oppression and its instruments.

Borer and Erde's journey is accompanied by the voice of Darwish, the Palestinian poet. In the performance, when Borer cites Darwish's poem (excerpted above), she does so in Hebrew, not in its original Arabic. Borer and Erde do not just examine actual political borders, they also explore the boundaries of their personal and collective thoughts and imagination. In other words, they examine the language in which they participate, a language that is always, by definition, politically tainted by preconceptions, stereotypes, and ideologies. They turn to the translation of Arabic into Hebrew to search for and express what lies outside of contemporary Israeli thought. As Jacques Derrida declared: "My language, the only one I hear myself speak and agree to speak, is the language of the other."[28] Even though here he refers to different historical events and to the Franco-Maghrebian identity, his approach to language influences Borer and Erde's attempt to move between languages—just as they move between mediums and places—as well as their effort to extend our vision as the audience. This is because, when approaching the language of the other ("at once invisible and almost impassable"), Derrida reminds us, "this is the strange and troubling part, the other as the nearest neighbor. *Unheimlich* [uncanny]."[29]

In one of the scenes in *ANA*, Borer dances in front of an enormous video clip that shows her placing notes on a wall. This video was first presented in a previous artistic collaboration between Borer and Erde entitled *Isaura Hun* (2009).[30] This work presents dreams, each addressing a different psychological and corporeal interest, represented by five dancers onstage: Borer, the dreamer, and four other dancers—Vera Goldman, Michal Gil, Yousef Swaid, and Roi Sandrovich—who act out various aspects of Borer's dreams. The work deals with themes of imprisonment inspired by Darwish's poem "A State of Siege":

> In siege, life is the time
> between the remembrance of its beginning
> and the forgetfulness of its end.[31]

The sense of siege in *Isaura Hun* (and later in *ANA*) is manifested through the documentation of the deserted spaces and the living conditions in the Palestinian villages behind the Separation Wall. At the same time, *Isaura Hun* presents personal existential dreams and anxieties buried deep in the unconscious. As in *ANA*, the performance occurs both on video and onstage, thus creating an intense tension between the spiritual, abstract, and fictional dream atmosphere and the documentaries (and staged documentaries) reflecting the ferocious political reality.

The video with Borer placing notes on a wall is part of "The Imprisonment" dream. Interestingly, the *Isaura Hun* version of the video clip uses different music than in *ANA*. The soundtrack of the dream in *Isaura Hun* is the well-known Israeli song "Yerushalim shel zahav" ("Jerusalem of Gold"), written by Naomi Shemer in 1967. After the Six-Day War, Shemer added a final verse to the song to celebrate Jerusalem's reunification after almost two decades of Jordanian control. The new version became a sort of a Zionist hymn and is considered to be one of the most popular songs among Jewish Israelis to the present day.[32] While the ideological resonance of the song is incorporated into *Isaura Hun*, by locating it in the contexts of their photographic journey Borer and Erde challenge some of its major conceptions. Shemer's song voices a Zionist perspective that celebrates what it considers the unification of Jerusalem, whereas Borer and Erde's context expresses a different Israeli perspective. This viewpoint sees the 1967 "unification" as a defining moment in the Israeli occupation, and it is concerned with the political, cultural, and ethical consequences of this historical moment.

Moreover, the wall in the video clip in the background is greatly reminiscent of the Kotel (the Western Wall), but in fact it was shot from the Palestinian side of the Separation Wall in Abu Dis, a Palestinian town bordering Jerusalem. Visitors to the Kotel customarily place a note with a prayer or request into the cracks of the ancient wall. In a provocative manner, Borer inserts her notes—actually small bags of spices—into the cracks of the Separation Wall (also known as the Israeli West Bank Wall), which was built by Israel in 2002 to separate Palestinians of the West Bank from Israel—linking it symbolically to the Western Wall (figure 12). In fact, many members of the Israeli audience experience it as the Western Wall, and hence are forced to project their warm feelings and hopes associated with the Kotel to the Separation Wall, prompting them to rethink its meanings and implications.

Borer's onstage dance integrates with the video, which is projected onto the back wall of the stage, and we see her leaning against the wall, as if trying to hold or lift it, and then slowly putting her hands in her pockets, pulling out her notes, and throwing them in despair and fatigue. Deborah Friedes Galili suggests that Borer's arms in this scene are raised in a gesture that reads alternately as a plea or a surrender.[33] Borer's unique bodily position is very interesting, as she sways firmly, neither sitting nor lying down. She is acting out the collapse of the wall, the imagined cultural moment in which the wall, with everything it represents, ceases to exist. Moreover, she embodies the Kotel and the Separation Wall as an extension of her own disabled body, thus revising the cultural and political significance of both. In other words, Borer invites us to think about the unification of Jerusalem or about the Separation Wall as a kind of a "new body," a prosthesis in the sense of David Wills's *Prosthesis*, in which the prosthesis is "about nothing if not placement, displacement, substituting, setting, amputating, supplementing."[34]

Conflating the Western Wall and the Separation Wall, hope and despair, as well as the ancient and the contemporary, provokes our encounter with a complex and dense political reality, and hence

FIGURE 12. Borer inserts a small white bag resembling a note in the wall in *Isaura Hun*. (Photographed by Tamara Erde. Courtesy of Tamar Borer.)

encourages us to rethink our own political, emotional, and existential position. By blurring the boundaries between one of the most sacred places for the Jewish people and one of the central symbols of hostility, Borer and Erde create a unique cultural space for Israelis to reflect upon their own walls of hope, anticipation, and expectation, as well as upon walls of hatred, anger, and aggression that separate and alienate them from each other and from their Palestinian neighbors. To adopt Derrida's notion of the lie as containing the potential to ruin the credit of rhetoric, the artificial, fictional, performative gesture of placing the two walls together unveils and ruins the rhetoric of the occupation, of Israeliness in the 2000s.[35]

The Disabled Angel of History: Disability and the National Abled Bodies

Whenever I'm on wheels . . . I come to know the intimate geography of a place.

—Julia Watts Belser

FIGURE 13. Image from *Isaura Hun*. (Photographed by Tamara Erde. Courtesy of Tamar Borer.)

In 2003, Tamar Borer engaged in a performance called *Gaza*, cochoreographed and performed with Inge Zommer, the Norwegian-born Israeli dancer. *Gaza* takes up the reality of the occupation and addresses the tension between fundamental existential values and the terror and occupation. The piece is divided into four sections, each focusing on a different key figure: a widow, a hedonistic female presence, Adam (man), and an angel. One of the most striking images within this performance is the magnificent white angel, designed by Shira Borer, Tamar's sister, roaming the streets of Gaza in a wheelchair (figure 14). The angel onstage corresponds to the image of an angel in the lyrics of a song that runs throughout the show:

> Hovering
> over the mightiest [Aza, Gaza] city
> in the country,
> a silent angel,
> an angel sees
> fire.[36]

The image of an angel gazing upon a horrific scene brings to mind Walter Benjamin's angel of history from his "Theses on the Philosophy of History." A direct encounter of Borer with Benjamin's angel of history can be found in her cooperation with the scholar, curator, and documentary filmmaker Ariella Azoulay, in which Borer created the choreography for one part of Azoulay's 2000 film *The Angel of History*.[37]

As Benjamin examines Klee's 1920 painting *Angelus Novus*, he evaluates a visual representation of the angel of history, choosing this particular image to embody an "angel" whose "face is turned toward the past. Where we perceive a chain of events, he sees one single catastrophe which keeps piling wreckage upon wreckage and hurls it in front of his feet."[38]

The ability to see the destruction and the ruination, stripped of the forced narratives of restoration and innovation, serves as the basis of Benjamin's historiography. As Shoshanh Felman claims, "[The] 'Theses on the Philosophy of History,' written shortly before Benjamin's death in 1940, represent his ultimate rethinking of the nature of historical events and of the task of historiography in the face of the developments of the beginning of the Second World War."[39] She suggests that in this work Benjamin advances "a theory of history as trauma" in that it deals with the role of *the historian* of his era.[40]

FIGURE 14. Borer, adorned with white wings, resembles an angel in this image from *Gaza*. (Photographed by Efrat Turgeman. Courtesy of Tamar Borer.)

In this context, Borer reveals her artistic sensibilities as appealing to the role of *the artist* of his, her, or their era. If the poetic position depends on the exchanging of gazes between the artist and the world, how can an artist—like the open-eyed angel of history—express themself? What can an artist do when the gaze of nature is usurped by a vision of horrors and atrocities? When it is only catastrophe reflected back into those eyes, how can an artist work to shape an understanding of the appropriate medium, form, and language?

Whereas Benjamin leaves his angel frozen, unable to face his own era, Borer awakens hers, conjuring up a corporeal representation.[41] Her embodied reactions to wandering on the streets of Gaza in a wheelchair challenge the frozen gaze Benjamin uses to express his notions of traumatic histories.[42] In other words, Borer's angel of history offers another interpretation of historiography and activism stemming from the angel's disabled experiences.[43] Julia Watts Belser, a rabbi, scholar, and activist, argues that it is not enough to speak about disability only in terms of legalities or care; rather, she suggests that "communities need the insights that emerge out of disability experience, they need the voices, contributions, imaginings, and aspirations of people with disabilities. . . . Communities need the critical sensibility that comes from resisting ableism, from refusing the stare, from sloughing off stigma, from spitting out sentimentality and pity, from rejecting daily assaults of injustice and indignity, from claiming disability as a vibrant powerful source of possibility and pride."[44]

In this discourse that claims the power of disability to create social change, it is doubly important to note that *Gaza* was the first time in her career that Borer brought her wheelchair onstage. She explains that it made sense in this piece because of the angel's helplessness while hovering over Gaza; in spite of its inherent goodness, "the heavy stone lying on its wings" pulls the angel down, impeding its flight.[45] Borer stresses this point: "Gaza (Aza) in oxytone means mighty. I had a strong sense that I had to cry out to the people seemingly living like in a cage, like animals in this tragic conflict we live in. Everyone is unable to find common ground. From this place I felt that the wheelchair was very appropriate. The chair is also a kind of a cage and a very extroverted definition of limitation, helplessness and inability."[46]

Borer's depiction of the wheelchair as a cage captures a visceral, lived experience illustrating the tremendous shift in her own physical capacities. My analysis, however, offers a different interpretation that does not make the wheelchair into a symbol of weakness. Rather, I believe that the wheelchair stimulates conceptual and political alternatives. This approach is highly influenced by various disabled dancers who have thoroughly critiqued existing cultural tropes of a wheelchair as something that traps or deadens a person. These dancers and dance companies—such as Candoco Dance Company, AXIS Dance Company, and Stopgap Dance Company—use their wheelchairs and bodies to very different effect.[47] Thus Borer's angel gives up its privileged position and its heightened perspective, allowing itself to experience Gaza from the position of a wheelchair. Perhaps for the first time in the history of Israel and Israeli dance, Israeliness enters Gaza in a wheelchair, and the glorified abled Zionist body gives way to a different position.[48]

Borer offered this artistic representation in 2003: two years after 9/11, three years after Israel withdrew from Lebanon, and after the failure of diplomatic negotiations at the 2000 Camp David Summit. She offers vulnerability as a political point of departure during the Second Intifada, also known as the Al-Aqsa Intifada. As Borer works to bring her performance to the stage, the State of Israel conducts Mivtza Homat Magen (literally, "Operation Defensive Wall") in 2002, and it begins to build the Separation Wall. In such a conflicted political environment, what does it mean to visit Gaza in a wheelchair?

"Whenever I'm on wheels," says Julia Watts Belser, "I come to know the intimate geography of a place."[49] Being in a wheelchair requires full physical and emotional attention to the environment—to a misplaced stone, to a steep sidewalk, to a narrowed bypass. In his writings on spatial stories, Michel de Certeau claims that the "solar eye," the empowered gaze from the top of a skyscraper, cannot thwart the alternative spatial stories that emerge as a consequence of seeing from below with a gaze that is limited and blocked. This gaze from below both requires and enables alternative ways of experiencing space, making it possible to subvert the panoptic gaze.[50] Orly Lubin adds a gendered and political dimension to de Certeau's argument in her discussion of feminist/political stakes. She employs the term "low gaze" to challenge the (masculine) cultural positionality of the "high" and unfettered gaze. By allowing significant space for actual, concrete, mundane experiences, the low gaze challenges extensive historical narratives and becomes a disruptive force in national justifications. The low gaze is limited by the eye's receptive abilities and by spatial elements, making it a gaze focused upon space, not time.[51] The low gaze does not erase time; rather, it experiences space as it appears only after time has been etched into it. It recognizes that time cannot be fixed and that only space can be repaired. Since one cannot fix what was—only what is—the low gaze provides the space for potentially radical change, that is, "the space that the past is etched into."[52] In what might sound paradoxical to a Western abled ear, Lubin offers this modest position of limitation as a political device. By giving up any pretensions of changing time or atoning for the past, the low gaze provides a space for an assessment of limitations that might in fact foster radical change as it cannot evade accountability and responsibility.[53]

It is important to note that when Borer rejects the serene and static position of Benjamin's angel of history and puts in its place a variation of the low gaze—while the low gaze and the disabled experience are related, they are not parallel terms—she does not offer a subversive option to Zionism or to nationalism; in fact, she presents a much more radical position by renouncing the historical perspective in favor of the spatial one.[54] The national project is characterized by its attempts to establish memory and to ascribe historical context to the nation. The historical perspective, the rewriting of time, stages the nation as an integral part of a historical continuum that leads to the present. In other words, the past is narrated by the interests of the present as well as the aspirations engendered by the future. Incorporating gender and disability, Borer offers an experience of history through space rather than time. Rather than rebuilding the past by repossessing memory, she suggests employing the space, meaning working through the geopolitical space and what the past has engraved upon it. The low gaze of her angel of history lies in space; it sees Gaza as it is while he or she wanders within it.[55] Accordingly, the change it enacts is not to adjust the past, but rather to modify space in a way that will not erode the past or its implications. The national narrative is entwined with the historical; the one ratifies the other. Borer does not ignore this Gordian knot, but she does not embed herself within it either. Her project does not wish to anchor herself or her surroundings in history. Rather it reacts to, and illustrates, her political space, a space stained with all the etchings of the past within it, and thus creates a future of change.[56]

Consequently, it should probably not come as a surprise that despite Borer's astonishing performance and her sophisticated challenges represented through the juxtaposition of history, nationalism, and the body, her disabled angel was not received with open arms. The dancer, scholar, choreographer, and dance critic Ruth Eshel often writes about Borer's work, usually with sensitivity and sympathy, but her reaction to *Gaza* was fundamentally different. In her harsh (not to say vicious) newspaper review of *Gaza*, "On the Verge of Amateur," Eshel criticizes the banality of the show, its amateur dancers, and Borer's mediocre performance. If indeed, as Eshel herself states, she has been following Borer's career for over a decade, why did *Gaza* arouse such strong feelings of disgust and aversion? It seems that exposing Israeli vulnerability as well as negation of the performance's radical political potential are at stake here. As long as Borer is "a wretched young woman," identified as an artist who suffered personal trauma and loss, she deserves the attention of audiences and critics. But once she claims her disability and choreographs an alternative that challenges the abled national body, she is banished to the realm of the (female, disabled) "amateur."[57]

In sum, Zionist history is experienced as a sequence of events that lead to change, reconstruction, and a *tkuma* (recovery and revival). The Zionist healthy, vigorous body comes to symbolically represent the overcoming of historical obstacles by the Jewish nation and the fulfillment of the Zionist dream. Borer's work includes the insights and critical sensibility that emerge out of disability experience. She invites us to think about this Zionist dream in light of the disabled body, and hence prompts us to rethink national stability and national abled bodies.

5

"A SNIPER SHOT MY HAND"

Disability in Documentaries
About Occupied Palestine

Imagining Disability Justice for Palestine

Sins Invalid, founded in 2005 by Patricia Berne and Leroy F. Moore Jr., is a disability justice–based performance and movement-building project that centers disabled people of color as well as queer and gender-nonconforming individuals with disabilities. It has formulated and catalyzed disability justice as a distinct concept, articulating it as a social movement and organizing framework distinct from single-issue disability rights approaches. While these ideas have deep, complex roots in the work of many organizers and activists, Sins Invalid has been instrumental in naming and framing this paradigm through its art and performance.

In August 2014 Sins Invalid released a statement detailing their choice to cancel their participation in the Vancouver Queer Film Festival because "the festival had accepted advertising from an organization known for 'pinkwashing.'" This "Disability Justice for Palestine" statement was partially an acute reaction to the 2014 Gaza War, also known to Israelis as Operation Protective Edge—a military operation launched by Israel in July 2014 in the Gaza Strip, ruled by Hamas. The attack, one of the deadliest conflicts in the region in decades, resulted in many deaths and injuries, mostly Palestinians but some Israelis. It also caused the destruction of residential buildings in Gaza and impacted vital systems, causing damage to the supply of electricity, food, water, and medical equipment.

The statement of Sins Invalid, released together with a *Disability Justice for Palestine* video and the "To Exist is to Resist" graphic, expresses their opposition to "the occupation and mass murder of Palestinian people" and to the global effort to "pinkwash" Israel's image. The statement emphasizes the connection between state violence against Palestinians and subsequent disability: "Of the thousands wounded from this current assault [in Gaza], many will be permanently disabled in a place where the basic necessities of daily life are stopped at the border, and basic medicine . . . is beyond reach."[1]

This campaign not only referenced disabled Palestinians living under the Israeli occupation, it also highlighted the struggles of queer Palestinians and Palestinians who became disabled as a result of injuries sustained during the occupation, those "whose bodies most directly bear the burdens of occupation and state violence, and most obviously show its scars."[2]

Sins Invalid's statement, made by queer artists, poets, and performers with disabilities, centralizes disability within a geopolitical context and therefore addresses the connections between disability, global power dynamics, and geopolitical violence, simultaneously challenging the common notion of disability as ahistorical by directly addressing the violence in Gaza and its long-lasting results.[3] More specifically, the statement rejects any assumed separation between disability culture and questions of political justice for the Palestinian people; for Sins Invalid, sexuality, disability, and art are not only interconnected but inherently related to social justice. In other words, their perception of disability is not rooted solely in identity politics, but instead relates mainly to disability justice. Although disability is (or can be) an individual experience and identity, it is also inextricably interconnected to other intersections of political identity, such as (but not limited to) race, queerness, gender, national affiliation, geographical location, and other layers of experience. Thus the aims of disability justice are not only to uncover ableism or resist oppression, but also to seek out and address institutionalized ableism and question the ways in which disability interacts with white supremacy, male supremacy, enforced heteronormativity, settler colonialism, state violence, and so on, all in hopes of resisting and working against systemic oppression.[4] In the context of the present chapter, Sins Invalid addresses accessibility to nationhood as one of these axes of intersectionality. To quote Liat Ben-Moshe, "Having an inclusive movement is not just about wheelchair accessible gathering space. It is a much larger movement that needs to be cognizant of access, very broadly defined, including land use itself."[5] Access to the land—ownership of it, the right to travel through it, being able to traverse from rivers to seas, from city to city—as well as the ability to seek medical attention, spend time with family, and essentially enjoy opportunities and experiences that many are so cruelly cut off from: these issues of justice and access most certainly need to be considered and prioritized.

In this chapter, I embrace this call to action and investigate this tripartite commitment—to disability, to social justice in the context of Palestine, and to art—as expressed in Palestinian and Israeli documentaries that depict the experiences of people with disabilities in occupied Palestine. I am interested in the ways in which the directors (in this case, people who do not publicly identify as living with disability) both relate to and present disability, and what questions about the experience of living with disabilities in occupied Palestine they raise in their documentaries. At the same time, I also seek to trace discourse about the occupation that is evoked by the lived experiences of disabled people who are filmed (and who sometimes film themselves) in the same documentaries and to analyze how both the intersections and discrepancies in these representations can be brought to the fore. I aim to highlight questions about the broader issue of accessibility in the occupation by discussing the ways in which physical disability presents barriers and limitations. I intend also to underscore the importance of understanding cinematic moments of movement as another form of access in the Israeli occupation, as many of these documentaries showcase how often travel is viewed as a rare opportunity rather than as an intrinsic right.

Tamar Kay: *The Mute's House*

On Cameras, Schnitzel, and Political Domination

The Mute's House is a thirty-two-minute documentary directed by Jewish Israeli director Tamar Kay. The documentary was produced in 2015 as her final project at the Sam Spiegel Film and Television School in

Jerusalem. The film focuses on Sahar Rajabi, a deaf Palestinian, and her eight-year-old son Yousef, who was born with one hand and has mobility limitations. The two live in a building in Hebron that other Palestinian residents had to leave in 1997 following the signing of the Hebron Agreement (also known as the Protocol concerning the Redeployment in Hebron or Hebron Protocol), which divided Hebron into two parts: one under Israeli control and the other under Palestinian control.

The film offers a vignette into the life of Yousef, who moves between his home in the Jewish settlement in Hebron and the Palestinian area, where his school is located and where many of his friends and family members live. It follows Yousef's daily routine—from his journey to school and his interactions with Israeli soldiers at the checkpoint near his house—and focuses on his familial relationships, especially with his father, who is in and out of prison, and with his mother and uncle, with whom he communicates in sign language.

In one interview, Tamar Kay stated, "I'm not a political person, I am a people's person. . . . I still believe in human beings, in looking in another's face, in the potential of opening hearts and minds."[6] She echoes this sentiment in other interviews as well: "I'm a believer in human beings and I feel change does come from inside, from people understanding that the other side may not be so different. . . . I tried in this film in a metaphoric way to create a closeup—with all the chaotic narratives and stories [about Hebron]—and just to get to know one story, one family, one child."[7]

Indeed, despite the violent political reality underpinning the life of the Rajabi family, the film depicts a close, warm relationship between the Israeli director and the Palestinian subjects of her film; at times, the film itself feels like a small, tentative step toward change—a kind of small-scale vision of peace between the two peoples.

Given the built-in power dynamics inherent in the relationship between an adult Israeli director and a young Palestinian boy, Kay gives Yousef a camera. She states: "I made a decision that the film would be aware of itself, aware of the fact that it's a film. Hence, my voice will be present, the characters will ask me direct questions, even regarding the film itself. . . . My decision to break away from the traditional 'fly on the wall' filmmaking, along with reality (Yousef was fascinated by the camera from the beginning), led me to give Yousef his own camera, making him an active participant in the telling of his story."[8] However, despite good intentions to make Yousef an "active participant in the telling of his story," the reality of how he got the camera starkly presents the imbalanced nature of their dynamic. Yousef asks the photographer Zvi Landsman if his camera is new and if it came "with cardboard and everything." Kay then asks Yousef if he also wants a camera and in response, he points to the professional camera, clarifying, "Such a camera?" She replies, "No. A small camera. For you."

That unbalanced power dynamic inherent in the creation of the film is therefore echoed in the relationship between the two cameras in the film, between Yousef's "small camera" and the professional camera that guides the narrative of the film; it underscores Yousef's voice as an "official voice about Palestine but not of a Palestinian."[9] The lack of equality between the authority and control of the two cameras disrupts the notion of Kay's desire to empower Yousef as an "active participant": for now Yousef captures pieces of his life through the lens of his small camera while the director holds a professional camera, documenting his life and the impact of Kay's gift, before eventually editing the film, deciding what pieces of his story are most fit for the narrative she seeks to tell. Yousef's small camera, then, although meant to give him agency and power in the context of the filming, perhaps inadvertently serves as his "weapon of the weak," becoming a tool in the service of the Israeli director.[10] The so-called authenticity of his story, therefore, is undermined, revealing yet another story about Palestinians from a Jewish Israeli perspective.

Despite the Israeli appropriation of Yousef's camera, glimpses of his truths and his story manage to break through the Israeli lens, becoming highlights of the film. In one scene, Yousef wanders around his home filming. He shows Kay the goats they raise indoors. In Arabic, Kay asks him what they are and he answers, "It's *maaah maaah*," mimicking a goat bleating. Still in Arabic, she goes on to ask the names of the goats but Yousef replies in Hebrew that the goats have no names. After a moment, he smiles and makes a joke of naming the goats: "This is Hummus, this is Fūl [fava bean], and this is Schnitzel."

In this charming and childish way, Yousef inadvertently reveals the massive chasm between a Palestinian family who lives with its food animals and how Yousef imagines the experience of a Jewish Israeli child, who eats hummus, beans, and schnitzel. In naming the goats, he names the economic gap between a Palestinian child living with goats as a source of food ("It's *maaah maaah*") and an Israeli child whose food arrives on a dining table, prepared and ready for consumption. His simple joke actually highlights the chain of political and economic privileges enabling the sheer existence of schnitzel, such as open shops, working refrigerators, water supply, reliable electricity, and so forth, and thereby exposes the gaps and controlled dynamic between Israeli Jews and Palestinians.[11] Thus, in fact, Yousef testifies about the "unchilding" of Palestinian children by the Zionist enterprise. Nadera Shalhoub-Kevorkian, who coined the term, defines it as "the authorized eviction of children from childhood."[12] This process, as seen in the case of Yousef, "delegitimizes Palestinian children while simultaneously rewriting the pathways for Jewish national control not only over Palestinian land and space but also over the intimate spaces where children live: their homes, their schools, and even . . . their own bodies."[13]

In a way, this conversation refers back to the national-political power relations represented by the cameras. This dynamic—where Yousef speaks Hebrew and the director asks her questions in somewhat broken Arabic—challenges Tamar Kay's claims of being a "people's person" rather than "a political person," because the dialogue in this supposedly amusing scene about naming animals reveals Yousef's understanding of the relationship between him and the director, despite their closeness. Although the director asks questions in basic Arabic (Tamar Kay learned Arabic for this film), Yousef responds in her language of Hebrew, because she is the one in control of the situation. As a director she dictates his camera ("his" story), and as a Jewish Israeli she is in a position of privilege and dominance in almost every aspect of his life.

Gazing at the Occupation, Staring at Disability

The tension between Israeli and Palestinian narratives told through the lens of the camera weaves its way throughout the film, and often Yousef's perspective seems to haunt the film in spite of the director's obvious advantages in constructing the story. The director asks Yousef to film the Palestinian area of Hebron—an area that she and her photographer do not have access to as Israelis. Yousef wanders on the Palestinian side, enthusiastically photographing the houses and mostly deserted streets, sometimes coming across goats or people as well, as he excitedly exclaims, "Look at my camera, photographing the whole world!" At the end of this filmed excursion, Yousef comes to a room within a house and with an air of spontaneity, he dances on the bed, excited, lifting up his shirt to reveal his upper body, focusing on his one hand.

Tamar Kay's invitation to gaze at the occupation through Yousef's camera is therefore shifted by Yousef, morphing into an invitation to stare at his disabled body. Unlike gazing, an oppressive and subordinating act, staring, according to disability studies scholar Rosemarie Garland-Thomson, is not a one-way act but rather a starer/staree interaction, "an intense visual exchange that makes meaning."[14] Staring creates a mutual and interactive space that enables Yousef to introduce himself on his own terms. By presenting his visibly disabled body without shame, Yousef creates a deliberate and relatively safe space to communicate his identity—to both himself and his viewers.

In filming himself Yousef creates an open invitation to staring, presenting the reality of his disability and his life experience in occupied Palestine. The editing work done by Tamar Kay, however, shifts this powerful moment of connection and celebration; Kay connects the scenes with his other shots of the occupation, therefore drawing a connection between Yousef's disabled body and the Israeli occupation. Yousef's disability becomes a *symbol* of occupation through her editing. Thus Yousef's celebration of self, his call to stare at his disabled body, is effectively turned on its head by the director's ableist gaze, molding an ableist symbol out of a real-life experience.

Kay uses this cinematic device to criticize the occupation, but she does so in an inherently ableist manner; in an ableist society, disability is perceived as a deficit or lack and so becomes a useful symbol to describe the occupation—another "problem" within the "abnormal" national condition. The film draws a parallel between what Tamar Kay calls the "surreal situation"—the "abnormal" life of Yousef and his family, as well as the lives of many other Palestinians—and Yousef's "abnormal" body.[15] Somewhat patronizingly, she calls for the audience to understand that "the other side may not be so different," yet through her actions in directing and editing, *The Mute's House* ends up speaking over Yousef's own filmed story, simultaneously erasing the actual experience of disability from Yousef and his family, using it instead as a narrative prosthesis.[16]

The Journey to Jaffa

What makes the aspect of disability-as-symbol so much more noteworthy, however, is its manifestation in an earlier iteration of the film. In 2012, Tamar Kay prepared a sixteen-minute human interest documentary feature as part of her studies at the Sam Spiegel Film and Television School—a piece that also focuses on the story of the Rajabi family.[17]

The approach to deafness in this feature, however, seems to have a very different tone than the film—one that is markedly less political and more patronizing. The emphasis on the deaf members of the Rajabi family speaking sign language is undercut by the focus on "touching" moments, such as Sahar and Yousef going to watch a performance by deaf and blind actors in the Na Laga'at Center in Jaffa in December 2011, a trip coordinated by the Israeli production team. Basically, the entire feature is fraught with paternalistic "feel-good" undercurrents that place it squarely within that voyeuristic, ableist genre of "fulfilling a dream for the disabled." This genre works with the intention to evoke compassion for disabled people, but often does so at the expense of dignity; it relies on feelings of pity and superiority in nondisabled people who "enable" a disabled person to realize a dream. Oftentimes, that "dream" is simply an ableist fantasy that assumes the value of an experience for a disabled person who might not necessarily find it as meaningful or as useful it is intended to be.

In the particular case of the Rajabi family, this skewed representation of disability, already rife with paternalism and condescension, coincides with a sense of privilege that the Israeli filming contingent can provide in aiding Palestinians on this journey from Hebron to Jaffa. As Palestinians are prevented from moving freely between Jaffa and Hebron because of the occupation, Tamar Kay and her crew not only enable passage but, in some warped sense, seem proud to "allow" them this opportunity, which compounds the problematic nature of this feature.

In one scene, Tamar Kay gives Rasmiya, Sahar's sister who is also deaf from birth, the permits to move from Hebron to Jaffa, and it is Kay who narrates the voice-over, dramatically intoning: "Today they are carrying documents they have never seen before of official exit papers from Hebron on which their names are written." This journey is described as exciting and happy for the Rajabi family and the narration of events lacks any self-awareness about the blatant injustice inherent in issues of travel for Palestinians and in deploying an ableist, charity model of disability, which is expressed in the cinematic expectation that the viewers will be deeply moved by the "kindness" of the Israeli production team toward this poor, disabled family. The narrative of disability in this feature is not used to help educate on issues pertaining to disability or to promote disability justice; instead, the story the filmmakers tell upholds and inadvertently venerates the framework of oppressive geopolitical injustice. Furthermore, the emphasis on travel permits and the way they are presented not only demonstrates the production team's arrogance, it also highlights their relative economic and political privilege; the ease with which the Israeli crew is able to secure permits stands in stark contrast to the harsh day-to-day reality of travel for most Palestinians, who do not have such access.

"It's Scary Here"

One of the emotional peaks of the 2012 feature, in which the production team clearly overlooked problematic political and ableist moments communicated in their filming and editing, deserves this same criticism. The clip shows Yousef and his mother in attendance at the Na Laga'at performance, which features a cast of deaf, blind, and deaf and blind actors. The camera narrows in on Yousef and Sahar as one of the actresses in the performance speaks in the background: "I asked my father why am I deaf? He told me it's from God. The problem is that when I'm alone and people knock on the door I cannot hear them and know if there are people outside. Sometimes this scares me." Editing the close-up on Sahar together with the actress's lines (figure 15) inextricably links the actress's experiences with Sahar's; the editing assigns these emotions and experiences to Sahar. But just as *The Mute's House* inadvertently undercuts Yousef's own claiming of his disability and shifts away from the narrative he initiates in filming such a moment, here too is a moment where Sahar's direct words from earlier create a more complicated, nuanced, and intense counternarrative to the one the director Tamar Kay tells.

At the beginning of the clip, Sahar speaks in sign language: "I have lived in this building for seven years, since I got married. My husband used to live with us and then he left for Palestine Hebron. It's scary here so I prefer to stay at home. When [Israeli] soldiers come, asking questions, or when [Jewish] settlers throw rocks, I send Yousef down and he tells them that there is nobody home" (figure 16).

While the actress's lines give the audience a clear but generalized sense of the existential anxiety felt by a deaf woman living her life in a world made for hearing, the anxiety and terror Sahar describes when she speaks directly is much more concrete and specific: a fear of Israeli soldiers and settlers in the midst of an unstable political situation experienced by a woman with intersecting positions of social vulnerability.[18] Sahar is deaf, a Palestinian, a battered woman, and a single parent; these intersections so clearly articulated in the clip at the beginning of the film depict the real-life experience of a human living in constant fear related to very specific vulnerabilities along the axes of gender, disability, and nationality.

The editing of the film actively attempts to undermine this colossal distinction by assigning a broader sense of fear to Sahar in this moment; it neutralizes specific experiences that juxtapose disability and state violence perpetrated by Israel. Once more we see disability appropriated to symbolize the injustices of the occupation, situating the narrative in a firmly Jewish perspective; the film takes concrete and real fears and portrays them with an almost abstracted political wrongness.

Indeed, in an interview with Nirit Anderman about *The Mute's House*, Tamar Kay states: "I really did not want to make a film that would talk about Hebron and the occupation, things I can no longer see. I wanted experiential observation and felt that Yousef could be a good storyteller in this context."[19] Kay's insistence on "experiential *observation*" subverts Yousef's agency as a storyteller even as she helps to "share" his story, and here, the dubious honor of the *possibility* of being "a good storyteller in this context" undermines the charm and naivety that Yousef demonstrates on-screen, subtly shifting the attention back to his disability-as-narrative-prosthesis once more. In a similar way, by withholding Sahar's experience, Kay neutralizes and sanitizes disability by stripping it from its lived experience. She thus turns it into a symbol that

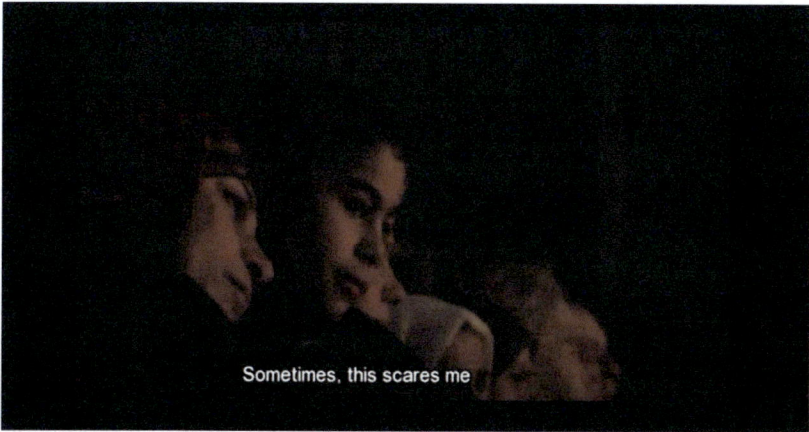

FIGURE 15. Sahar and Yousef Rajabi during the Na Laga'at performance in Tamar Kay's short film *Hebron* (2012).

FIGURE 16. Sahar Rajabi in her home, featured in Tamar Kay's short film *Hebron* (2012).

allows her to make a film about Hebron and Jaffa supposedly removed from the context of the occupation.

In contrast to this symbolic representation of disability, depicting it as a real-life experience of Palestinians living under Israeli occupation allows for the exploration and deconstruction of the mechanisms that sustain the injustices of occupation. The rest of the chapter will focus on this real-life approach to disability, examining how Palestinian directors Mohammad Bakri and Ramzi Maqdisi take more substantial steps toward this goal in their respective documentaries.

Mohammad Bakri: *Jenin, Jenin*

"The Silent Cry"

The documentary *Jenin, Jenin*, directed by the prominent Palestinian Israeli actor and filmmaker Mohammad Bakri, was filmed in the Jenin refugee camp in the occupied West Bank right after the IDF's 2002 military operation in the camp. In the film, the tale of the camp's destruction is told by its inmates, many of whom lost loved ones and are still living among the debris of the attack, which Jewish Israelis called Operation Defensive Shield.

The film includes testimonies from Jenin residents immediately following the Israeli incursion, and it opens with the testimony of a man who is mute as he runs through the ruins of Jenin; his story is told through sign language and body gestures. Throughout the film we meet him a few more times, although his name—like the names of most who testify in the film—remains unknown to us. Various scholars have referred symbolically to his muteness, arguing that he symbolizes the conflicted struggle of needing to testify about the atrocity while being unable to communicate it thoroughly. Muteness therefore comes to symbolize the limitation of the testimony at the heart of the film. Hamid Dabashi suggests that "in a sense, the deaf and dumb man is Palestine: having witnessed but not able to bear witness to the crime he has seen. He has to invent, to will, a language, to speak out against a massive propaganda machinery that denies its very existence."[20] Yael Ben-Zvi Morad notes that silence is a recurring theme in Palestinian cinema; there is a marked "silent cry" in the face of difficult events; paradoxically, the Palestinian national story is told through silence.[21] Yael Friedman offers a similar interpretation. She explains that a critical element of the Palestinian national narrative is the ethos of resistance movement, which was shaped by Palestinian calls for national liberation as early as the 1960s and 1970s. In this narrative, the second generation of the Nakba (the 1948 Palestinian Catastrophe) needs to repair the initial mistake of the Nakba generation, that is, their escape and surrender. Friedman locates the character who is mute within this ethos, but comes to understand him through the proxy of a highly verbal girl in the film. Without fear, the girl—the representative of the second generation—speaks the words he cannot utter.[22]

These interpretations offer a symbolic understanding of the character who is mute that is deeply rooted in ableism. People who are mute are by no means "silent"—they often communicate by using sign language, vocalizations, bodily gestures, and so on—but these interpretations seem bent on understanding the muteness of this man in *Jenin, Jenin* as deficient, as unable to express at all what the girl and the other witnesses in the film express in words, as lacking the agency to tell his own story.

Instead of referring to him as a person who signs, these interpretations refer to him as someone who doesn't speak. While I do not rule out the possibility that the director of the film intentionally set the stage for this interpretation of symbolic representation, it seems clear that the identity of the person who is mute can be treated neutrally—we should not assume a symbolic meaning to his muteness. After all, people who are mute live in Jenin, so it only makes sense that they are included in the numbers of those who testify in the film. But more significantly, we can understand Mohammad Bakri's choice to open the film with this specific testimony not as an evidence of Bakri's symbolic understanding of disability, but rather as an artistic and political (conscious or unconscious) choice that directs the audience to engage with and investigate questions of the lived experience of disabled people. And if so, the film actually calls on us to examine the life experiences of Palestinians with disabilities under occupation, while also exploring, in part, how these various narratives can help us better understand occupation.[23]

The Right to Maim

Jenin, Jenin opens with this specific testimony, but it is not the only narrative of disability or injury that the film examines. Another unnamed woman tells the story of an IDF soldier shooting at her feet: at the time, she was eight months pregnant and deeply worried about the safety of herself and her children during the attack, so she ran with her children to the safety of her brother-in-law's house. On the way, a sniper positioned on a hill shot at her feet and hit his target. Wounded, she cried for help and her relatives picked her up and took her to the hospital, where her baby was delivered via caesarean section. Although the baby was born healthy, her injury compromised her health so she was unable to take care of him for a while.

An elderly man interviewed at the hospital tells his own similar story of being fired upon by an IDF soldier: "I was sleeping, when at midnight, I heard the loud speakers ordering us to gather in the school courtyard. I dressed and went outside. On my way, at about one and a half meters away, a sniper shot my hand from a window. I fell to the ground, under shock. The soldier ordered me to get up and go away. I told him I couldn't get up, he then threatened to kill me, after which he shot me again in the foot." These testimonies stand in stark contrast to the interpretations of "muteness as a symbol" for the inability to express the national catastrophe of occupation, as they bear witness to both the cruelty of the occupation and the implementation of a particularly horrific militaristic tool of the Israeli occupation, a mechanism that Jasbir K. Puar called "the right to maim."[24]

Puar argues that the Israeli military injures Palestinians as part of a tactical strategy to enforce rule. By shooting to maim instead of to kill, Israeli power becomes visible on the Palestinian body. The deliberate debilitation of a population is carried out to maintain Israeli control over Palestinian people and lands, and many Palestinians become permanently disabled without access to the resources they need to achieve autonomy.[25] Puar uses the term *debility* (not "disablement") to emphasize a type of injury that is endemic—a sanctioned tactic that becomes part and parcel of biopolitical population control.[26] The right to maim is "the weaponization of debilitation," the conscious political choice to make certain populations disabled in order to maintain oppressive dynamics.[27] The right to maim thus is not a byproduct of the occupation but one of its deliberate mechanisms to maintain control.[28] Tanya Reinhart also discusses "Israel's systematic policy of injuring Palestinians," pointing out that "specially trained Israeli units . . . shoot [Palestinians] in a calculated manner in order to cripple, while keeping the statistics of Palestinians killed low."[29] As Liat Ben-Moshe explains, since the IDF (or the U.S. in Afghanistan) supposedly does not aim to kill Palestinians with their shots, maiming "makes Israel seem humanitarian, while justifying occupation and settler colonialism."[30]

Unlike other disability scholars in the Global North who address disability as a universal and inevitable condition of life, Puar discusses disability as something that is *done* to people by other people; disability is something *produced*—a deliberate product of exploitation within a biopolitical context. Similarly, Dina Kiwan argues that decolonizing disability is crucial for our understanding of citizenship, as it underscores how disability has been created in the Global South to exclude certain groups from being recognized as human and as citizens.[31] It is within this context that Puar pushes back against the tendency to consider disability mainly as a source of pride, claiming that this approach "does not take into account the politics of debilitation that render some populations as definitively unworthy of health and targeted for injury."[32] Purposeful or intended debilitation as a means of subduing or controlling a population, therefore, is viewed outside the normal boundaries of conversations on ableism, pride, and disability, as other concerns, rooted in geopolitical conflict or oppression, become the focus of Puar's work.

The Demonstration at the Jalame Checkpoint

Mohammad Bakri's focus on the specific acts and tactical decisions that caused the destruction in Jenin, and especially on the soldiers' targeted shootings (their "right to maim") may also be related to his own life experiences. In his 2005 documentary *Since You Left* (*Min Yum Mahrucht*) Bakri tells about the event that motivated him to film *Jenin, Jenin*:

> We went, me and Valentina, my "daughter" [in Federico García Lorca's play *The House of Bernarda Alba* performed at the AL-Maiden theater in Nazareth] . . . to a demonstration that took place north of Jenin, at the Jalame checkpoint. We were hundreds of people, Arabs and Jews. An Israeli soldier passed by us and began shooting at us. Valentina was hurt. She was standing beside me. And I went nuts. I said: if the soldier passes by and shoots at us like that, when we are standing, how will he behave inside, in Jenin? It was at that moment that I decided to enter Jenin with a film camera.[33]

In January 2021, about sixteen years after Bakri discussed his moment of resolve and determination in *Since You Left*, the Pluralistic Spiritual

Center in Neve Shalom conducted a virtual interview with him. Bakri retold the story of the shooting at the demonstration, but this time he added specific details. Bakri said that the weapon fired at demonstrators was an M16 rifle and that he suspected the IDF soldier had been targeting him specifically, as he is a well-known figure in Israel for his activism. Bakri also shared details about Valentina's injury, describing how he witnessed the bullet striking her elbow at close range, with her blood splashing on him.[34]

It took Bakri a decade and a half to process and articulate the trauma and its consequences, but he has used this experience of witnessing firsthand the geopolitical production of debility among Palestinians through direct and deliberate shooting to guide his filming, interviews, and editing of *Jenin, Jenin*. In other words, being the presumed target of an IDF soldier's bullet and subsequently witnessing an injury caused by IDF gunfire (not knowing whether it was intended to kill or injure) gave him direct, concrete exposure to the tactic of deliberate shooting guided by these violent strategies. Thus, Bakri is both the director who has painstakingly documented and catalogued the testimonies of the victims in Jenin and an individual who has testimony of his own to give regarding the "right to maim." His commitment is not to giving a broad overview of the occupation more generally, but instead to document the specific mechanisms of oppression and violence—some of which he has experienced firsthand—that reinforce the occupation.

Disability as a Political Force

Bakri has processed his personal experience as part of a broader Palestinian one—the individual event that he suffered through and his private thoughts on that no longer belong solely to himself but to a wider national group. He redirected these experiences into his work as an artist and activist, using film to depict a multitude of personal testimonies whose tellers remain mostly unnamed, possibly in an attempt to weave them into a larger Palestinian narrative. The compilation of testimonies in *Jenin, Jenin* stands, then, as a means of Palestinian national recollection through the creation of a political film of resistance, a visual "J'accuse" that at its heart aims to expose the violence inherent in the IDF's arsenal of weapons and methods of attack[35]

Haim Bresheeth argues that while *Jenin, Jenin* contextualizes the events in Jenin within the context of the Nakba, because it is yet another link in a chain of traumatic events that echo the founding national trauma, the film also posits that what Palestinians are experiencing currently is even worse.[36] This positioning of the film relies on an understanding of *Jenin, Jenin*—as well as other Palestinian films from that period, such as *Chronicle of a Disappearance* (Elia Suleiman, Europe and Palestine, 1996), *1948* (Mohammad Bakri, Israel, 1998), and *Ustura* (Nizar Hassan, Israel, 1998)—as "trauma agents," or socio-cinematic mechanisms for processing the manifold traumas in Palestinian society that originated from the Nakba and the years of continuous occupation.[37]

However, I argue that certain testimonies, such as the ones of the elderly man and the woman in *Jenin, Jenin*, move away from the discourse of trauma and the association of present atrocities as a repetition or reembodiment of the Nakba and instead shift the discussion to a new political context, focusing upon the IDF's current and evolving techniques for preserving and maintaining the occupation and therefore controlling Palestinians.

Many times, depictions of disability link it with passivity, with an absence of agency—which, in this case, renders Palestinian lives legible and grievable.[38] As Laura Jordan Jaffee shows, "Palestinians become grievable only when portrayed as apolitical objects of pity, via depictions that reinforce dominant assumptions about disability, not subjects fighting for autonomy."[39] The manner in which *Jenin, Jenin* both exposes Israel's state-sanctioned violence and categorizes it as tactical disabling—a method of sustaining the occupation by disabling Palestinians and restraining resistance—also defies outside labeling of that disability. In other words, Bakri's representation does not preserve the perception of disability as a political inferiority, but rather makes disability itself a political force. The Palestinian maimed body becomes a visible marker of the invisibility of impairment production. Disability is thus not only real and material, it carries a powerful demand for justice in the face of the injustices of geopolitical power.[40]

The Palestinian debilitated body, thus, reclaims its disability not as an individual identity (as is the case in many approaches to disability in the Global North) but as a political apparatus that testifies to political injustice.[41] Demanding transnational justice for impairment, explains

Karen Soldatic, might seem problematic for the disability movement, but it is in fact a solid part of a larger global claim to intervene in injustices with the hope of transforming geopolitical dynamics of power. In these cases, impairment is not an individualized claim that assumes deficit, but a shared claim for justice.[42]

A Palestinian Cinematic Arsenal: A Conclusion

One of the other testimonies in *Jenin, Jenin* comes from a father who discusses the gradual shift in his son's understanding of the Israeli occupation and their weapons—how his ability to "tell the difference between the 500- and 800-caliber bullets, all the tanks, the M16 missiles, Kalashnikovs, NATO, etc."—helps his eight-year-old son to cope with his fear and react with courage and confidence to the inhumane conditions of his childhood. From the father's perspective, the son not only carries the initial trauma of the Nakba as part of a generational and national burden, he is also keenly aware of the specific methods the Israeli army deploys to harm the residents of Jenin. Footage of this appears throughout the film: Jenin residents are photographed near their destroyed homes, we see clips of aerial bombardment of the camp, ground invasion, bombed and falling houses, and bulldozers demolishing houses; there are photographs of a destroyed school, of bombed UN vehicles, of IDF helicopters in the air, and tanks and soldiers in the camp. The film is saturated with images of bullets and empty cartridges scattered on the floors of houses in the camp next to empty boxes with Hebrew labels of bullets and hand grenades. We hear testimonies about a young man being crushed beneath a tank when he holds his arms up in the air, children being used as human shields, Palestinian men who were forced to undress, and Israeli soldiers urinating in the cooking pans of a Palestinian family.

This film does not deal with "the bureaucracy of the occupation" or its "control system," and it does not try to understand the systemic and structural logic of the "occupation regime."[43] Instead, it deals with the concrete mechanisms and tools that enable and maintain the occupation—strategic terrorizing as a method of control and debilitation. Through the testimonies and footage of violence, and the focus on produced disablement, the film concretizes the brutal reality in

Jenin—the woman's foot being shot, the gunshot wounds to the elderly man's hand and foot, and the young boy's extensive knowledge of IDF weaponry and what it sounds and looks like. These become the center of Bakri's narrative, and they are the core of the Palestinian testimony.

While both *The Mute's House* and *Jenin, Jenin* act as "cultural weapons," disability in *The Mute's House* functions as a means for the director to make a film about Hebron "without talking about the occupation," but disability in *Jenin, Jenin* reveals its underpinning in the discussion of concrete mechanisms and tools of oppression (such as "the right to maim," weapons, tanks, and so on).[44] In short, *The Mute's House* becomes a cultural weapon preserving a Zionist viewpoint while *Jenin, Jenin* constitutes a weapon of resistance to the Israeli occupation—a Palestinian "cinematic arsenal."[45]

In an article analyzing the history of Hebron in films and media, director Ra'anan Alexandrowicz explains that watching films and videos about Hebron with no historical and political context leaves the viewer feeling that the Israeli occupation is a terrible chaos, a hopeless situation beyond all comprehension. He argues that this rhetoric is misleading and harmful; while the occupation is a system that produces arbitrary evil as a matter of routine, it has its own logic and its own structured patterns. If the purpose of the documentation is to make the reality of the occupation accessible to the viewer, that viewer must also be exposed to the logic of the existing situation.[46]

The transition from a narrative of horrific trauma on some grand, incomprehensible scale to a discourse that focuses on how the occupation is realized and maintained reveals the occupation's own logic, and it does not allow viewers to treat the occupation as a kind of generalized or unchangeable evil. In contrast to films such as *Waltz with Bashir* (2008) by the Jewish Israeli director Ari Folman, the documentary *The Invasion* (2002) by Palestinian Israeli director Nizar Hassan, and the feature *Divine Intervention* (2002) by Palestinian director Elia Suleiman—which respectively portray the Israeli soldier as a confused child, as a character too weak to oppose violence, and an occupier to be ridiculed—*Jenin, Jenin* exposes the Israeli occupation as a well-oiled machine that knows how to maintain its power and does not hesitate to deploy the weapons in its arsenal. The soldiers in *Jenin, Jenin* loot Palestinians' savings, purposefully humiliate the camp's inhabitants, demolish houses with weapons of war, and shoot at Palestinians to injure and maim.[47]

Ramzi Maqdisi: *Defying My Disability*

Unlike *Jenin, Jenin* and *The Mute's House*, which feature disability prominently but as part of a larger narrative, the documentary *Defying My Disability* (2016) explicitly deals with the lives of people with disabilities as the main focus. The film was made by Palestinian director Ramzi Maqdisi, who was born in 1980 in Jerusalem, Palestine. The film follows the lives of seven Palestinians with physical disabilities who live in Gaza and the occupied West Bank.

The people in the film, some born with disabilities and some living with disabilities as a result of IDF violence, discuss their lives, their dreams, and the myriad challenges they face. They describe their hopes for the future while also addressing the inaccessibility of their towns, the occupation, and their limited access to resources that could significantly improve their lived experiences of disability. In exploring this documentary and its connections to the other films I've discussed, I am particularly interested in the attitudes expressed toward disability and how enmeshed these perspectives are in both reality and the cinematic representation of life under political occupation.

Shown surrounded by paintings, canvases, gouache paints, and color palettes, artist and photographer Zyad Deeb explains in *Defying My Disability* that his injury was caused by an IDF explosion that led not only to the amputation of both of his legs but also to the deaths of most of his family members. He emphasizes that his disability is the direct result of the political struggle between Israelis and Palestinians. As in *Jenin, Jenin*, the editing of *Defying My Disability* highlights this dimension by the images it presents in between the interviews. Before Deeb's first interview, the audience views an image of bombs falling on Gaza from the air. This shot and similar clips and photos that recur throughout the film were taken during the Gaza War, a three-week armed conflict between Gaza Strip Palestinian paramilitary groups and the Israel Defense Forces that began in December 2008 and ended in January 2009. Known in the Palestinian world as the Gaza Massacre and in Israel as Operation Cast

Lead (Mivtza Oferet Yetzuka), the conflict resulted in between 1,166 and 1,417 Palestinian deaths and 13 Israeli deaths.

Speaking of his dream to one day have his own gallery, and to reflect his love of Gaza and Palestine in his art, Zyad Deeb says: "Gaza is beautiful to its people. I can say I want to get out of Gaza, that it's not nice, that life here is difficult. The reality of living in Gaza is hard for a person with disability. I want to travel. I think of traveling outside of Gaza for one reason only. That's to be able to move and go to places freely and easily. This doesn't exist in Gaza, of course. Gaza is not equipped for people with disability. My own house is not equipped for me to live in. Imagine going to a place that's not yours?" Deeb's words can be understood in two ways. First he names the difficulty of maneuvering in Gaza and the inaccessibility of its infrastructure, but then he highlights the fact that in Gaza all Palestinians find it difficult to move from place to place because of the restrictions imposed by the Israelis. Is Zyad Deeb's sense of his own impairment related to his disability or to his national affiliation and his location? Is his home unsuitable for his needs because it is physically inaccessible, or because it has been made inhospitable by the conditions of the occupation, including constant bombing by the IDF? Most important: is it at all possible to separate the two? This tension—between questions addressing the lived experiences of disability and how they're inextricably intertwined with occupation—is a common thread throughout the film.

Apolitical Disability

The film showcases a wide range of disabilities, featuring people in a way that the other two films do not. While we know that artist Zyad Deeb's disability was caused by an IDF explosion, the disabilities of the children and some of the adults in the film appear to be congenital. The film does not distinguish between them; it instead focuses on the barriers that Palestinian people with disabilities face, including the inaccessibility of public and private spaces and widespread stigma against visibly disabled people.[48] One man, for instance, dreams of an elevator that will enable him to get to his apartment by himself, and another girl wishes for a motorized chair that will enable her to go to school. This highlighting of the lack of accessibility is unique to this film of the three reviewed here.

However, the documentary does not explicitly link the lack of accessibility in Gaza and the occupied West Bank to the political situation. While it does show how disability in Palestine is entwined with poverty and stigma, it focuses on physical inaccessibility. It does not highlight the fact that many experiences of disability in Palestine are hugely affected by limited resources due to Israel's regulations and Palestinian authorities' policies.[49] The Israeli occupation and neglect by Palestinian authorities both significantly encumber the day-to-day life of Palestinians with disabilities. Furthermore, insufficient prenatal and postnatal care, malnutrition, and inadequate medical services all contribute to illness and disability. Restrictive policies limit access to assistive devices (such as wheelchairs and hearing aids), health care, and electricity—all of which can be essential to people with disabilities. The lack of adequate services is thus the result of both the Israeli blockade and occupation and the ongoing neglect by Palestinian authorities—together preventing Palestinians from accessing food, medications, and essential services.

The uncritical positionality of the film and its lack of a direct link between the myriad challenges of disabled experiences and the political situation was later echoed, in a sense, by the public response expressed in a promotional video for the film. In these promotional clips, we learn that "Ramzi Maqdisi's film about the challenges of disability for Palestinians in Gaza has inspired Portuguese football manager André Villas Boas to provide help. . . . The Portuguese football manager André Villas Boas saw the film and contacted the film-maker Ramzi Maqdisi. Improved equipment and treatment are being provided and dreams supported. His help will improve quality of life, but their [Palestinians with disability] positive attitudes despite the hardships are the main source of strength here."[50] This promotional video melds the charity model of disability, depicting people with disability as victims of circumstance in dire need of pity and care, with the inspirational model, which basically makes nondisabled people feel better about themselves for not being disabled. Furthermore, and more significant to our discussion, this clip contributes to the continued separation of disability from its geopolitical context. The assistance provided by André Villas Boas is at the level of equipment and is therefore not related to the political context in which the people it assists live.[51] Despite its importance, as Rita Giacaman aptly states, "it does not make sense to offer humanitarian aid, alleviate daily suffering and support Palestinian resilience so that they can cope, adapt and accept unacceptable conditions without also calling for justice to Palestinians."[52]

"My Dream Is to Go to Jerusalem"

While the overall tone of the film highlights questions of disability over the brutalities of occupation (or, even more specifically, the production of disability from the occupation), it should be noted that the film does intrinsically address many of these issues. The film begins to draw to a close with what can only be called the journey of Idriss Awaad, a schoolboy from Hebron, who has difficulty walking as he makes his way to his uncle's house. The film depicts this walk as an epic journey of sorts, during which the child heroically overcomes the difficulties he faces: we see him cling to the stones of a wall between two houses with immense effort before stumbling and then continuing on, limping slowly and steadily. The close-up of Idriss Awaad's struggling body both reveals the physical inaccessibility of the streets of Hebron and sets a focus upon the boy's own willpower—that is, how his determination of spirit allegedly overcomes the limitations of his body. The film, in this moment, is devoid of any critical stance in relation to this ableist discourse of the supercrip—someone who overcomes their disability in ways that are often seen by society as inspiring, a stereotype that neutralizes any social and political responsibility for disability.[53]

In the midst of Idriss Awaad's journey, the film moves to a shot of another Palestinian boy, running barefoot with a Palestinian flag in his hand toward the Palestinian side of the Separation Wall that was built by Israel in 2002 to separate Palestinians of the West Bank from Israel, climbing it quickly and with ease. The film seems to position this child, whom the audience has not met, as a kind of symbol for the children of Palestine and for the future of Palestine. When he reaches the top of the wall, Jerusalem is revealed in all its glory in a bird's-eye view, and we see the Dome of the Rock in the center and the Al-Aqsa Compound.[54] The sky is cloudy, but rays of sunlight penetrate through the cover, which contrasts with the bombed sky we saw glimpses of throughout the film.

This political vision is underscored then, yet again, by a voice-over in this cinematic moment in which artist Zyad Deeb declares, "My dream is to go to Jerusalem, but Israel won't allow me to. It's my right as a Palestinian to enter Jerusalem, but the Israelis don't allow me to."

The editing of these moments together clearly links a child's determination to "overcome" physical disability and limitations with a political journey of the Palestinian people to cross or destroy the Israeli Separation Wall. It can be argued that Maqdisi turns the actual disability allegedly at the center of his film into symbolic disability with these "profound" and inherently ableist moments created during the editing process. It is as if Idriss Awaad, the child with disability, symbolizes the condition of the Palestinian people in the present, and the able-bodied child who manages to climb the wall symbolizes the Palestinian people's overcoming the present oppression and rising into their future political victory.[55] This further pits a depiction of disability as something lacking or left wanting against a vigorous and able-bodied future.

However, the connection between Idriss Awaad's disability, the scene of the Separation Wall, and the voice of Zyad Deeb, who was wounded in an IDF attack, actually strengthens the film's political argument about the right to maim as a key mechanism in maintaining the occupation. It highlights the fact that whether the disability is congenital or a product of political violence, it is impossible to really separate the disability of the characters from the Separation Wall and Jerusalem, which symbolize the occupation and Palestinian aspiration for national independence. That is, the film does not allow separation of the experience of life with disabilities from the experience of life under continuous occupation. This is particularly noticeable in light of Ramzi Maqdisi's cinematic allusions to *Jenin, Jenin*.

The juxtaposition of Idriss Awaad's journey with the footage of the barefooted boy climbing the Separation Wall (figure 17) bears remarkable similarities to a scene in *Jenin, Jenin* in which we see a barefoot child climbing slowly, and with great difficulty, over the ruins of a house shortly after a doctor provides testimony of his young son dying in front of him during the bombings of Jenin (figure 18). Although *Defying My Disability* came out fourteen years after *Jenin, Jenin*, and although the two scenes take place in different locations, the editing in *Defying My Disability* connects the invasion of Jenin to the occupation in Hebron,

Jerusalem, and the Gaza Strip. It thus creates a narrative that connects Palestinians living in different areas of occupation, but it also links *Jenin, Jenin*'s discussion of the right to maim with the political argument regarding the link between disability and the oppression of the Palestinian people in *Defying My Disability*.

The symbolic treatment of disability in *The Mute's House* and the scene featuring Idriss Awaad in *Defying My Disability* follow similar approaches, but with radically different goals. While the symbolic approach to disability has allowed Israeli director Tamar Kay to obscure the centrality of the occupation, Palestinian director Ramzi Maqdisi uses the symbolism of disability to express Palestinian hope for national liberation. And in some ways, *Defying My Disability* continues *Jenin, Jenin*'s cinematic perspective of treating disability as a real-life experience that is a product of concrete occupation mechanisms.

Defying My Disability refuses to address disability as a general, "universal" identity component of individuals with disabilities, instead offering a cinematic discourse in which Palestinian identity and disability intersect. While implementing ideas from the social model of disability that emphasizes the socially created barriers experienced by people with disabilities, the movie extends this approach. By focusing on intersectionality and geopolitics, it explores how disabled Palestinians living under Israeli occupation experience their lives. By offering an intersectional lens, therefore, the movie emphasizes the relationship between disability and Palestinian nationhood, as well as the potential for justice for occupied Palestine and movements of disability justice. Palestinians face state-sanctioned violence that at times results in living with a disability, and at the same time, Palestinians with disabilities are disproportionately impacted by the structural violence of the occupation.

All three documentaries discussed in this chapter show us, in cinematic language, that the layers of disability and national affiliation do not exist separately from each other and cannot be separated; instead, they intersect and can even magnify the brutality people experience, while feeding into their perception of disability, nationhood, and justice.

FIGURE 17. A barefoot Palestinian boy climbs the Israeli Separation Wall in *Defying My Disability*.

FIGURE 18. A barefoot Palestinian boy climbs the ruins of a destroyed building in *Jenin, Jenin*.

In Conclusion: Sea Under Siege

Throughout the film *Defying My Disability* the audience is given glimpses of the sea on the shores of Gaza and Jaffa. Haneen Abu Ayash, a student with physical disability from Hebron, is brought to the promenade along the ocean in Tel Avi–Yafo, and in the background is the mosque in Jaffa. Other children are brought to the shore of Gaza. The sea seems to draw a narrative parallel to the stories of disabilities—at times it seems as if all the people in the film are united not by their disabilities but through their love for the sea. The characters are brought to the ocean as part of the film's production and are filmed as they watch the ocean with amazement and longing, aware that this is an extraordinary, perhaps unique, event in their lives. The sea in the film, then, is an object of observation and passion, a site that has not yet been achieved, rather than a place of relaxation or entertainment—or even a symbolic site that one sails on in order to reach the homeland, as we find in Zionist texts—and as such, it becomes a potent political symbol.[56]

Throughout the film the sea functions as a politically blocked site that one strives to reach—the ultimate expression of political borders and barriers that Palestinians cannot overcome. The sea highlights the fact that Palestinians from certain areas cannot reach it, and that in areas that do have access to it, it is a dangerous place due to restrictions and attacks by Israel. At the same time, in the fictional narrative the documentary paints, the sea allows freedom of movement that does not exist in reality, and it acts out overcoming those political limitations by showcasing shots of it. In addition, the way this cinematic narrative comes together expresses a geopolitical conception of the unification of Palestinians that are currently scattered in Gaza, Hebron, Jaffa, and Jerusalem. The divided homeland and the scattered people are united in the cinematic work.[57] Although the people in the film live in different places and they certainly cannot meet or move freely from place to place because of the occupation, they share a common space that reflects and realizes their political-national truth while on the screen. In other words, it is not just a hope or a dream of a future in which Palestinians and Palestine will be united; it is a political statement of a reality in which, despite the political limitations, Palestine *is* united. If anything, the cinematic editing of these different moments in which people encounter the

sea on the various shores of Palestine shows Palestine as a unified homeland. As Yael Ben-Zvi Morad has shown, despite the barriers that divide
Palestine, it exists in a complete and unified way in cinema.[58]

The function of the sea as a political statement stands out in light
of the contrast between how these images are deployed in *Defying My
Disability* and *The Mute's House*. In the former, in the moment depicting
Haneen Abu Ayash on the promenade of Tel Aviv–Yafo, the camera shifts
its focus from the buildings of Tel Aviv to the mosque in Jaffa, proactively moving our attention from current Jewish Israeli Tel Aviv toward
Palestinian Jaffa. In contrast, in Tamar Kay's early investigative feature,
which ends with Yousef and his mother visiting the ocean in Jaffa, the
camera focuses on Yousef and his mother talking in sign language, but
the shot includes Israeli flags fluttering before the buildings of Tel Aviv
in the background. In addition, when the camera narrows in on the sea,
we hear Tamar Kay's voice-over: "The way back [from Jaffa to Hebron] is
much faster. Within an hour, Yousef and his mother will be back on the
other side. They will cross the Tarkumiya border terminal and return to
Hebron to the 'house of the mute woman.'" Thus, in Ramzi Maqdisi's
film, the sea is a key point in a cinematic sequence that links the Palestinian people and their envisioned demilitarized homeland; in Tamar
Kay's, the sea serves to strengthen and preserve the geographical separation between Jaffa and Hebron while tacitly highlighting the existence
of the State of Israel. Although the film "brought" Yousef and his mother
to Jaffa, it also makes sure they return to "the other side." And although
in the scene we see Yousef's mother and other Palestinian relatives who
joined the journey taking many pictures, the perspective on the sea—and
its political significance—remains that of the Jewish Israeli director. As
was the case with the symbolic struggle between Yousef's "small camera"
and the director's professional camera, the power dynamics remain
clear and defined.

Both films' choice to end with scenes in which disabled people ful-
fill their dream of going to the sea follows the cliché of inspirational
symbolism and stresses the films' use of disability in order to advance
political agendas, even if those agendas differ. But then again, within this
narrative, the voices of the people living with disability break through
the "inspirational" veneer of ableism to present political possibilities for
interpretation stemming from their lived experiences.

In *Defying My Disability*, artist Zyad Deeb speaks of the sea in Gaza; while he refers to its beauty, he mainly experiences the sea as yet more evidence of Israeli control.[59] He does not refer to the sea as a political symbol, but he locates it in the larger context of his life under surveillance, observed and policed by militarized systems of control:

> I love Gaza. I try to look for the nicest things in it. I try to find the most beautiful thing. Thank God we still have the sea. Gaza's sea is under siege. [The other day] I sat in a chair, on the shore, and saw the gunboats, I saw the battleships, far away. After sunset, Israeli spotlights flashed on us. When I saw the light, I got scared. I felt like there was an eye watching us.
>
> Why? You go to a place to enjoy the beach with friends or family or sometimes alone. Suddenly there's bombing nearby or a spotlight on you. You feel horrified. You start saying, "I'd rather leave before something happens."

The director's dominant perspective is therefore converted by the point of view of Deeb, who creates a narrative of self-representation that resists attempts to turn either disability or the sea into a symbol; instead, it insists on locating his experience of living with a disability in a particular geopolitical context. He describes sweeping Israeli control, military activity, and specific militarized technologies as well as his fear and desire to avoid harm as much as possible. The sea for him, as for many other Palestinians, is a looming threat of militarized action upon Palestinian bodies and minds. His narrative wraps together space, nationhood, and disability, and illustrates how, through debilitation and disablement, power is exercised over Palestinians, forcing them to limit their movement and political struggle. All three documentaries, then, in different ways, raise questions about the politics of representing disability, as well as displaying how discourse around disability has the power to change and shape a new political conversation regarding geopolitical injustice and endemic violence against Palestinians.

EPILOGUE

Embodiment and the Contours of Israeli Disability Culture

Cognitive Disability in the Context of Israeli Disability Culture

Disability culture has always had a presence in Israel, but often it remained concealed, relegated to the background of events, with limited visibility or acknowledgment in a wider cultural perspective. Events that might display or celebrate artwork from disabled communities included exhibitions in "special" institutions, art integrated into therapeutic practices, ceremonies held at schools for students with disabilities, and the like. Consequently, the work of disabled artists wasn't always acknowledged as art or, in fact, even theorized or discussed in the context of disability culture. In some ways, the artistic expression(s) of disability culture has been largely amorphous and widely variable—as the ideas of "art" and the idea of "disability" are both wont to be—but I feel nonetheless that there are certain shapes and contours that suggest the interplay of disabled artistic embodiment in Israeli culture.

Although *The Un-Chosen Body* has a scope set on disability culture in the 2000s, focusing particularly on the creative works of women who, to some extent, received recognition within the disability community, I want to conclude by highlighting a poem from an earlier period of disability culture that went largely unrecognized, perhaps as a symbol of that which might remain undiscussed—but not unacknowledged—in my own work. The poem is not well known or widely discussed; in fact, I myself only heard it after it appeared in a 1983 documentary about an inclusive community called Kfar Tikva. Discussing the poem in this epilogue serves a dual purpose. It is an illustrative example of disability culture that existed in a period preceding the book's primary focus, allowing us to take a retrospective approach. Simultaneously, it embodies an internal critique of Israel's disability culture by an artistic creator with a cognitive disability and therefore sparks discussion on how we draw lines around definitions of art and disability.

Kfar Tikva (literally meaning "village of hope") was founded in 1964 as an inclusive community and lifelong home for over 220 adults with cognitive, developmental, and emotional disabilities. The community is dedicated to promoting resident autonomy and offers a wide range of personalized care and services, including diverse activities, employment opportunities, and integration into the broader community at different stages of life.[1] The documentary *Kfar Tikva*, which offers an intimate portrayal of the lives of several Kfar Tikva residents, was directed by Aran Patinkin, whose sister lived in Kfar Tikva during the making of the film. Without narration or an interpretive soundtrack, the film features only individuals associated with the village, mainly the *haverim* or members, but also counselors and parents.[2] It provides an engaging glimpse into the daily routines, work, decision-making processes, challenges, mutual support, and relationships among the community members of Kfar Tikva.

Throughout the film, viewers are immersed in the detailed preparations for Kfar Tikva's Hanukkah celebration, to which families of the residents are warmly invited. The film concludes with selected segments of the performance prepared by the residents. The introductory words of the ceremony, articulated by members of Kfar Tikva, immediately establish it as a ceremony deeply rooted in state-Zionist values: "Good evening! It's our custom to celebrate Hannukah together. The Maccabees lead us from the conquest of the land [of Israel] to the present. We dedicate this Hannukah night to the love of Israel." The ceremony proceeds with lively folk dances set to the melody of "Stalks in the Field" ("Shibolet Basade"), accompanied by participants dressed in blue and white. The performers also sing Israeli folk songs, including "Beautiful Land of Israel" ("Eretz Yisrael Yaffe") and "We Don't Need More Than That" ("Yoter Mize Anachnu Lo Tsrihim"). As the ceremony nears its conclusion, a remarkable moment occurs. One of the members of Kfar Tikva begins to recite a personal poem written as a heartfelt letter to his mother:

> Mother, soon I will enter the world.
> I know that you have waited a long time for me.
> Nine months you waited and imagined how I would look.
> But Mother, I have something to tell you:
> I'm not exactly whom you awaited—
> you see, I'm not exactly what you wanted.
> I'm different.
> I'm afraid, Mother.
> I really want you to want me.
> I would love for you to love me
> the way you love little Yafit,
> and Eli who is in the army already.
>
> I see, I already see light, I'm out.
> I have arrived, Mother. Hug me.
> Hold me close.
> You are crying, I know—so am I.
> You will get used to me.
>
> But I ask you, Mother:
> Help me,
> help me not to give up.
> I can,
> I can, Mother,
> I can do much more than you think
> and much more than they all know.
> And if it's hard for you—I'll fight alone.
> I will show them all, Mother, that I can,
> that I can grow and flourish,
> that I can straighten up and stand on my feet.

So maybe I won't stand so straight,
maybe they won't understand what I say,
perhaps they won't always grasp
precisely what I'm saying.
But tell them, Mother,
tell them I don't want their pity.
I don't want pity from anyone.
I demand respect,
speak to me as [you would with] any other person.
I'm twenty seven—don't fondle my head and ask:
"How are you, honey? How do you feel?"
"Hello"—that's enough for me.

I have difficulties, Mother, and I don't always succeed.
But inside me, Mother, beats a heart that knows how to love, that
    knows how to hate,
that hurts and breaks out laughing—just like any other person.

I am a person, mother, like any other.
I am a person.
Expect me to walk the path like any person
and I will follow the path.

I found I can
and now I will start to stand up straight.
I can, Mother,
I can.[3]

אמא, אני עוד מעט אצא לעולם.
אני יודע שהרבה זמן חיכית לי.
תשעה חודשים חיכית לי ודמיינת איך אראה.
אבל אמא, יש לי משהו להגיד לך:
אני לא בדיוק מי שאת מחכה לו–
את מבינה, אני לא בדיוק מה שרצית.
אני אחר.
אני מפחד, אמא.
אני מאוד רוצה שתרצי אותי.

הייתי מאוד רוצה שתאהבי אותי,
כמו את יפית הקטנה,
כמו את אלי שכבר בצבא.

אני רואה, אני רואה כבר אור, אני בחוץ,
הגעתי, אמא, תחבקי אותי.
תחזיקי אותי קרוב אליך.
את בוכה, אני יודע—גם אני.
את תתרגלי אלי.

אבל אני מבקש ממך, אמא:
תעזרי לי,
תעזרי לי לא להכנע.
אני יכול
אני יכול, אמא
אני יכול הרבה יותר ממה שאת חושבת
וממה שכולם יודעים
ואם קשה לך—אלחם לבדי.
אני אראה לכולם, אמא, שאני יכול,
יכול לצמוח ולפרוח.
אני יכול להזדקף ולעמוד על רגלי.
אז אולי אני לא אעמוד כל כך ישר,
אולי לא תמיד יבינו את מה
שבדיוק אני אומר.
אבל תגידי להם, אמא,
תגידי להם שאני לא רוצה את הרחמים שלהם.
אני לא רוצה את הרחמים של אף אחד.
אני דורש שיכבדו אותי,
שידברו אלי כמו כל אדם אחר.
אני בן עשרים ושבע—שלא ילטפו לי את הראש
וישאלו: "מה שלומך, מותק? איך אתה מרגיש?"
"אהלן" זה מספיק לי.

יש לי קשיים, אמא, ולא תמיד אני מצליח.
אבל בתוכי, אמא, פועם לב שיודע לאהוב, שיודע לשנוא,
שכואב ופורץ בצחוק—כמו כל אדם אחר.

אני אדם, אמא, כמו כל אחד אחר,
אני אדם, אמא,
אני אדם.
תצפו ממני ללכת בַּדרך ככל האדם
ואני אלך בדרכו.

גיליתי שאני יכול
ועכשיו אתחיל לעמוד זקוף.
אני יכול,
אני יכול, אמא.

The speaker addresses his mother at three distinct stages: as a fetus in utero, during/immediately after his birth, and as a twenty-seven-year-old man. Each stage reveals different facets of his self-identity and the expectations he has, both for himself and for his environment. During the birth phase, a connection is established between the crying mother and the newborn baby ("You are crying, I know—so am I"). The language in the poem is markedly unclear about the emotion(s) motivating the tears—if they signify excitement or disappointment or worry. Nonetheless, the son seeks comfort from his mother, his initial request being for touch, connection, and love. This desire for closeness is expressed while he simultaneously reassures her with the heartbreaking line "You will get used to me." This consolation doesn't negate his otherness or promise a change in his situation but rather suggests a transformation in hers—it is the mother who needs to adapt to her son.

Speaking with the perspective of an adult later in the poem, he appeals to his mother for assistance. The request for help isn't rooted in a sense of dependence or inferiority; rather, it stems from a need to have his independence and capability acknowledged: "But I ask you, Mother: / Help me, / help me not to give up. / I can, / I can, Mother / I can do much more than you think / and much more than they all know. / And if it's hard for you—I'll fight alone." Essentially, the speaker seeks his mother's support to resist yielding to the low expectations set for him, to refrain from surrendering to the societal mindset that associates disability with a bleak future. While this rather barren vision of a future might be considered natural and self-evident, given various socially limiting factors, the poem's speaker challenges this perception boldly—much like the women highlighted in *The Un-Chosen Body*. While the poem's lines "Nine months you waited and imagined how I would look" reflect the mother's perspective, mirroring the societal gaze that idealizes a social norm that assumes a dim future for individuals with disabilities, the poem underscores the obvious fact that "I can do much more than you think / and much more than they all know."

The emphasis on his capabilities challenges and blurs the power dynamics while redefining the caregiver–cared for relationship between the speaker and his mother; it essentially recontextualizes the tension at the heart of the poem. Even the perspective of the baby seeks to provide comfort and reassurance to his mother—a message to his caregiver but one that extends to other parents of disabled individuals. The speaker offers solace to the one most closely associated with a caregiving role, effectively establishing what Tyler Zoanni describes as "care in the middle voice": "Care in the middle voice is not simply care turned intransitive. Differences between the caregiver and the cared-for persist but are not fixed positions; they vary depending on the situation. Viewing care in the middle voice brings attention to the dynamic aspects of care where clear, unchanging lines between the subjects and objects of care break down."[4] From an external perspective, the residents of Kfar Tikva and similar communities may seem like individuals who are primarily cared for and who are reliant on others due to their cognitive disabilities. However, as they navigate their daily lives, these individuals become enmeshed in intricate networks in which they both offer and receive care.

In offering care to his mother, the speaker takes on the role of caregiver—for his mother, for his own self, and for the audience. The growth depicted in the poem doesn't revolve around striving for normalcy or an adjustment of a disabled individual to their surroundings. The poem doesn't hinge upon seeking accommodations to "fit" into a place in society but instead seeks substantive change in the social foundations of *expectation* itself. The speaker expresses, "I will show them all, Mother, that I can, / that I can grow and flourish, / that I can straighten up and stand on my feet. / So maybe I won't stand so straight, / maybe they won't understand what I say, perhaps they won't always grasp / precisely what I'm saying." Even the language here, signifying an uneven posture and incomprehensible or confused speech, stands as clear signposts to the diversity the speaker embodies. Furthermore, the poem serves as a call to action to the audience, which includes peers from Kfar Tikva, counselors, families attending the ceremony, and those of us viewing the film—with or without disability.

Simply put, these lines contain a powerful appeal for a sense of humility and decency from the audience. The poem calls for the acknowledgment that there are times when others can't fully understand him or his life—from the very literal words he speaks to the perspective he brings to bear as a person. In a society where people with intellectual or cognitive disabilities are often viewed as lacking knowledge and social understanding, this call advocates for a more equitable framework.[5] In theory, this framework would be scaffolded upon appreciation of the fact that the responsibility for knowledge and understanding (or lack thereof) is not the sole responsibility of an individual with intellectual disabilities—it is a duty shared by support systems, parents, caregivers, and counselors.

The speaker doesn't ignore the challenges he faces and admits that he doesn't always succeed. However, he staunchly defends himself and his humanity, which is not (and should never be) diminished in any way by his failures. He affirms, "I have difficulties, Mother, and I don't always succeed. / But inside me, Mother, beats a heart that knows how to love, that knows how to hate, that / hurts and breaks out laughing—just like any other person." In societies shaped by ableism, people with cognitive disabilities are sometimes dehumanized, often because they are viewed as deviating from the normative path of development—the progression from childhood to adulthood and eventually old age. In ableist cultures that exalt self-sufficiency and functionality, individuals with intellectual disabilities, who may not engage in traditional employment or live independently, are erroneously seen as lacking growth or development. Instead, they are perceived as perpetual children. The poem spotlights this ableist stance and advocates for the right of people with cognitive disability to mature and gain recognition as adults in their own right, without ableist benchmarks for "success" or "independence" that often serve to patronize and infantilize. It is nothing less than a brilliant critique of cognitive ableism; the speaker highlights that even as a twenty-seven-year-old man, he is still subjected to being patted on the head and treated like a child. It is societal treatment that perpetuates a perception of childlike dependency rather than his actions, his desires, or his behaviors.

Consequently, when the speaker insists on being respected, he articulates it as "Speak to me as any other person" ("sheyedabru eli kmo kol adam aher") rather than the grammatically correct "Speak to me as you would with any other person" ("sheyedabru eli kmo el kol adam aher") as typically expressed in standard Hebrew. This apparent linguistic oversight may be construed as marking the speaker as someone who doesn't have full command of language, often interpreted as a consequence of disability. However, this analysis unfairly prioritizes linguistic normativity associated with neurotypical individuals and a socially agreed-upon standard for spoken and written language. If we refrain from characterizing the omission of "as you would" as a linguistic error, instead choosing to acknowledge the agency of the speaker, we can understand the sentence differently. In this new light, the sentence isn't just about the speaker's demand to be spoken to respectfully, as anyone should be, it conveys a far more inclusive notion: authenticity. The sentence comes to suggest that the speaker is urging every person to communicate with him uniquely, and thus encouraging people to speak in their own distinct and authentic manner, rather than adhering strictly to conventional and normative communication.

Furthermore, if we take into account that the poem's author has a cognitive disability, his message can be seen as a plea to give prominence to cognitive issues and use the insight he offers to outline a more comprehensive disability culture, giving shape to something that more fully prioritizes cognitive considerations.

The Cripping (and Critiquing) of the Gallery

In many respects Kfar Tikva was ahead of its time in its approach to community life for individuals with intellectual and cognitive disabilities. It recognized the importance of home, intimate relationships and sexuality, family, and community for its members. Moreover, it emphasized the rights of its members to make decisions regarding various aspects of their lives—issues that remain central to the ongoing struggles of individuals with disabilities. However, it's essential to acknowledge that Kfar

Tikva was initially founded as a Zionist collective model. This implies that it reflects national values that prioritize productivity and the relative independence of its members. This inherent tension characterizes the attempt to celebrate and normalize disability culture in Israel from its inception. The poem stands as an emblem, representative of the ongoing endeavor to distinguish a distinctive and affirmative culture of disability within the confines of a national environment with its own values. It dares to demand more, paving the way for the possibility of making broader demands and addressing the acute concerns of Israeli disability culture in the 2000s, including the act of cripping spaces within the arts, as well as conversations about gender and sexuality and geopolitical justice.

More specifically, this poem is part of a long-standing tradition that still persists today at Kfar Tikva, where members continue to share their art both within the village and outside of it. In February 2021, the exhibition *Extraordinary* (*Yotse min haklal*), curated by Ilan Beck, was held in Kiryat Tivon at the Kiryat Gallery of Artists located within the Deganiot Community Center. This exhibition was dedicated to the works of artists with a range of disabilities, primarily cognitive and emotional. Several members of Kfar Tikva also participated. In an interview for community television in Tivon, Danny Shein, a member of Kfar Tikva, discussed his contribution to the exhibition. He referred to one of his photographs featuring a peacock:

> I am thrilled to present these photographs for the second time. This is a special shot of how to capture [the Hebrew verb here is *litfos*, which can also mean "grasp"] this peacock. How I caught him for the first time just as he opened his wings. It's something very . . . It's in the village [Kfar Tikva] we have it. It's something that not everyone can capture [or grasp, with their camera]. The interesting thing is that I caught it at the right moment. It's art, it resembles a painting I think, but it's on a canvas that looks like a painting.
>
> Kfar Tikva has been on the Zeid Hills for fifty-five years and it—we have huge spaces and I also, apart from photographing it, I also do articles for the village in the village's media. This is the main job and [I] also edit things that I photograph. . . . That

the village is also included in such a gallery, that's what's beautiful about it. That also special people are given a place.[6]

Shein's words do more than merely emphasize the unique aspects of his photography—they invite us to consider the symbolic significance of his contribution. His description of having captured the peacock with wings spread wide alludes to concepts such as flying, growth, freedom, and independence. His statement "It's in the village we have it. It's something that not everyone can capture/grasp" can refer to more than the opportunity to photograph a remarkable moment; it also carries a more poignant, subtle message about his experiences. Danny Shein's description, seems to convey that not everyone comprehends the unique freedom and opportunities to "spread one's wings" that Kfar Tikva offers its members.

Shein expresses his appreciation for the exhibition by highlighting the fact that "the village is also included in such a gallery." While "such a gallery" evidently pertains to the professional and conventional venue of an art gallery, it sheds light on what it means to have the village integrated into this gallery. While Shein might be referring to images of the village and the peacock quite literally, there is also a firm underlying message about the integration and inclusion of works created by artists with cognitive disabilities into a space of esteem—a space from which they are typically excluded.

It's crucial to understand that in Israel, the majority of disabled artists who have work showcased in more traditional settings, in prominent galleries and museums, are individuals with physical or psychiatric disabilities. Art by those on the autistic spectrum or individuals with cognitive disabilities, if it is displayed at all, often finds a place on social networks, in experimental venues, or within the rehabilitation and welfare system.[7] Consequently, the inclusion of Kfar Tikva members' works in the gallery setting differs from exhibitions by people like physically disabled artist Tamar Getter (born in 1953), whose art has been consistently featured in established galleries and museums across Israel.[8] This distinction arises from the fact that Getter's work has always been recognized as art, while the works of Kfar Tikva artists have traditionally been perceived (and in many cases are still seen) as amateur creations completed during village recreational classes or as part of art therapy. These works are viewed as valuable primarily for the personal empowerment of their creators, shifting the focus to the therapeutic and rehabilitative power of art for disabled individuals rather than acknowledging the possibility that their art might be valuable as art itself.

The integration of Kfar Tikva members' works within the gallery environment effectively calls into question a range of assumptions concerning the distinctions between "professional art" and "amateur or therapeutic art." It extends a challenge to the role of the traditional art gallery as a promoter or collector of art by highlighting the myriad social, communal, and political functions of art. Simply put, it prompts us to reconsider not only *what* but also *how* and *for what purpose* art might be displayed.[9]

Cultural aesthetics are not only arbitrary, they also seem to have an intrinsically "in-crowd" tendency that is necessary to underscore in the epilogue of a book delving into disability culture and art; the distinctions between what is "art" and what is "therapeutic and rehabilitating artistry" seem to both converge and diverge in such discussions. My intention isn't to revisit discussions of high versus low art or the center versus the margins, as these undoubtedly important conversations have been well discussed in their own right.[10] Instead, I aim to elucidate the space in which Israeli disability culture exists, though at times veiled or concealed, through artistic representation.

Throughout the book, I have consciously avoided differentiating between "high" art and literature and art and poetics on the fringes, between professional filmmakers and self-taught or untrained photographers. This choice was made in order to create an inclusive space where all these works could coexist, each in its own unique way. It was a deliberate decision that challenged the dichotomies between the political and the aesthetic—between the amateur and the professional. It's likely that had I chosen to exclude works that traditionally don't find their place in galleries or academic discourse, the book's content would have been vastly different, with many works (and therefore representations of lived experiences in disability culture) left unrepresented. This choice was not arbitrary; it emerges from the hierarchical reality that permeates our society, in all of its myriad facets, and potential challenges to it.

In the introduction, I alluded to how gender, ethnicity, and economic factors impact the cultural visibility or invisibility of the artists featured in this book. However, it is also essential to consider the tensions between different disabled communities and the informal social hierarchies among and/or within various disabilities. These factors influence the boundaries and definitions of disability culture. In essence, when we endeavor to explore disability culture conceptually, we must "recognize disability in terms of a socially uneven geography."[11] In other words, even though disability culture as a whole opposes ableist perspectives, it is imperative to acknowledge that not all differences and disabilities are equally visible, historically, culturally, or socially—and not all differences and disabilities are treated with similar levels of sensitivity and accommodation.

Within this cultural context, cognitive disabilities frequently face significantly more exclusion and discrimination, and they tend to receive far less recognition from scholars in the field of disability studies and disability rights activists.[12] Sara Lige points out that within the disability arts movement, there has been a notable lack of emphasis on artists with intellectual and developmental disabilities.[13] Petra Kuppers also highlights that in the disability arts community, cognitively disabled artists maintain a unique historical status in that they have struggled for equal rights within discourse frameworks that predominantly articulate a rhetoric of independence. However, these frameworks often leave little room for the rights and needs of individuals who do not fit within the confines of this rhetoric as proficient speakers of political language.[14]

Furthermore, while art, in theory, can exist in a realm devoid of words, artists rely on articulate language to promote and elucidate their work. Consequently, disability culture in Israel, whether consciously or unconsciously, tends to exclude artists with cognitive disabilities who possess distinctive modes of communication and expression. The predominance of embodiment and physical disability within the field is well documented. However, beyond the need to include a wider range of disabilities, Benjamin Fraser raises a significant question: "Are the insights generated by disability studies with a primary focus on physical disabilities applicable to the study of cognitive disabilities?"[15] Positing an answer to this question is beyond the scope of this book, but reversing the question is not; indeed, how might insights from the realm of cognitive, neurological, and mental disabilities (encompassing intellectual, developmental, and psychiatric disabilities) enrich or enhance the insights we've gained from the study of physical disabilities?[16] And how might we suggest a shift in discussions currently dominated by a focus on physical disabilities, which (inadvertently) obfuscate or deny the broader shapes and lines of a wider disability culture—one not focused solely on embodiment?

"It's Something That Not Everyone Can Grasp": Sketching Out the Future of a More Inclusive Discipline

To refine my questions, I will return to the interview in which Danny Shein from Kfar Tikva discusses the inclusion of his photograph of a peacock in a gallery and once more highlight the following quote: "It's in the village we have it. It's something that not everyone can capture/grasp." The underlying message here, once again, might refer to the opportunity for liberation and growth that Kfar Tikva offers. "Spreading your wings" in a typical sense might be seen as actions with the goal of progressing toward an independent life, which stands in contrast (or at least in contradiction) to the freedom Shein describes through his art—growth within a supportive framework tailored to both his needs and his abilities. The act of flourishing he describes is very different from the ableist myth of independence. The discussion regarding the inclusion of the village in the gallery, to use Danny Shein's language, or cripping the gallery, as some might say today, thus raises this fundamental question, which itself is a paradox: one to which I offer no answer here, but also one that this book is incomplete without.

While *The Un-Chosen Body* celebrates crip beauty and creativity, communicating this sentiment through the discussed artistic productions, I wonder what insights I might have gleaned if my investigations had focused on art removed from the gallery—for example, work done in programs involving therapeutic services, activities in recreational workshops and disabled adult day centers, and other things that might be culturally relegated to what many might consider "arts and crafts." In what way would this have changed my understanding of the contours of contemporary disability culture in Israel? What shapes might my ideas have taken if my focus had instead been directed toward the creative agency of Danny Shein and his fellow artists from Kfar Tikva? What might have been discerned about artistic composition and contributions in the amorphous form of Israeli disability culture?

The Un-Chosen Body presents disability culture as it is understood in light of its poetic and artistic contributions such as books, films, photographs, and performances. Each piece, I can testify after spending some years sitting with and reflecting upon this art, is more beautiful and more perfect than I had originally thought. But at the same time, each of them is embodied in the world as a real and finished product: the books were edited and published, the films participated in festivals, and the performances were presented on stages in front of an audience. In other words, in their final phases, they all conform to the social expectation of productivity and tangible performance. Thus, contrary to Danny Shein's call to integrate the village into the gallery according to the criteria of the village (as "we have it" in the village), that is, to contain different criteria for the definition of art and culture in the gallery (or in an academic book), my book in some ways inherently preserves neo-capitalist liberal values of what culture is, what a finished product is, where art might be found, and what is appropriate to write about. Therefore, as Danny Shein may imply, my book is limited in its understanding of the boundaries of disability culture in Israel.

The speaker in the poem with which I began this epilogue shared with us that "perhaps they won't always grasp / precisely what I'm saying." I conclude this book with a sense of wonder—and a deep curiosity to fathom the expressions of those who, like him, do not always conform to conventional standards, and how they challenge the confines and possibilities of Israeli disability culture. What's important isn't what we miss when we concentrate our understanding on embodiment, though that is certainly the case, but also how prominent works within Israeli disability culture perpetuate a form of cognitive ableism, even while doing radical and revolutionary work. This ableism is evident in the prejudice against individuals with cognitive disabilities as well as in the fact that the mindsets and lifestyles of people with cognitive disabilities do not significantly impact our fundamental notions of disability culture, art, and aesthetics.[17] In sum, there is so much more to attempt to capture/grasp in terms of understanding the contours of Israeli disability culture, and further investigations can only enrich and add dimension to such a varied and spectacular body of work.

NOTES

Introduction

1 Chen, Kafer, Kim, and Minich, *Crip Genealogies*, 3.
2 The expectation to overcome disability is probably why the film takes place in a physical therapy room. The wounded in Israeli culture almost never go beyond the confines of hospitals or rehabilitation centers. When they return to Israeli society they do not bring disability with them in the sense of an alternative culture. They "overcome" their disability before returning to society. For more on the subject, see my "'Do Not Bandage the Wounded" in *Flesh of My Flesh*.
3 Kafer, *Feminist, Queer, Crip*.
4 My use of "bodymind" rather than "body and mind" is influenced by Margaret Price, who explains that "mental and physical processes not only affect each other but also give rise to each other—that is, because they tend to act as one, even though they are conventionally understood as two—it makes more sense to refer to them together, in a single term." Price, "The Bodymind Problem and the Possibilities of Pain," 269. For a thorough discussion of how Black women's fiction complicates conventional understandings of bodyminds, see Schalk, *Bodyminds Reimagined*. In chapter 3, I explore and define the concept of the bodymind in greater detail as it applies to my examinations within the book.
5 Given the scarcity of literature on disability culture in the early stages of the Zionist movement, it is imperative to highlight Sarah Imhoff's important biography of the esteemed Zionist writer Jessie Sampter (1883–1938). Sampter, who contracted polio as a child, endured chronic weakness and illness throughout her life. As Imhoff

mentions, Sampter's Zionism did not quite adhere to traditional norms: "While Zionists elevated productive bodies that worked, built, and farmed, Sampter could rarely work with her hands apart from tending flowers and writing; while Zionism applauded reproductive (women's) bodies, Sampter never married or bore children—in fact, she wrote of homoerotic longings and had same-sex relationships we would consider queer." Imhoff, *The Lives of Jessie Sampter*, 69. Marco Di Giulio also addresses disability during mandatory Palestine and the early years of the State of Israel. See "Beyond Silenced Voices"; "Motherhood, Mental Incompetence, and the Denial of Reproductive Autonomy"; "Killing out of Compassion."

6 The phrase is the title of chapter 11 in Paul Longmore's book *Why I Burned My Book*. It originated as a keynote address delivered at "This/ Ability: An Interdisciplinary Conference on Disability and the Arts" at the University of Michigan on May 19, 1995. Mitchell and Snyder, *Vital Signs*; Gill, "A Psychological View of Disability Culture."

7 Puar, *The Right to Maim*.

8 The logic of sacrifice in relation to nationalism is not unique to the Zionist case. For a discussion of another example, disabled veterans' sacrifice-mediated relationship with state sovereignty in Turkey, see Aciksoz, *Sacrificial Limbs*.

9 In this sense, Rona Soffer's film actually participates in what Stacey Park Milbern deemed "access washing," that is, "leveraging 'accessibility' as justification to harm communities of color and poor & working-class communities." Milbern, "Notes on 'Access Washing.'" Laura Jaffee, on the other hand, focuses on access washing in U.S. and Israeli settler colonialisms. Jaffee, "Access Washing at the Imperial University." For further discussion on access washing, see also Chen, Kafer, Kim, and Minich, *Crip Genealogies*, 31 and onwards.

10 Weiss, *The Chosen Body*.

11 I feel the need to temper the assertion regarding the uniqueness of the Israeli case. While the relationship between gender and disability in Israeli society has unique elements—related to Zionist ideology and mandatory military service—the link between heterosexual masculinity and countering the feminization of the wounded soldier's body is not exclusive to Israel. For more on these connections, see Kim, "'A Man, with Same Feelings.'"

12 Chen, Kafer, Kim, and Minich, *Crip Genealogies*, 15.
13 Many important studies address the privileges and whiteness of disability studies. See, for example, Bell, "Introducing White Disability Studies"; Chen, Kafer, Kim, and Minich, *Crip Genealogies*.
14 Barthes, "The Death of the Author."
15 Grech and Soldatic, *Disability in the Global South*, xiv.
16 Nguyen, "Critical Disability Studies at the Edge of Global Development." Similarly, through her exploration of female physical illness and disability in Arab literature from the Levant and Egypt, Abir Hamdar addresses the tension between Western and Arab cultural perceptions of illness and disability. Hamdar, *The Female Suffering Body*.
17 Meekosha, "Decolonising Disability." Fiona Kumari Campbell has coined the term "geodisability knowledges." See Campbell, "Geodisability Knowledge Production and International Norms."
18 Kleege, *More Than Meets the Eye*, 10.
19 Garland-Thomson, "Misfits."
20 I should probably use the plural form, Israeli-Palestinian conflicts, because, as Liron Mor explains, the Israeli-Palestinian conflict is not a single one. It consists of "multiple conflictual mechanisms and conditions that the singular label 'conflict' obscures." Mor, *Conflicts*, 17–18.

Chapter 1

Shiri Oved's poems were translated by my brilliant friend Shira Szobel, who also happens to be my beloved sister-in-law.

1 Broyer and Ita Tal-Or, *Take a Seat* (Israel: Holon Institute of Technology, 2004), https://www.youtube.com/watch?v=faGyBWpCW5s.
2 Mitchell and Snyder, *Narrative Prosthesis*.
3 Garland-Thomson, "Misfits."
4 Kafer, *Feminist, Queer, Crip*.
5 Black, "Sheila Black's Six Poets with Disabilities"; Black, Bartlett, and Northen, *Beauty Is a Verb*.
6 Garland-Thomson, "The Case for Conserving Disability," 343.
7 Sandahl, "Disability Arts," 2.
8 Estrin, "The 'Edgiest' Singer on the Israeli Airwaves."

9 Jacobson, "Interview with the Voice Artist Victoria Hanna."

10 Tausinger, "Victoria Hanna."

11 Hadar, "Victoria Hanna"; Victoria Hanna, "Hebrew Vowels Demonstration," performance at the international conference "Music and Brains: The Surprising Link—An Interface Between Music Cognition and Neuroscience," Jerusalem, February 10–13, 2013, https://www.youtube .com/watch?v=fGliOFFUkoQ.

12 Garland-Thomson, "The Case for Conserving Disability," 341.

13 Ibid.

14 For further exploration of embodiment and rituals in Jewish traditions of learning the Hebrew alphabet, consider Ivan G. Marcus's book *Rituals of Childhood*. Marcus examines the rite of passage whereby medieval Jewish boys initiated their education, which included, among other things, the teacher smearing honey over the Hebrew letters on a tablet and asking the child to lick it off.

15 Marc Shell provides an engaging interpretation that draws a connection between his personal experience as a stutterer and the theological, performative, and linguistic dimensions of the Hebrew language, as well as the diverse interpretations of the biblical narrative of Moses. Shell, "Moses' Tongue."

16 Garland-Thomson. "Misfits," 597.

17 St. Pierre, "The Construction of the Disabled Speaker," 9.

18 Hanna, *Twenty-Two Letters*.

19 Hadar, "Victoria Hanna."

20 Mitchell and Snyder, *Narrative Prosthesis*. In her groundbreaking article, "Politics of Silencing," Hannah Naveh explores blindness as a symbolic element, offering a radical feminist interpretation of Jacob Steinberg's story "The Blind Woman" within the context of Jewish literature and Israeli society. Kevin Paterson argues that the field of disability studies has not yet fully engaged with speech impairments. In his view, even though norms of communication discriminate against people with speech impairments, scholars of disability studies have not yet theorized this discrimination. Paterson, "It's about Time!"

21 Deleuze, "He Stuttered," 27.

22 Henig, "Stammering Hebrew," 229; Pedaya. "Gam-ve-gam (gimgum)," 38.

23 Siebers, *Disability Theory*, 8–9.

24 Bauman and Murray, "Deaf Studies in the 21st Century," 247.

25 Oved, *Chiseling My Own*, 5. Unless I state otherwise, all the translations in the book are mine.

26 Ibid., 10.

27 Siebers, *Disability Theory*, especially 1–33.

28 Various scholars and activists have written about the ableist attitude that assumes that able-bodied identities and bodies are preferable. See, for example, Linton, *Claiming Disability*; and McRuer, *Crip Theory*.

29 Oved, *Chiseling My Own*, 13.

30 To quote Robert Murphy, "The notion that one is better off dead than disabled is nothing less than the ultimate aspiration against the physically impaired, for it questions the value of their lives and their very right to exist." Murphy, *The Body Silent*, 230. It is important for me to clarify that my aim is not to evade or downplay the pain and frustration present in Shiri Oved's poetry or the work of disabled poets in general. While I delve into the intricacies of these emotions in the next chapter, it's worth noting here that Julia Watts Belser eloquently describes writing about the loss associated with disability as the most challenging aspect for her, as "the one [story] I'm still not sure I dare to tell." This hesitation stems from the way society tends to interpret disability loss and pain in a way that feeds ableist worldviews (Watts Belser, *Loving Our Own Bones*, 100). For more discussion of pain and its complexity in relation to disability politics, see Eli Clare's *Brilliant Imperfection*.

31 Oved, *Chiseling My Own*, 27.

32 Preston, *Fantasy of Disability*.

33 Oved, *Chiseling My Own*, 14.

34 Ibid., 24.

35 Kafer, *Feminist, Queer, Crip*, 1–2.

36 Oved, *Chiseling My Own*, 23.

37 Ibid., 25, 24.

38 Ibid., 29, 35.

39 Ibid., 39.

40 Ibid., 51.

41 Ibid., 53.

42 Ibid., 45.

43 Ibid., 44.

44 Ibid., 15.

45 See, for example, Perske, "The Dignity of Risk and the Mentally Retarded"; Wolpert, "The Dignity of Risk."

46 Pulrang, "Disabled People Have Unique Perspectives on Risks and 'Reopening.'"

47 Bluwstein Sela, *Rachel's Poetry* (*Shirat Rahel*), 34.

48 Yudkoff, *Tubercular Capital*, 51, 52.

49 Rice et al., "Imagining Disability Futurities," 221.

50 Jerusalem Talmud, Tractate Yoma 27a:3. I would like to thank Professor Lynn Kaye, an expert in rabbinic literature and thought, for helping me with this translation.

51 Brown, *Investigating a Culture of Disability*.

52 Finkelstein, "Disabled People and Our Culture Development."

53 Ibid., 3. Colin Barnes and Geoff Mercer also mention the constant concern that disability culture "will be assimilated into mainstream culture with the result that its political significance is neutralized." Barnes and Mercer, "Disability Culture," 531.

54 Broyer, "Stigma and Unconsciousness," 31. Nissim Mizrachi interviewed key figures working to advance the status of people with disabilities in Arab communities in Israel. He concludes that while concepts such as integration and accessibility are widely supported among people with disabilities and activists, there is a reluctance bordering on real opposition to concepts that emphasize specific positive dimensions of disability. Mizrachi, "Translating Disability in a Muslim Community."

55 Mizrachi, "On the Social Boundaries of the Critical Discourse on Disability."

56 This generalized affirmation of the celebration of the unique dimensions of disability in the U.S. should perhaps be tempered by Robert McRuer's comment, "Although it is changing rapidly, it is still possible to say that, after other fields (feminism, critical race theory, queer theory) have sharply critiqued inclusion, tolerance, or multiculturalism, or have moved to more radical questions about the limits of tolerance or about figures who are always already excluded from, or sacrificed by, multiculturalism, the disability movement (in and out of the academy) at times remains a project largely indebted to liberalism." McRuer, "No Future for Crips," 70.

57 Oved, *Chiseling My Own*, 18.

58 Ibid., 17.

59 Ibid., 13. While I interpreted the laxative as an allusion to self-harm, one of my anonymous readers pointed out that since one takes a laxative to expel something, it might have an almost opposite meaning. Similarly, the line "when will I cease, when will I desist" from the same poem is powerfully ambiguous. Does it mean "When will I cease to exist?" or "When will I cease and desist from self-hatred?" These are very different possibilities that could lead to different interpretations of the poem. To maintain the rawness and ambivalence of the physicality in Oved's poetry, I believe we don't need to choose between these options. Instead, we can recognize that the ambivalence itself is central to the poem.

60 Barnes and Mercer, "Disability Culture," 530–31.

61 Cameron and Swain, "Unless Otherwise Stated," 70.

62 Samuels, "My Body, My Closet," 243. While Samuels interprets passing as a subversive practice that allows for the establishment of a nonlinear identity (and not an internalization of oppression), she mentions, "This dynamic may also be observed from the role of passing in transgender contexts, in which the ability to pass for a new or different gender, or to present an ambiguous gender, is often experienced as a validation of radical identity rather than as assimilation or misrecognition" (253 n.34).

63 Slava Greenberg and nili Broyer analyzed Dana Diment's 2014 film *Tifkud Gavoah* (*High Functioning*) as a cinematic narrative of coming out of the autistic closet that is possible in this case only because of Diment's "high-functioning" autism. Greenberg and Broyer, "Staring Back."

64 Cameron and Swain, "Unless Otherwise Stated," 76–77.

65 Samuels, "My Body, My Closet," 237.

66 Garland-Thomson, *Staring*, 52.

67 Broyer, "Through the Restroom Mirror," 1490.

68 Ibid., 1496.

69 Ibid., 1495.

70 Broyer, "Through the Restroom Mirror," 1496.

71 Garland-Thomson, "Misfits," 592–93.

72 Carroll, *Through the Looking-Glass*, 9.

73 Deems, "'We're All Mad Here,'" 68.

74 McRuer, *Crip Theory*, 2. For more on the concept of "compulsory able-bodiedness," see also Kafer, "Compulsory Bodies." For an analysis of the ways in which disability arts provide a critical response to the experience of social exclusion and marginalization, see Barnes and Mercer, "Disability Culture."

75 Bhabha, *The Location of Culture*.

76 Alster, "The Amazing *Miss Vertigo* [*sic*]," 3.

77 Rice et al., "Imagining Disability Futurities," 223–24.

78 Garland-Thomson, "Misfits," 593.

79 Ibid., 595. Garland-Thomson mentions that she has borrowed the phrase "shape carries story" from medieval historian Caroline Walker Bynum.

80 Dolmage, *Disability Rhetoric*, 2–3; Kafer, *Feminist, Queer, Crip*, 9.

Chapter 2

I thank Shira Szobel, my beloved and smart friend and sister-in-law, for the enormous help with the translations in this chapter.

1 The entire anthology is available to view: poets.org, March 2022, https://poets.org/anthology/disabled-and-ddeaf-poets-anthology-curated-leah-lakshmi-piepzna-samarasinha.

2 Other examples of collections of poetry written by disabled poets include Alland, Barokka, and Sluman, *Stairs and Whispers*; and Black, Bartlett, and Northen, *Beauty Is a Verb*.

3 Hebrew literature is saturated with writers who dealt with a variety of emotional disabilities: Devorah Baron, Yona Wallach, and Dahlia Ravikovitch are certainly among the best-known examples.

4 Shabat-Nadir, "A Boy Without a Face," 115–46.

5 Noticeable exceptions within this trend are Tamar Gelbets's *Last One* (*Haaharon*) (Tel-Aviv: Modan and Ḥargol, 2023) and Ruti Zooaretz's *Eaten* (*Ahulot*) (Or Yehudah: Kinneret, Zmora-Bittan, Dvir, 2008). These two pseudo-autobiographical novels explore women's illnesses and were authored by the women themselves, offering first-hand accounts of their experiences with cancer and eating disorder respectively.

6   Marton, *To Be Trapped in My Body*, 41, 20, 37, 44, 47.
7   Addressing Eliza Suggs's 1906 memoir *Shadow and Sunshine*, Andrew
     Walker-Cornetta grapples with the question of how scholars might
     approach subjects whose concepts of disability don't necessarily align
     with the models we tend to use. He wonders how, for example, in
     an era of celebrating disability, we should respond to subjects whose
     experiences are incompatible with "disability pride"; and how, in
     a field that prefers subjects who enact forms of agency, we should
     interpret disabled individuals who embody religious submission.
     Walker-Cornetta, "Without the Lord." Inspired by models of nega-
     tivity in queer studies, Black studies, and crip theory, J. Logan Smilges
     provides a critical assessment of liberal disability politics. Smilges,
     Crip Negativity.
8   Crow, "Renewing the Social Model of Disability," 3–4.
9   Price, "The Bodymind Problem and the Possibilities of Pain," 274.
10 Love, *Feeling Backward*, 4.
11 Ibid., 8.
12 In my reading of Orit Marton's poetry, I keep in mind Sue Lanser's call
     against the idealization of pain and suffering: "Perhaps because I grew
     up before gay was proud (or even gay), I worry about romanticizing
     shame and pain in the name of a grief that I also acknowledge as
     justifiable." Lanser, "Review of Heather Love's *Feeling Backward*," 545.
13 Ailam, "On the Poetry of Orit Marton," 31; Hakak, "Orit Marton's
     Poems Are the Victory of Spirit over Matter," 30–32.
14 Ngai, *Ugly Feelings*; Smilges, *Crip Negativity.*
15 Vig, "Being Imprisoned in My Body."
16 Ibid.
17 Kelly, "Building Bridges with Accessible Care," 792.
18 Fink, *All Our Families*, 7.
19 Piepzna-Samarasinha, *Care Work*, 26.
20 Ibid., 22.
21 In her autobiographical work *The Cancer Journals*, Audre Lorde under-
     scores the importance of having a community of women in her jour-
     ney of coping with breast cancer. She writes about the significance
     of "knowing that my work is part of a continuum of women's work, of
     reclaiming this earth and our power, and knowing that this work did
     not begin with my birth nor will it end with my death. And it means

knowing that within this continuum, my life and my love and my work have particular power and meaning relative to others" (6).

22 Malatino, *Trans Care*, 58–59. Questions regarding the power and authority of archives also arise of course in the context of Black history and enslavement. For a fascinating work that focuses on the experience of girls and young urban Black women in Philadelphia and New York at the beginning of the twentieth century that goes against the limits the archive sets on what can be known and whose perspective matters, see Hartman, *Wayward Lives*.

23 Britton, Floyd, and Murphy, "Overcoming Another Obstacle," 222. See also White, "Crippling the Archives"; and Brilmyer, "Archival Assemblages."

24 Milbern, "On the Ancestral Plane."

25 Ibid.

26 Marton, *To Be Trapped in My Body*, 7.

27 Vig, "Being Imprisoned in My Body."

28 Marton, *To Be Trapped in My Body*, 41.

29 Although I mention the influence of Leah Goldberg on Orit Marton's ars poetic concept, the notion of poetry as being committed to the mundane is also deeply influenced by the poetic position formulated in Natan Zach's well-known essay "Reflections on Alterman's Poetry" (1959). This polemic essay became a kind of generational manifesto that called for the writing of concrete poetry—a poetry of the here and now. It was a call to write in simple, everyday language, use accurate images from the poet's world of experience and emotion rather than general symbols, escape pathos, and above all, use free internal rhythm that arises from the poem and not from an artificial rhythmic framework. Zach, "Reflections on Alterman's Poetry."

30 Goldberg, *The Courage for the Mundane*, 165–70. This work has received extensive interpretations. See, for example, Weiss, "A Man with His Life at Both Ends of Time"; Weisman, "After All of This, I Will Have to Muster All of My 'Courage for the Mundane'"; Gordinsky, "Essayistic Writing as an Everyday Art."

31 Goldberg, *The Courage for the Mundane*, 168.

32 Marton, *A Woman, After All*, 7.

33 Gill, "Becoming Visible." See also Broyer, "Stigma and Unconsciousness," 19.

34 Friend and Sandbank, *Flowers of Perhaps*, 45.

35 Soker-Schwager, *Excess Thought*.

36 Marton, *A Woman, After All*, 59.

37 Bluwstein Sela, *Rachel's Poetry*, 111.

38 Olmert, *Predicaments of Writing and Loving*, 72–73. See also Tsamir, "The Pioneers' Sacrifice."

39 Olmert, *Predicaments of Writing and Loving*, 86.

40 Gill, "Becoming Visible," 7. See also Garland-Thomson, "Feminist Disability Studies."

41 Sachs, "Yona Explores the Life of a Poet Who Turned Madness into Verse."

42 The translation is taken from Ziv, "'Our Virgin Friends and Wives?'" 342. For a different English translation of the poem, see Cohen, "*Loosen the Fetters*," 66–67.

43 Cohen, "*Loosen the Fetters*," 70.

44 For feminist interpretations of Yona Wallach's poetry, see, for example, Rattok, *Angel of Fire*; Tsoffar, "Staging Sexuality"; Tsamir, *In the Name of the Land*; Stav, *Reconstructing Daddy*.

45 Feminist disability studies exposes women and gender studies' neglect of disabilities. See, for example, Smith and Hutchison, *Gendering Disability*; Garland-Thomson, "Feminist Disability Studies"; Hall, *Feminist Disability Studies*; Ben-Moshe and Magaña, "An Introduction to Race, Gender, and Disability."

46 While there are a number of personal narratives available written by disabled people who voice their own feelings of being the object of fetishistic desire, this experience remains virtually unstudied. See Kafer, "Amputated Desire, Resistant Desire"; *Encyclopedia of Sex and Gender*, "Disability, Fetishization of."

47 Lauf, "Uncovering the Mad Woman."

48 The interview that Helit Yeshurun conducted with Yona Wallach in 1984 is unusual in that it took place while Wallach was in the Tel Hashomer Hospital. Parts of the interview were published in the periodical *Hadarim*, edited by Yeshuron, and almost three decades later it became the basis for Yair Qedar's documentary *The Seven Tapes*.

49 Marton, *A Woman, After All*, 21.

50 Ravikovitch, *The Complete Poems*, 46; Ravikovitch, *Hovering at a Low Altitude*, 76–77.

51 Szobel, *A Poetics of Trauma*, 73–76.
52 Ravikovitch, *Hovering at a Low Altitude*, 76–77.
53 Hirsch, "Review of *Dahlia Ravikovitch*."
54 Stevens, "Structural Barriers to Sexual Autonomy for Disabled People," 62–63; Broyer, "Disabled Fashion Models vs. Cripsex."
55 Gill, "Becoming Visible," 15.
56 Love, *Feeling Backward*, 147. For a fascinating reading of Jewish women's poetry written in English, Yiddish, and Hebrew through Love's queer model of "feeling backward" and "backward future," see Weiman-Kelman, *Queer Expectations*.
57 Lev-Ari, "Inbal Eshel Cahansky."
58 Eshel Cahansky, *Samael My Beloved*, 28.
59 Ibid., 77.
60 Khanmalek and Rhodes, "A Decolonial Feminist Epistemology of the Bed," 35. In a somewhat similar way, Mel Y. Chen explores the connection between their illness and their couch in the context of animacies and intimacy: "The couch and I are interabsorbent, interporous, and not only because the couch is made of mammalian skin. These are intimacies that are often ephemeral, and they are lively; and I wonder whether or how much they are really made of habit." Chen, *Animacies*, 203.
61 Kim, *Curative Violence*, 6.
62 Pett, "Rash Reading," 26.
63 Woolf, *On Being Ill*, 3.
64 Ibid., 12.
65 Piepzna-Samarasinha, *Care Work*, 44.
66 Ibid., 12.
67 Eshel Cahansky, *Samael My Beloved*, 83.
68 Bailin, *The Sickroom in Victorian Fiction*, 27.
69 Yudkoff, *Tubercular Capital*, 54, 52–53.
70 Ibid., 63.
71 Ibid., 65.
72 Hedva, "Sick Woman Theory." An earlier version of this essay was published in *Mask Magazine* in January 2016. This virtual text is adapted from Johanna Hedva's lecture "My Body Is a Prison of Pain So I Want to Leave It like a Mystic but I Also Love It & Want It to Matter Politically," delivered in Los Angeles on October 7, 2015.

73 Piepzna-Samarasinha, *Care Work*, 11.

74 Hedva, "Letter to a Young Doctor."

75 Eshel Cahansky, *Roaring in an Infinite Loop*, 13.

76 Golgotha as an allusion to Jesus and as a place of suffering also recurs in Inbal Eshel Cahansky's poem "In the Kingdom of the Body and the Sky" from the same book. The poem opens with the speaker's call, "When you finally come to Golgotha / to take me down from the cross of my body's deformity, / you will cradle me with great compassion / and weep over my suffering that has ended" (*Roaring in an Infinite Loop*, 69).

77 Patsavas, "Recovering a Cripistemology of Pain," 213. For a related discussion on the topic "What might we learn about crip genealogies in their moves?" see Chen, Kafer, Kim, and Minich, *Crip Genealogies*, 18.

78 Wallach, *Let the Words*, 157.

79 Wallach, *The Unconscious Unfolds like a Fan*, 285.

80 Sarna, *Yona Wallach*, 291.

81 Not surprisingly, Yona Wallach's poem was published around the same time as Audre Lorde's famous statement "Caring for myself is not self-indulgence, it is self-preservation, and that is an act of political warfare." Lorde's sentence captures the amalgamation of personal experience with the political significance of self-care (Lorde, *A Burst of Light*, 95). Lorde's sentence is quoted at the beginning of Lin's dissertation "Freud's Jaw and Other Lost Objects." For further exploration, see Inbar-Weiss, "'That the Pain Not Be Wasted,'" 185.

82 Bluwstein Sela, *Rachel's Poetry*, 25, translated from the Hebrew by Friend in *Found in Translation*, 35.

83 Eshel Cahansky, *Samael My Beloved*, 27.

84 Hedva, "Sick Woman Theory."

85 Ravikovitch, *The Complete Poems*, 112; Ravikovitch, *Hovering at a Low Altitude*, 127.

86 Hever, "Alone with the Poems."

87 Ravikovitch, *The Complete Poems*, 112; Ravikovitch, *Hovering at a Low Altitude*, 127.

88 Patsavas, "Recovering a Cripistemology of Pain," 213. See also Holmes, "Pain."

89 Reflecting on his personal experiences of writing an illness memoir and contemplating what makes such storytelling possible, Arthur W.

Frank argues that "even the most personal story is a reconfiguration of other stories." Consequently, he suggests that "perhaps humans are best thought of as dependently creative." Frank, "An Illness of One's Own," 3.

90 The poetic archives produced by disabled poets in their genealogy can be referred to as "offended archives." Discussing the tension between hegemonic and marginalized groups in Israel through the lens of the camera, art critic Adam Baruch juxtaposes what he terms "photographed Israel" and its "offended archives," "the archives of the minorities, the rejected, the immigrants, the bottom deciles, who refused to be expelled from 'photographed Israel.'" Baruch, "How Are Things at Home," 20.

91 Malatino, *Trans Care*, 7.

92 Ibid., 54.

93 Patsavas, "Recovering a Cripistemology of Pain."

94 Siebers, "Disability, Pain, and the Politics of Minority Identity," 114.

95 Patsavas, "Recovering a Cripistemology of Pain," 205.

96 Price, "The Bodymind Problem and the Possibilities of Pain," 279.

Chapter 3

1 Hands, "An Interview with Israeli Star Hanna Azoulay-Hasfari."

2 Munk, "Fate and Choice in Post-Colonial Feminist Cinema."

3 Loshitzky, *Identity Politics on the Israeli Screen*, 77.

4 Ibid., 86.

5 Anidjar and Funkenstein, "Jewish Mysticism Alterable and Unalterable."

6 Lubin, "On the Way to Mommy," 206.

7 While my discussion in this chapter focuses on Pnina, there are other disabled characters depicted in offensive and ableist ways in the film. For example, the blind father is portrayed as dysfunctional and violent. According to Yael Munk, he represents male authority that has lost its power ("Fate and Choice in Post-Colonial Feminist Cinema," 22). The father's blindness, according to this interpretation, symbolizes his alienation in Western society and his lack of authority in the family—the filmmakers, in other words, use his blindness to

signal weakness and helplessness. His blindness not only functions on a purely symbolic level, rather than referencing his experiences of disability, it is also primarily shaped in an ableist form in which blindness is negative and inherently limiting.

8 Mitchell and Snyder, *Narrative Prosthesis*, 49.

9 Azoulay-Hasfari, *Sh'Chur*, 148.

10 Michal Friedman suggests that Pnina represents the fear of madness that hovers over female existence ("The Beyond Dimension," 231).

11 Chesler, *Women and Madness*; Gilbert and Gubar, *The Madwoman in the Attic*; Foucault, *History of Madness*.

12 For a comprehensive and up-to-date survey of the field of mad studies, see Beresford and Russo, *The Routledge International Handbook of Mad Studies*. For a discussion on madness in Black radical art, see Bruce, *How to Go Mad Without Losing Your Mind*.

13 Garland-Thomson, *Extraordinary Bodies*, 6.

14 In an analysis of Michal Aviad's film *Invisible*, Raz Yosef explains that "even if spectators do not identify with the male perpetrator on the screen, or even if they feel empathy toward the female victim, it is what Kaplan calls 'empty empathy' . . .—an emotional reaction that does not give rise to ethical-social refection on the viewer's part—both because the rape is embedded within a melodramatic sentimental narrative that reduces the terror and because the voyeuristic look at the spectacle of rape works to distance the spectator from the victim's suffering, thereby preventing onlookers from ethically examining their own privileged viewing position." Yosef, "Conditions of Visibility," 927.

15 It is worth noting the play *Spoon of Gold* (*Kapit shel Zahav*, 2010) by the Kenafayim ("Wings—Because in art there is no disability") organization, created by and with actors with cognitive disabilities. Co-written by Shira Gefen and directed by Rina Padwa, the play features a monologue from one of the actresses addressing past experiences of sexual violence. The segment is accessible online: https://www.youtube .com/watch?v=CDu-slB2eHY.

16 Valenti-Hein and Schwartz, *The Sexual Abuse Interview*; Shapiro, "The Sexual Assault Epidemic No One Talks About."

17 Hamutal Maapil Varsano argues that "Pnina's character represents the unbridled female sexuality that threatens to violate the existing

order and overtake it" (*A Blue and White Movie*, 150). In contrast to this interpretation, I would argue that Pnina's characterization functions in two ways: she represents the way that asexuality is ascribed to the disabled female body, a cultural deprivation of sexual agency and autonomy, but also how that body is at risk of being excessively exposed to sexual danger—this creates an inherently problematic and ableist understanding of how women with disabilities relate to or connect with their own sexualities.

18 On representations of Mizrahi women's sexuality, see Dahan Kalev, "Made to Be Inept"; and Naaman, "'Everyone Knows Yemenites Are Great in Bed.'"

19 Pnina becomes pregnant as a result of the rape, and her mother performs *sh'chur* on her to abort the fetus. The film actually depicts two abortion-related scenes, radical in Israeli (and not only Israeli) cinema, where representation of abortion on-screen is rare. One of these occurs at the beginning of the film, when Shlomo's girlfriend considers getting an abortion, and the other is Pnina's abortion. Shlomo's girlfriend, as the able-bodyminded woman, does not abort, while Pnina is forced to have the abortion. In a way, the film erases the possibility of motherhood for Pnina as a disabled woman, but the able-bodyminded woman could not possibly be willing to abort and therefore not choose, or delay choosing, motherhood.

20 Margrit Shildrick claims that there is a strange paradox in Western society that "alternates between denying that sexual pleasure has any place in the lives of disabled people, and fetishising it. Both responses constitute a refusal of sexuality as a regular element in disability experience, an effective silencing that damages not just self-esteem, but . . . all aspects of the capacity for self-becoming" (Shildrick, *Dangerous Discourses*, 60). While Israeli culture does indeed deny the sexuality of disabled people, it has almost no expressions of fetishizing disability. Instead, as mentioned, the disabled body, especially the female disabled body, is described as vulnerable and constantly exposed to sexual danger. For a discussion of one of the canonical representations of sexual danger to a disabled male body in Yoram Kaniuk's 1966 novel *Himmo, King of Jerusalem*, see Szobel, *Flesh of My Flesh*, 69–99. For further discussions about people with disabilities as either hypersexual or asexual, see Finger, "Forbidden Fruit"; Murphy,

The Body Silent, 195–96; Kim, "A Man, with Same Feelings"; Kulick and Rydström. *Loneliness and Its Opposite*, 4–11; Greenberg, *Animated Film and Disability*, 82.

21 Duvdevani, "*Next to Her.*"

22 Utin, *Lessons in Cinema*, 124–51. Shmulik Duvdevani points out that *Next to Her* has a dark, disturbing, even threatening tone that invokes the 1962 film *What Ever Happened to Baby Jane?*, directed by Robert Aldrich, a film with a plot that centers on a former Hollywood star who abuses her disabled sister who lives with her ("*Next to Her*").

23 Director Asaf Korman in a conversation with Pablo Utin, *Lessons in Cinema*, 145.

24 The actors with disability who participate in the film are actors from the Wings (Knafaim) association directed by Rina Padva: Yehiel Cohen, Tzachi Zeif, Tali Hirsch, Sivan Selma, and Idan Avigal.

25 The term "fantasy of disability" was coined by Jeffrey Preston, and it refers to representations of disability that do not express the true lived experiences of people with disability, but rather dominant cultural projections, "the unconscious fantasies circulating in representations of disability" (Preston, *Fantasy of Disability*, 9). My previous work on literature featuring wounded Israeli soldiers as characters explored Zionist "fantasies of disability," showing the extent to which Israeli culture invests in suppressing the experience of disability and neutralizing its rebellious potential (Szobel, *Flesh of My Flesh*, 69–99).

26 Limor Ashkenazi in Krimolovski, *Selfie in a Limited Edition.*

27 Limor Ashkenazi's portfolio (2022). I thank Limor Ashkenazi from the bottom of my heart for very generously sharing her portfolio with me. The portfolio includes photographs of her rich artistic work, accompanied by brief explanations she wrote.

28 Crip theory of sexuality is used as an analytical, artistic, or practical framework to identify, challenge, and politicize sexual norms and practices. Robert McRuer notes in *Crip Theory* that, as with the term *queer*, the choice of *crip* is meant to be provocative and to offer an opportunity for reclamation of the word. "Crip" is short for "cripple," generally regarded as a strongly derogatory word. Instead of being addressed as someone different, such as "functionally impaired" or "differently abled," the choice is there to claim the term *crip* for oneself and experience pride. Crip theory thus affirms lived, embodied

experiences of disability and the knowledges (or *cripistemologies*) that emerge from them. *Cripping* offers a critical process, considering how certain bodily, mental, emotional, or neurological experiences have been marginalized or invisibilized, made pathological or deviant.

29 I borrow the term "countercultural approach" from Alison Kopit's thesis "Toward a Queer Crip Aesthetic," 15.

30 As is the case with most selfies, whether it is admitted or not, those in this exhibition were staged; for obvious reasons pertaining to physical ability, however, they were not always physically photographed by their subjects.

31 Feuerstein, *Breaking Through the Glass Wall.*

32 Gordon-Chen and Teomi Sela, *Breaking Walls.*

33 Alhadaz, "Breaking Walls."

34 Ibid. In an interview I conducted with Limor Ashkenazi after completing this chapter, we further explored how BDSM influences her art. See Szobel, "Crossing Boundaries."

35 Sheppard, "Using Pain, Living with Pain," 57. See also Langdridge, "Speaking the Unspeakable"; Langdridge and Barker, "Situating Sadomasochism."

36 Segersky, "People Don't Realize That a Disabled Person Is Also Sexual."

37 For a thorough analysis of how people living with chronic pain find a space for the reestablishment of their subjectivity through BDSM, see Sheppard, "Using Pain, Living with Pain."

38 Mark Hay claims that the intersection of BDSM and disability has received little attention, even within the kink world. And if this is the case in the United States, it is all the more true in Israel. (Hay, "The Pleasure and Pain of Being Disabled in the BDSM Community.")

39 In the early 2000s, there was a small but significant trend of Israeli artists and activists foregrounding conversations dealing with intersections of sexuality and disability. For example, Dani Garmise founded his groundbreaking internet discussion group, "Disabled and Sexy" (having borrowed the name from Iddo Gruengard's fashion show); Limor Ashkenazi's play *Other Person* (*Zulat*) was performed in 2008, and in 2010 Rona Soffer's pioneering documentary *Love Davka*, about the sexuality of disabled women, was released. At the same time, a similar preoccupation with crip sexuality was also prompting discourses within the United States and the United Kingdom.

In the early 2000s there was an increasing call among both activists and theorists—Tom Shakespeare in the UK and Tobin Siebers in the U.S., for example—to seriously address issues of sexuality and sexual agency within the disability community. While it might seem that the Israeli trend was influenced by the concurrent American and British ones, many conversations with artists active during this time reveal that most of them were not familiar with these international works (many of which were not then available to Hebrew speakers).

For a comprehensive and detailed discussion of this period in the United States and United Kingdom, with an emphasis on the works of Tom Shakespeare, Diane Richardson, Mark Sherry, and Tobin Siebers, see Shildrick, "Sexual Citizenship, Governance and Disability."

40 Broyer, "On the Margins of Femininity," 15.

41 Adams, *Sideshow U.S.A.*, 4–5.

42 Ibid., 10.

43 Adams, "Disability and the Circus," 16.

44 Moser, *Standard Mark* (*Tav Teken*).

45 The title of the photograph overtly alludes to the 1984 romantic comedy *The Woman in Red*, directed by Gene Wilder, in which Charlotte (Kelly LeBrock), a beautiful woman clad in a red dress, crosses over a ventilation gate—gusts of wind cause the dress to billow up and over her head, creating an iconic image that represents sexuality, desire, and temptation.

46 Segersky, "People Don't Realize That a Disabled Person Is Also Sexual."

47 Ibid.

48 Garland-Thomson, "Staring Back," 335.

49 For a similar move in the Disabled and Sexy fashion show organized by Iddo Gruengard, Roni Viner, and Talia Gal-Ed in 2004 in Tel Aviv, see Broyer, "Stigma and Unconsciousness," 19–31.

50 Shildrick, "Sexual Citizenship, Governance and Disability," 140.

51 Butler, "Is Kinship Always Already Heterosexual?" 18.

52 Ibid.

53 Shakespeare, "Disabled Sexuality," 163.

54 Although the images Ashkenazi presents are radical in the Israeli social context, it is hard to ignore their heteronormative nature. Despite the feminist criticism that can be attributed to Ashkenazi's adaptation of Jessica Rabbit, it could be argued that the project itself preserves a

heteronormative sexist beauty ideal. Similarly, the use of BDSM as a liberating crip and feminist practice can be challenged due to the duality inherent in BDSM. While the power dynamics and exchanges seem to make BDSM a means to break free from traditional patriarchal sexual roles, one might argue that it is still a heteronormative fantasy rooted in masculinity, and it does not necessarily represent female crip sexuality. By the same token Audre Lorde argues that "S/M is not the sharing of power, it is merely a depressing replay of the old and destructive dominant/subordinate mode of human relating and one-sided power, which is even now grinding our earth and our human consciousness into dust" (Lorde, *A Burst of Light*, 6). In other words, Limor Ashkenazi's works set up a multifaceted movement between heteronormative sexuality and crip sexuality.

55 Weeks, "The Sexual Citizen," 37.

56 I borrow the term "sexual justice" from Morris B. Kaplan's book, *Sexual Justice*, which deals with the connection between citizenship and rights for queer people.

Chapter 4

1 Butoh is a form of Japanese dance theater that encompasses various philosophies, motivations, and techniques. It arose after World War II through collaborations between its two key founders, Tatsumi Hijikata (1928–86) and Kazuo Ohno (1906–2010). A Butoh dancer seeks to free herself from the shackles of rigorous technique; she looks for ways to break out and to abandon ready-made methods that focus on muscular strength, the lengthening and stretching of the body. Relinquishing rigid structure offers both dancers and viewers a raw encounter with the state of simply being, of "is-ness." It allows meditation on the mental, political, and existential condition without being caught in the past or haunted by any predicted future. It also enables the participants to take a leap into unfamiliar territory and to unveil "the body's hidden truths." See Ohno and Ohno, *Kazuo Ohno's World*, 65.

2 Some of the biographical information is taken from Tamar Borer's website, "Tamar Borer: About the Artist."

3 "About the Choreographer: Tamar Borer," *Choreographers*, accessed September 21, 2018, http://www.choreographers.org.il/798 (no longer available). For more on the award, see "Token of Grace" ("Ot hachsed"), Beit Issie Shapiro, accessed November 14, 2018, https://www.beitissie.org.

4 Albright, *Choreographing Difference*, 56. See also Albright, "Strategic Abilities." Among other explanations, the favoring of the able and stable body is related to the fact that, as many have argued, the visual presence of the disabled body disrupts hegemonic notions of normalization and reveals repressed anxieties about the mortality and vulnerability of the human body. See Smith, "Shifting Apollo's Frame," 81; Linton, *Claiming Disability*; Garland-Thomson, *Extraordinary Bodies*, 6.

5 The term "Apollonian frame" is taken from Owen Smith's analysis of dance, aesthetics, and normativity. Here it is employed as a code for the social preference of postural uprightness and verticality. Social and moral judgment often uses the site of the human body for such association; the vertical is associated with nobility and virtue, and the curved, bent, or otherwise socially "broke" body with subordination and dependence. Smith, "Shifting Apollo's Frame," 73–85.

6 See films *The Women Pioneers*, directed by Michal Aviad; and *Living for Tomorrow*, directed by Lilach Dekel; and the texts Shapira, *Land and Power*; Boyarin, *Unheroic Conduct*; Gluzman, *Ha-guf ha-tsiyoni*; and Presner, *Muscular Judaism*.

7 Weiss, *The Chosen Body*, 4. Mitchell and Snyder coined the term *ablenationalism* to describe the conflation of nation and ableism emerging in the late eighteenth century. Mitchell and Snyder, "Ablenationalism and the Geo-Politics of Disability," 124.

8 Rebecca Rossen discusses the emphasis on Jewish fortitude and the endurance of the Jewish people in Zionist dance in *Dancing Jewish*, 189–233.

9 Sandra M. Sufian and Natan M. Meir argue that Zionism displayed intricate sentiments regarding the disabled Jewish body and mind from its inception. On one hand, these individuals symbolized the persecuted and ailing condition of the Jewish nation, invoking sympathy and concern. Simultaneously, however, they were perceived as embodying the degeneracy of the Jewish people, necessitating their elimination through the regenerative processes promised by Zionism.

Sufian, "Mental Hygiene and Disability in the Zionist Project"; Sufian, *Healing the Land and the Nation*; Meir, *Stepchildren of the Shtetl*. For insights into the intertwining of crip and queer experiences in the early stages of the Zionist movement, see Imhoff, *The Lives of Jessie Sampter*.

10 Grosz, *Volatile Bodies*, ix.

11 See, for example, Feldman, *No Room of Their Own*; Lubin, "Body and Territory"; Naveh, *Israeli Family and Community*; Halpern, *Guf belo nachat*.

12 The works of Dina Roginsky, Orly Baor, and nili Broyer about Israeli disability dance are highly appreciated exceptions to this generalization. See Roginsky, "On the Symbolic and Physical Body"; Broyer, "Wearing the Mask of Dis-Dance"; Baor, *Disabled and Dancing*.

13 Baor, *Disabled and Dancing*. For a fascinating critical analysis of soldier-dancers in Israeli society, see Roginsky, "On the Symbolic and Physical Body."

14 Tsamid is Jerusalem's municipal organization for people with special needs.

15 For a survey about the growing interest in the field of disability studies in Israel, see Ben-Moshe and Colligan, "The State of Disability in Israel/Palestine."

16 Kafer, *Feminist, Queer, Crip*, 9.

17 Linton, *Claiming Disability*, 113.

18 Butler, "Rethinking Vulnerability and Resistance."

19 Butler, "Vulnerability and Resistance."

20 Ibid.

21 Butler, "Rethinking Vulnerability and Resistance." By approaching the body as articulate matter, Susan Leigh Foster demonstrates "the central role that physicality plays in constructing both individual agency and sociality" ("Choreographies of Protest," 395). My examination of the juxtaposition of disability and politics in Borer's dance is also informed by Foster's previous work, in which she discusses dance as a socially encoded discursive practice, and explores an aesthetico-political alternative in dance: *Reading Dancing*.

22 Butler, "Vulnerability and Resistance."

23 Linton, *Claiming Disability*, 113.

24 Borer, *ANA*.

25 Ibid.

26 Ibid.

27 Ruth Eshel refers to "A Story Like a Tale," choreographed by Amir
Kolben and Ofra Dudai in 1982, as the first dance performance that
dealt with the political situation in Israel. Eshel, "To Dance with the
Times," 16. Included among the scarce Israeli choreographers who
address political commentary through bodies are Rami Be'er, Ohad
Naharin, Liat Dror, Nir Ben Gal, Yasmeen Godder, Arkadi Zaides,
Hillel Kogan, Niv Sheinfeld, Oren Laor, and Ehud Darash. See also
Aldor, "The Borders of Contemporary Israeli Dance"; and Rotman,
"The Jewish-Arab Conflict in the Works of Amir Kolben, Rami Be'er,
and Ohad Naharin."

28 Derrida, *Monolingualism of the Other*, 25.

29 Ibid., 37.

30 Isaura is the city of a thousand wells from the much-admired book by
Italo Calvino, *The Invisible Cities*.

31 Borer and Erde, *The Making of "ANA."*

32 The Israeli singer and international recording artist Ofra Haza was
invited to perform the "Tikva," the national anthem of Israel, in
Paamoni ha Yovel (Bells Jubilee), the official celebration of the fiftieth
anniversary of the State of Israel, held on April 30, 1998. While
accepting the invitation to perform, she asked to sing "Jerusalem of
Gold" instead of the hymn. Not surprisingly, her performance became
the iconic image of these national celebrations. For a discussion
about the special status of the song "Jerusalem of Gold" in Israel, see
Gavrlely-Nuri, "The Social Construction of 'Jerusalem of Gold.'"

33 Friedes Galili, *Contemporary Dance in Israel*, 105.

34 Wills, *Prosthesis*, 9. He is quoted also in Jacobs, "Hebrew Remembers
Yiddish," 297. For a brilliant discussion of how the Hebrew translation of Yiddish serves as a prosthetic in the poetry of the Jewish
poet Avot Yeshurun, and his characterization of modern Hebrew as
a linguistic body disabled by hegemonic monolingualism, see Jacobs,
Strange Cocktail, 135–66. In her book *Prosthetic Memory* Alison Landsberg invites her readers to imagine memory as a site of possibility for
progressive politics based on empathy. Despite the relevance of this
argument to the Israeli–Palestinian conflict, I do not use the notion
of prosthetic memory here in the way that Landsberg coined it, as

referring to experiences "not strictly derived from a person's lived experience" (25). This is not just because for Borer the Israeli occupation is a personal and lived experience, but mainly because of the implied assumption in Landsberg's project about the prosthesis as an already missing appendage—a notion Borer's performances and dancerly philosophy constantly challenge. What many would perceive as "lacking" or "faulty" becomes in Borer's work a visceral and physical representation of a constantly changing, growing, and biodegradable world.

35 Derrida, *Monolingualism of the Other*, 3. The lie in Derrida's thought is related to the juxtaposition of political history, imagination, and time: "The lie is the future, one may venture to say. . . . To tell the truth is, on the contrary, to say what is or what will have been and it would instead prefer the past." Derrida, *Without Alibi*, 66.

36 The song "Gaza" is taken from Mafatal's album *Telling Pictures* (1994), written by Anat Lane. Mafatal, established in 1993 by Ronit Rosenthal and Ilana Tsabari, expressed a radical voice in the Israeli context both musically and socially. They combined different musical styles and songs, and along with independent pieces, they performed a Yemenite folk song by the Egyptian singer Umm Kulthum. They sang and played a variety of instruments, from bass guitar, drums, and piano to the cans. In a particularly unusual and political move, their album cover included Arabic titles.

37 Azoulay, *The Angel of History*. See also Azoulay, *Once upon a Time*.

38 Benjamin, "Theses on the Philosophy of History," 257.

39 Felman, *The Juridical Unconscious*, 25.

40 Ibid., 33.

41 Lutz Koepnick refers to the angel of history as an allegorical figure that represents failure and incompetence. He claims that the angel does not represent active intervention, but rather a melancholic recollection that turns its back on the future and is unable to assist and support the victims. Koepnick, *Walter Benjamin and the Aesthetics of Power*.

42 The reference to Benjamin's urban wanderer is clear; unlike his white, European, abled, male wanderer, Borer's "wanderer" is a disabled Israeli female dancer in a wheelchair. While both are wandering

observers who gaze upon history, it is the wanderer in Borer's work who offers new perceptions about gender, space, and history.

43 Interestingly, while Borer danced her radical political suggestions to Israeli society—literally embodying her perspectives—another movie was inspired by Benjamin's angel of history, as another artist implemented it to search for political alternatives. Udi Aloni's film *Malach Mekomi* (*Local Angel*) documents Aloni's attempts to face and unpack the post-9/11 reality, especially with the escalating violence in the Middle East. The resemblances in the all-encompassing perspectives of Aloni's cinematic exploration and Borer's dancerly examination are striking, as we see in their challenge to normative notions of history as well as in their rejection of the privileged. Similar to the way Borer posits the disabled position as a point of departure for a discourse not caught up in the repressive hegemonic historical narrative, Aloni suggests the image of a fragile God—a God in need of people's help and compassion—as a starting point for a radical change. Nancy Eiesland's notion of the Disabled God merges Borer's and Aloni's suggestions, as she argues that "Christians do not have an abled-bodied God as their primal image." She draws on the image of a Disabled God to challenge social constructions of disability. This image provides a different outlook on society—one that challenges the split between the providing abled body and the receiving disabled body. The Disabled God who provides grace and support to people through God's broken body offers a new model of subjectivity, compassion, and resistance to oppressive constructs of hegemonic embodiment. Borer relates to this model while inviting her disabled angel to offer a political alternative. Eiesland, *The Disabled God*, 11.

44 Watts Belser, "Familiarity and Difference." See also Watts Belser, "God on Wheels." Even though Watts Belser's argument refers specifically to religious communities, I adopt it here as a general social suggestion.

45 Tamar Borer, in Hirsch, "An Angel in a Wheelchair," 19. It is important to note that *aza* in Hebrew has a dual meaning, depending on the placement of emphasis in the word. It can mean Gaza as a place or it can mean "strong" or "mighty." This duality clearly informs Borer's work and the titling of it.

46 Tamar Borer, in Krymolowski, "Dancing from the Soul."

47 Candoco Dance Company is made up of disabled and nondisabled
    dancers. Based in London, it was co-founded in 1991 by Celeste
    Dandeker-Arnold and Adam Benjamin. AXIS Dance Company is a
    physically integrated dance company founded in 1987 by Thais Mazur,
    and is based in Oakland, California. Stopgap Dance Company started
    in 1995 as a community dance project that brought together disabled
    and nondisabled members of the community. The choreography was
    led by University of Surrey (England) graduate and founding artistic
    director Vicki Balaam, who was mentored by Dave Toole and Kuldip
    Singh-Barmi. See "About History," StopgapDance.com, accessed Sep-
    tember 21, 2018, http://stopgapdance.com/about/history.

48 I take issue here with Gitit Ginat, who criticizes Tamar Borer for not
    "using her disability" to say something political about pain and injury,
    restriction of movement, and the inability to stand on two feet.
    Exploring Borer's depiction of the disabled angel in the context of the
    chosen Zionist body, I believe, unveils Borer's radical position. See
    Ginat, "Gaza Is Nothing."

49 Watts Belser, "Familiarity and Difference."

50 De Certeau, *The Practice of Everyday Life*, 91–110; de Certeau, "Practices
    of Space."

51 Lubin, "Low Gaze, Freed Gaze," 39. In a more recent article, Lubin
    develops and extends her argument about the low gaze as a political
    alternative. See "Space and Gaze." Even though Lubin does not men-
    tion de Certeau in her article about the low gaze, his writings seems
    very germane to her argument. I thank Professor Karen Grumberg for
    drawing my attention to this important influence.

52 Lubin, "Low Gaze, Freed Gaze," 37.

53 My use of the term *limitation* in the contexts of disabilities merits
    clarification. The social-construction model (unlike others, such as
    medicalized models and so on) locates disability within the context
    of a society made for and dominated by nondisabled interests and
    needs. Disability, thus, does not stand by and for itself. The dominant
    presence of the nondisabled environment is what makes disability
    experienced as a limitation. As Sandahl and Auslander argue, "It is
    the stairway in front of the wheelchair user, or written text in front
    of the blind person, that handicaps an individual, not the physical

impairment itself." "Disability Studies in Commotion with Performance Studies: Introduction," 8.

54   Even though Lubin ascribes the low gaze to women and to any position culturally coded as feminine, she does not include disability in her discussion. Situating Lubin's conversation in such a way that disability experiences might be influential has the potential to magnify the audience and intent of the gaze. In other words, it might be enriching "to explore the theoretical terrain opened up by reading disability into those queer narratives and feminist analysis that never use the word 'disability.'" Kafer, *Feminist, Queer, Crip*, 17.

55   The Israeli artist, photographer, and art curator Michal Heiman claims that by referring to the angel of history in a masculine form, Benjamin and his followers are missing the fact that the angel is wearing a skirt in Paul Klee's picture. The masculine and feminine aspects of the angel live side by side. See Heiman, "The Journey to Pictures Lost by Walter Benjamin."

56   Lubin, "Low Gaze, Freed Gaze," 36.

57   Eshel, "On the Verge of Amateur."

Chapter 5

1   The number of people who became disabled as a result of political violence is unknown, as are the types of disability, and there is certainly no sense of how people cope in the aftermath on a larger scale. For a study that reports and analyzes injuries associated with war in the Gaza Strip from July 8 to August 26, 2014, see Mosleh et al., "The Burden of War-Injury." For more studies about disabled people within the occupied Palestinian territories, see Nasser, Maclachlan, and McVeigh, "Social Inclusion and Mental Health of Children with Physical Disabilities in Gaza, Palestine"; and Downey et al., "Arts and Disability in Lebanon, the Occupied Palestinian Territories, and Jordan."

2   All quotes from the statement are taken from Sins Invalid, "Disability Justice for Palestine." In the years since this statement, other disability advocacy and awareness organizations have issued similar statements. See, for example, the statements put forth by the Autistic

People of Color Fund, "Condemning Israeli State Terror"; and by the Abolition and Disability Justice Collective, "Statement of Solidarity with Palestine."

3 Helen Meekosha calls scholars and activists "to be conscious about the lack of geopolitical specificity in disability studies and acknowledge the issues of access and exclusion inherent in the universalising tendencies of the discipline." This awareness should be part of a broader move by disability activists and scholars with the aim of preventing global atrocities in any form. Meekosha, "Decolonising Disability," 668, 678. Karen Soldatic also takes issue with the way disability "is represented as a cross-cultural singularization, positioned as ahistorical and abstract, decontextualized and disembodied" ("The Transnational Sphere of Justice," 749). While presenting ways in which the global disability movement addresses claims for justice at the transnational scale, Soldatic also presents a fascinating analysis of the limitations of the realm of transnational disability justice (744–55).

4 Activist, writer, and performance artist Leah Lakshmi Piepzna-Samarasinha criticizes the ways in which the term "disability justice" has been adopted and misused in recent years, writing, "And right now, we're at an interesting moment in the history of disability justice. It's one where white disabled people who are the reason we invented disability justice because they've ignored or actively excluded disabled Black and brown people for decades are saying, 'Hey, that's a fun term' and slapping 'disability justice' on their all-white crip conference or panel." Piepzna-Samarasinha, *Care Work*, 123.

5 Ben-Moshe, "Movements at War?" 59–60.

6 Tugend, "*Storm* Drifts off Oscar Map, but *Mute's House* Stands Its Ground."

7 Carey, "*The Mute's House.*"

8 Ibid.

9 Dabashi, introduction to *Dreams of a Nation*, 12.

10 In a fascinating review of the documentation of Hebron in film and media, director Ra'anan Alexandrowicz addresses the cameras provided by various organizations (such as Israeli NGO B'tzelem's 2005 project *Shooting Back*) to Palestinian residents in the West Bank with the aim of documenting the occupation from their perspective,

referring to these works as "the weapon of the weak": "The insider documentarians shoot back with the only weapon they have. After all, in Hebron, the last word belongs to the person with the M-16, not to the person with the camera. The camera is a weapon of the weak." Alexandrowicz, "50 Years of Documentation," 31.

11 For a fascinating analysis of the juxtaposition of the politics of food, loss, and homelessness in the context of the Israeli occupation of the West Bank, see Kotef, *The Colonizing Self.*

12 Shalhoub-Kevorkian, *Incarcerated Childhood,* 122.

13 Ibid., 126.

14 Garland-Thomson, *Staring,* 9.

15 Carey, *"The Mute's House."*

16 David T. Mitchell and Sharon L. Snyder explain, "Our phrase *narrative prosthesis* is meant to indicate that disability has been used throughout history as a crutch upon which literary narratives lean for their representational power, disruptive potentiality, and analytical insight." *Narrative Prosthesis,* 49.

17 Kay, *Hebron Short Film.*

18 For more about audism, see Bauman, "Audism."

19 Anderman, "Tamar Kay Presents Hebron Beyond Words." The quote here is my own translation.

20 Dabashi, introduction to *Dreams of a Nation,* 17.

21 Ben-Zvi Morad, "The Language of Resistance in Palestinian Cinema."

22 Friedman, "The Camera and the National Ethos," 132. Nadera Shalhoub-Kevorkian addresses the testimony of the young girl in *Jenin, Jenin* as one of many examples demonstrating "the power of children in the midst of destruction and loss." The girl's response to the injustice perpetrated by the Israeli forces asserts the justice of her cause and underscores the moral foundation of her claims, thereby highlighting the resilience and resistance of Palestinian children (*Incarcerated Childhood,* 132–33). Drawing on similar insights, Rita Giacaman's research on Palestinian resilience underscores the pivotal role of the collective recognition of the moral imperative—that Palestinians are the occupied and Israel the occupier, aggressor, and colonizer—in bolstering their resilience (Giacaman, "Reflections on the Meaning of 'Resilience' in the Palestinian Context").

23 More than a decade after the release of the film *Jenin, Jenin*, Mustafa Al-Nabih's documentary *Stronger Than Words* (2014) told the story of Gaza's deaf community in what seems to have been a response to the call inherent in *Jenin, Jenin* to portray the life of people with disabilities under occupation. *Stronger Than Words* portrays a multidimensional experience of deaf people in Gaza. It depicts a life of discrimination within the Palestinian community, the specific ongoing challenges of the occupation for deaf people (for example, the impact that repeated power outages have on children who speak sign language and cannot see each other when it gets dark), and the specific impact of the IDF bombings in July 2014 on the deaf community in Gaza.

24 Puar, *The Right to Maim*. Although Puar coined the term "the right to maim," she is not the first to point out disabilities caused by the IDF's violence. In his memoir *Moving Violations: War Zones, Wheelchairs, and Declarations of Independence*, journalist John Hockenberry, a wheelchair user, writes about the "young [Palestinian] people [who] had gotten spinal-cord injuries from the fighting [during the first Intifada]" (276). However, while Hockenberry leaves room for speculation as to the circumstances of these injuries, Puar treats the right to maim as a structured and intentional method.

25 While this chapter focuses on physical disability, state-sanctioned violence causes other disabilities and chronic issues as well; for a review of the literature and established studies concerning anxiety disorders and PTSD in Palestine, see Marie, SaadAdeen, and Battat, "Anxiety Disorders and PTSD in Palestine."

26 Julie Livingston also utilizes the term *debility* to encompass the diverse ways in which the shifts brought about by colonialism, industrialization, and capitalism have influenced alterations in bodily life and perspectives on health, illness, and disability. Livingston, *Debility and the Moral Imagination in Botswana*.

27 Puar, *The Right to Maim*, 70.

28 Yasmin Snounu, indigenous Palestinian born and raised in Gaza, presents in her work testimonies about Israeli maiming practice, that is, injuries caused by the IDF that lead to disabilities. Snounu, "Apartheid, Disability, and the Triple Matrix of Maiming in Palestine."

29 Reinhart, *Palestine/Israel*, 114–16.

30 Ben-Moshe, "Weaponizing Disability." In a similar way, Eli Clare
    argues, "Because disability is one of the major consequences of war,
    we need an anti-war politics that doesn't transform disability into
    a symbol of either patriotism or tragedy, a politics that thinks hard
    about disability. Who gets killed, and who becomes disabled? Who
    profits from that killing and disabling? Whose bodies are used as
    weapons, and whose are treated as expendable? . . . All the answers
    depend upon naming disability and committing to a multi-layered
    analysis of how white supremacy, capitalism, patriarchy, imperial-
    ism, and ableism work in concert." Clare, *Exile and Pride*, xxiv–xxv.

31 Kiwan, "Dis/abled Decolonial Human and Citizen Futures."

32 Puar, *The Right to Maim*, 68–69.

33 For a fascinating analysis of this scene emphasizing the cinematic lan-
    guage of *Since You Left*, as well as the connection between Lorca's play
    The House of Bernarda Alba and *Jenin, Jenin*, see Bahar, *Documentary
    Cinema in Israel-Palestine*, 32–33.

34 Trabelsi, "Creation, Protest, and Freedom of Expression."

35 Dabashi characterizes Palestinian documentaries as "a form of visual
    'J'accuse'—animated by a tireless frenzy to create an alternative record
    of a silenced crime, to be lodged in a place that escapes the reach of
    the colonizer as occupier" (introduction to *Dreams of a Nation*, 11). See
    also Hochberg, *Visual Occupations*, 118–19.

36 Bresheeth, "The Nakba Projected," 504–5. (Mentioned also in Fried-
    man, "The Camera and the National Ethos," 128.) Hamid Dabashi also
    claims that "the central trauma of Palestine, the *Nakba*, is the defining
    moment of Palestinian cinema—and it is around that remembrance
    of lost homeland that Palestinian filmmakers have articulated their
    aesthetic cosmovision" (introduction to *Dreams of a Nation*, 11). Simi-
    lar to this claim, Joseph Massad argues that "the unrepresentability of
    the Nakba in this aesthetic realm haunts Palestinian and Arab cinema
    like no other dimension of the Palestinian story. . . . The very unrep-
    resentability of the Nakba is what has structured Palestinian cinema
    all along" ("The Weapon of Culture," 41). For a thorough discussion
    of the profound impact of the Nakba on Palestinian art, see Ankori,
    Palestinian Art. More specifically, Nurith Gertz and George Khleifi
    claim that "the theme [in *Jenin, Jenin*] is the trauma of Jenin's destruc-
    tion, but the language, the style of depiction, and the terms used are

borrowed from another, earlier trauma—that of 1948." Gertz and Khleifi, *Palestinian Cinema*, 146.

37 While I explore the correlation between the Nakba and trauma here, I agree with Rosemary Sayigh's compelling argument that Palestinian suffering stemming from the 1948 Nakba and the ongoing Nakba has been systematically silenced and excluded from discussions about trauma. See Sayigh, "Silenced Suffering."

38 Jaffee, "Disrupting Global Disability Frameworks," 124. Jaffee refers here to Butler, *Frames of War*.

39 Jaffee, "Disrupting Global Disability Frameworks," 124.

40 Soldatic, "The Transnational Sphere of Justice," 749.

41 See, for example, Simi Linton's classic book *Claiming Disability*. For a comprehensive discussion about the power relations in disability studies between the Global North and the Global South, see Meekosha's article "Decolonising Disability."

42 Soldatic, "The Transnational Sphere of Justice," 751–52. For further exploration of the interplay between resilience, resistance, chronic exposure to violence, and justice in the Palestinian context, see Giacaman, "Reflections on the Meaning of 'Resilience' in the Palestinian Context."

43 Berda, *The Bureaucracy of the Occupation*. See also Berda, *Living Emergency*; Kimmerling, *The Israeli State and Society*, 161; Azoulay and Ophir, *The One-State Condition*.

44 Massad, "The Weapon of Culture."

45 I borrow the term "cinematic arsenal" from Joseph Massad, who claims that the films of Palestinian Israeli filmmaker Michel Khleifi "are not only *objets d'art* but also central parts of a growing Palestinian cinematic arsenal" ("The Weapon of Culture," 41).

46 Alexandrowicz, "50 Years of Documentation," 29–30.

47 The film *Jenin, Jenin* did not receive a warm reception from the Jewish Israeli public. The documentary was banned from public viewing in Israel soon after its release in 2002. Even though the Supreme Court overturned the ban in 2003, various people and institutions continued to pursue the film and its director Mohammed Bakri, and in 2021 the Lod district court made its decision in a libel lawsuit filed against Bakri by Israeli soldier Nissim Magnaji, whose participation in Israel's Operation Defensive Shield is portrayed in *Jenin, Jenin*. The

court ruled that *Jenin, Jenin* could not be screened in Israel and that all copies should be seized; it also ordered Bakri to pay damages to Nissim Magnagi. One might wonder why the film has haunted Israeli society for so many years. What about *Jenin, Jenin* leads Israelis to invest so much time, energy, and money in proving its supposed falsehood?

One answer may be related to the nature of the testimonies in *Jenin, Jenin* and the fact that it reveals to a Jewish Israeli audience the subjectivity of its victims, which is usually hidden. Bakri, to use Yael Monk's language, permits a glimpse of the other side—that which is usually hidden from view, removed from the frame (Munk, "Between Algeria and Palestine"). In other words, the Israeli audience is accustomed to cinema that centers the Jewish Israeli subject while Bakri emphasizes the subjectivity of Palestinians. Another answer that emerges from the present analysis is that the documentary reveals the apparatuses and mechanisms of control; the abstract occupation (as in *The Mute's House*, for example) is broken down into concrete tools and mechanisms, the materials from which the occupation is created. Israeli society, therefore, tries to conceal, silence, and ban the concrete nature of the occupation that Bakri reveals in *Jenin, Jenin*.

48 For an initial survey of the experience of people with disability living in the West Bank and Gaza, see Burton, Sayrafi, and Srour, "Inclusion or Transformation?"

49 Puar addresses the theoretical tension between disability as a universal condition and the geopolitical uniqueness of disability, claiming that "there is a productive tension . . . between embracing disability as a universal and inevitable condition, and combating the production of disability acquired under duress of oppressive structures of social injustice. While the former became necessary to push back against the exceptionalizing view of disability as a singular misfortunate and a private tragedy, disability should not then be conceptualized as a universal problem affecting everyone" (*The Right to Maim*, 70).

50 Al Jazeera English, "Palestinians Defy Their Disability Under Israeli Occupation." It is not surprising that the initiative to provide help to disabled people in occupied Palestine comes from an individual, André Villas Boas in this case, rather than an organization. As Burton, Sayrafi, and Srour note, there is a significant lack of consideration for

disability in humanitarian programs, despite the United Nations Convention on the Rights of Persons with Disabilities. In practice, both organizations and states often neglect the needs of disabled individuals, especially during post-conflict rehabilitation phases ("Inclusion or Transformation?" 814). For a similar argument, see also Kett and van Ommeren, "Disability, Conflict, and Emergencies."

51 Maria Berghs discusses how various humanitarian organizations embody apolitical approaches and ignore ongoing power imbalances that produce the disablement of people through geopolitical violence. Berghs, "The New Humanitarianism." Laura Jordan Jaffee also refers to this source in her article "Disrupting Global Disability Frameworks" ("Disrupting Global Disability Frameworks," 119).

52 Giacaman, "Reflections on the Meaning of 'Resilience' in the Palestinian Context," e372. Inspired by Giacaman, Bram Wispelwey and Yasser Abu Jamei also claim, "Humanitarian intervention and [mental health] treatment strategies that do not embrace the political realm risk being ineffective at best and may inadvertently prolong suffering by eschewing root causes." "The Great March of Return," 183.

53 For more about the supercrip trope, see Nelson, *The Disabled, the Media, and the Information Age*; Harnett, "Escaping the 'Evil Avenger' and the 'Supercrip'"; Kama, "Supercrips versus the Pitiful Handicapped"; and Schalk, "Reevaluating the Supercrip."

54 Yael Ben-Zvi Morad claims that in many Palestinian films, the Al-Aqsa Compound symbolizes the sovereign future. Often, characters or figures will look up to the compound and especially to the Dome of the Rock, which represents the Al-Aqsa Compound in its prestigious splendor. The gilded dome symbolizes the hope of liberation from the occupation, a return to the united homeland around Jerusalem, and the hope for a leadership that will unite the people and their space (Ben-Zvi Morad, "The Language of Resistance in Palestinian Cinema").

55 Friedman argues that children, as representatives of the next generation, have a central place in the Palestinian national ethos, and they embody the hope for a better future and national redemption ("The Camera and the National Ethos," 132).

56 For a discussion of the role of the ocean in Zionist contexts, see Hever, *Toward the Longed-For Shore*; and Greenberg, "Embodying Conflict."

57 For a discussion about "geographies of fragmentation" in Palestinian cinema, see Hedges, *World Cinema and Cultural Memory*, 71.

58 Ben-Zvi Morad, "The Language of Resistance in Palestinian Cinema."

59 For further reference to the symbolism of the sea in Gaza in the context of occupation, see Hass, *Drinking the Sea at Gaza*.

Epilogue

1 See Kfar Tikva's website: https://kfar-tikva.org.il/.

2 The word Kfar Tikva uses for its members is *haverim*, which could be translated in this context as residents or members—and indeed, on their website, Kfar Tikva chooses the language of "residents." *Haverim* is a fairly traditional and standard term used in nationalistic kibbutzim, but the root of the word (ח.ב.ר) has a broad semantic range that is most associated with ideas of friendship, fellowship, and participation in broader society.

3 Patinkin, *Kfar Tikva*. As the poem is cited in Hebrew in the film, the line breaks and the translation are mine. The poem, with minor modifications and some additional content, was also published under the title "Letter to Mother" in Aharoni, *From the Heart*, 127–28.

4 Zoanni, "The Possibilities of Failure," 69.

5 For a comprehensive theoretical discussion of justice for people with disabilities, particularly those with significant intellectual disabilities, see Nussbaum, *Frontiers of Justice*.

6 Quoted from a video of the community television in Tivon, March 2, 2021, https://www.video.comtv.co.il/?p=6399 (no longer available).

7 One notable case is the artistic expression of Eyal Shachal, an autistic activist, student, poet, and painter from Tel-Aviv. He utilizes a keyboard as his primary medium of self-expression, consistently sharing his work on various social networks.

8 Efrat, "On Disability and Formal Utopia in Tamar Getter's Work."

9 To explore analogous inquiries concerning the interaction between physical disability and museum environments, see Kleege, *More Than Meets the Eye*.

10 Lev-Aladgem, "History from Below."

11 Fraser, *Cognitive Disability Aesthetics*, 14.

12 Don Kulick and Jens Rydström critique disability studies for drifting
"from the least articulate people to the most articulate." While I
generally agree with their critique, I disagree with their assertion that
individuals in the former group are passive and "produce no cultural
artifacts, stage no protests, make few or no demands, write no poems,
[or] throw no balls"—a viewpoint I challenge throughout the book.
Loneliness and Its Opposite, 15–16.

13 Lige, "Adults with Intellectual Disabilities and the Visual Arts," 46.

14 Kuppers, *The Scar of Visibility*, 73.

15 Fraser, *Cognitive Disability Aesthetics*, 3–4.

16 For further exploration of the intersections and areas of divergence
between disability culture and mad studies, see Russo and Sweeney,
Searching for a Rose Garden; Frazer-Carroll, *Mad World*; and Beresford
and Russo, *The Routledge International Handbook of Mad Studies*.

17 Carlson, "Cognitive Ableism and Disability Studies."

BIBLIOGRAPHY

Abolition and Disability Justice Collective. "Statement of Solidarity with Palestine." May 20, 2021. https://abolitionanddisabilityjustice.com/2021/05/20/statement-of-solidarity-with-palestine-from-the-adjc/.

Aciksoz, Salih Can. *Sacrificial Limbs: Masculinity, Disability, and Political Violence in Turkey*. Oakland: University of California Press, 2019.

Adams, Rachel. "Disability and the Circus." In *The American Circus*, edited by Susan Weber, Kenneth L. Ames, and Matthew Wittmann, 3–18. New Haven: Yale University Press, 2012.

———. *Sideshow U.S.A.: Freaks and the American Cultural Imagination*. Chicago: University of Chicago Press, 2001.

Aharoni, Chanan. *From the Heart* (*Mimakor Rishon*). Hadera: Akim, 1993. [Hebrew.]

Ailam, Oren. "On the Poetry of Orit Marton." *Bitaon Shirah* 8 (2004): 30–33. [Hebrew.]

Albright, Ann Cooper. *Choreographing Difference: The Body and Identity in Contemporary Dance*. Middletown: Wesleyan University Press, 1997.

———. "Strategic Abilities: Negotiating the Disabled Body in Dance." *Michigan Quarterly Review* 37, no. 3 (1998): 475–501.

Aldor, Gaby. "The Borders of Contemporary Israeli Dance: 'Invisible unless in Final Pain.'" *Dance Research Journal* 35, no. 1 (2003): 81–97.

Alexandrowicz, Ra'anan. "50 Years of Documentation: A Brief History of the Audiovisual Documentation of the Israeli Occupation." In *Visual Imagery and Human Rights Practice*, edited by Sandra Ristovska and Monroe Price, 15–34. Cham: Palgrave Macmillan, 2018.

Alhadaz, Eitan. "Breaking Walls." *Haifa and the Outskirts Towns of Haifa News*, September 12, 2021. https://www.haifatimes.co.il/%D7%97%D7%93%D7

%A9%D7%95%D7%AA-%D7%97%D7%99%D7%A4%D7%94/%D7%A9%
D7%95%D7%91%D7%A8%D7%99%D7%9D-%D7%97%D7%95%D7%9E%D7
%A8%D7%99%D7%9D/. [Hebrew.]

Al Jazeera English. "Palestinians Defy Their Disability Under Israeli Occupation." YouTube, December 4, 2017. https://www.youtube.com/watch?v=
Px5bcYL2Zcl.

Alland, Sandra, Khairani Barokka, and Daniel Sluman, eds. *Stairs and Whispers:
D/deaf and Disabled Poets Write Back*. Rugby, UK: Nine Arches, 2017.

Al-Nabih, Mustafa, dir. *Stronger Than Words*. Gaza: Al Waha Production
House, 2014.

Aloni, Udi, dir. *Local Angel: Theological Political Fragments* (*Malach Mekomi*).
Local Angel LLC, 2002.

Alster, Paul. "The Amazing *Miss Vertigo* [*sic*]." *Jerusalem Report*, September 3,
2018. https://www.jpost.com/jerusalem-report/the-amazing-miss-vertigo
-565478.

Amihay, Ofra. *The People of the Book and the Camera: Photography in the
Hebrew Novel*. Syracuse: Syracuse University Press, 2022.

Anderman, Nirit. "Tamar Kay Presents Hebron Beyond Words." *Haaretz*,
December 17, 2015. https://www.haaretz.co.il/gallery/cinema/.premium-1
.2801093. [Hebrew.]

Anidjar, Gil, and Amos Funkenstein. "Jewish Mysticism Alterable and Unalterable: On Orienting Kabbalah Studies and the 'Zohar of Christian Spain.'"
Jewish Social Studies 3, no. 1 (1996): 89–157.

Ankori, Gannit. *Palestinian Art*. London: Reaktion Books, 2006.

Ashkenazi, Limor, and Nira Moser. *Other Person* (*Zulat*). Directed by Nira
Moser. Bat Yam Community Theater, 2008. Autistic People of Color Fund.
"Condemning Israeli State Terror and Ongoing Occupation of Palestine
Is a Disability Justice Imperative." Facebook, May 17, 2021. https://www
.facebook.com/autisticpocfund/posts/326566379097092.

Aviad, Michal, dir. *The Women Pioneers*. Herzliya: Eden Productions, 2013.

Azoulay, Ariella. *The Angel of History*. Herzliya Museum of Contemporary Art,
2000. DVD.

———. *Once upon a Time: Photography Following Walter Benjamin* (*Hayo haya
paam*). Ramat Gan: Bar-Ilan University Press, 2006. [Hebrew.]

Azoulay, Ariella, and Adi Ophir. *The One-State Condition: Occupation and
Democracy in Israel/Palestine*. Redwood City: Stanford University Press,
2012.

Azoulay-Hasfari, Hanna. *Sh'Chur: Screenplay and Seven Readings on the Film* (*Sh'Chur: Hatasriṭyeshevaḳeriot al hasereṭ*). Tel Aviv: Yedioth Ahronot Books and Chemed Books, 2009. [Hebrew.]

Bahar, Shirly. *Documentary Cinema in Israel-Palestine: Performance, the Body, the Home*. London: Bloomsbury, 2021.

Bailin, Miriam. *The Sickroom in Victorian Fiction: The Art of Being Ill*. Cambridge: Cambridge University Press, 1994.

Bakri, Mohammed, dir. *Jenin, Jenin*. Seattle: Arab Film Distribution, 2002.

——, dir. *Since You Left* (Min Yum Mahrucht). Israel: Ness Communication & Production, 2005.

Baor, Orly. *Disabled and Dancing: Dance on Wheelchairs* (*Nechim verokdim: machol al kisot galgalim*). Raananah: Kotarot, 2004. [Hebrew.]

Barnes, Colin, and Geoff Mercer. "Disability Culture: Assimilation or Inclusion?" In *Handbook of Disability Studies*, edited by Gary L. Albrecht, Katherine D. Seelman, and Michael Bury, 515–34. Newbury Park, CA: SAGE, 2011.

Barthes, Roland. "The Death of the Author." In *Image, Music, Text*, translated by Stephen Heath, 142–48. New York: Hill & Wang, 1977.

Baruch, Adam. *How Are Things at Home* (*Ma nishma babait*). Or Yehudah: Kinneret, Zmora-Bittan, Dvir, 2008. [Hebrew.]

Bauman, H-Dirksen L. "Audism: Exploring the Metaphysics of Oppression." *Journal of Deaf Studies and Deaf Education* 9, no. 2 (2004): 239–46.

Bauman, H-Dirksen L., and Joseph J. Murray. "Deaf Studies in the 21st Century: 'Deaf-Gain' and the Future of Human Diversity." In *The Disability Studies Reader*, edited by Lennard J. Davis, 246–60. Abingdon: Taylor & Francis Group, 2013.

Bell, Christopher. "Introducing White Disability Studies: A Modest Proposal." In *The Disability Studies Reader*, edited by Lennard Davis 275–82. Oxfordshire: Abingdon: Taylor & Francis: 2006.

Benjamin, Walter. "Theses on the Philosophy of History." In *Illuminations*, translated by Harry Zohn, 253–64. New York: Schocken Books, 1969.

Ben-Moshe, Liat. "Movements at War? Disability and Anti-Occupation Activism in Israel." In *Occupying Disability: Critical Approaches to Community, Justice, and Decolonizing Disability*, edited by Pamela Block, Devva Kasnitz, Akemi Nishida, and Nick Pollard, 47–61. Dordrecht: Springer, 2016.

——. "Weaponizing Disability." *SocialText Online*, October 25, 2018. https://socialtextjournal.org/periscope_article/weaponizing-disability/.

Ben-Moshe, Liat, and Sumi Colligan. "The State of Disability in Israel/ Palestine: An Introduction." *Disability Studies Quarterly* 27, no. 4 (2007). https://doi.org/10.18061/dsq.v27i4.41.

Ben-Moshe, Liat, and Sandy Magaña. "An Introduction to Race, Gender, and Disability: Intersectionality, Disability Studies, and Families of Color." *Women, Gender, and Families of Color* 2, no. 2 (2014): 105–14.

Ben-Zvi Morad, Yael. "The Language of Resistance in Palestinian Cinema." *Takriv: Online Magazine on Documentary Cinema* 4 (2012). https://takriv.net/ article/%D7%A9%D7%A4%D7%94-%D7%9E%D7%AA%D7%A0%D7%92 %D7%93%D7%AA-%D7%91%D7%A7%D7%95%D7%9C%D7%A0%D7 %95%D7%A2-%D7%94%D7%A4%D7%9C%D7%A1%D7%98%D7%99 %D7%A0%D7%99/. [Hebrew.]

Berda, Yael. *The Bureaucracy of the Occupation: The Permit Regime in the West Bank.* Tel Aviv: Van Leer Institute and Hakibutz Hameuhad, 2012. [Hebrew.]

———. *Living Emergency: Israel's Permit Regime in the Occupied West Bank.* Redwood City: Stanford University Press, 2017.

Beresford, Peter, and Jasna Russo. *The Routledge International Handbook of Mad Studies.* Abingdon-on-Thames: Routledge, 2022.

Berghs, Maria. "The New Humanitarianism: Neoliberalism, Poverty and the Creation of Disability." In *Disability, Human Rights, and the Limits of Humanitarianism,* edited by Michael Gill and Cathy J. Schlund-Vias, 27–43. Burlington: Ashgate, 2014.

Bhabha, Homi K. *The Location of Culture.* New York: Routledge, 1994.

Black, Sheila. "Sheila Black's Six Poets with Disabilities." *VELA—Written by Women,* n.d. http://velamag.com/sheila-blacks-six-poets-with-disabilities/ (accessed March 20, 2020).

Black, Sheila, Jennifer Bartlett, and Michael Northen, eds. *Beauty Is a Verb: The New Poetry of Disability.* El Paso: Cinco Puntos, 2011.

Bluwstein Sela, Rachel. *Rachel's Poetry (Shirat Rahel).* Illustrations by Abba Fenichel. Jerusalem: Ariel, 2001.

Borer, Tamar. *ANA. Tamar Borer: Performance Artist.* http://www.tamarborer .com/pages/ana.php (accessed September 21, 2018).

———. "Tamar Borer: About the Artist." *Tamar Borer: Performance Artist.* http:// www.tamarborer.com/pages/cv.php (accessed September 21, 2018).

Borer, Tamar, and Tamara Erde. *The Making of "ANA,"* 2010. DVD.

Boyarin, Daniel. *Unheroic Conduct: The Rise of Heterosexuality and the Invention of the Jewish Man.* Berkeley: University of California Press, 1977.

Bresheeth, Haim. "The Nakba Projected: Recent Palestinian Cinema." *Third Text* 20, nos. 3/4 (2006): 499–509.

Brilmyer, Gracen. "Archival Assemblages: Applying Disability Studies' Political/Relational Model to Archival Description." *Archival Science* 18 (2018): 95–118.

Britton, Diane F., Barbara Floyd, and Patricia Murphy. "Overcoming Another Obstacle: Archiving a Community's Disabled History." *Radical History Review* 94 (2006): 212–27.

Brown, Steven E. *Investigating a Culture of Disability: Final Report.* Las Cruces, NM: Institute on Disability Culture, 1994.

Broyer, nili. "Disabled Fashion Models vs. Cripsex: The Dangers and Opportunities in Making Disability Sexy." Lecture presented at the Beit Issie Shapiro's 6th International Conference on Disabilities, Unity & Diversity in Action, Tel Aviv, July 6–9, 2015. [Hebrew.]

———. "On the Margins of Femininity: Women Speak Disability." Edited transcript of International Women's Day Symposium, Beit Noam, Kiryat Ono, Israel, March 9, 2011. [Hebrew.]

———. "Stigma and Unconsciousness." Master's thesis, Hebrew University of Jerusalem, 2008. [Hebrew.]

———. "Through the Restroom Mirror: Accessibility and Visibility in Public Space." *Disability & Society* 35 (2020): 1483–1504.

———. "Wearing the Mask of Dis-Dance: Autoethnography of Israeli Wheelchair Folk Dancing." *Israeli Sociology* 13, no. 2 (2011–12): 331–52. [Hebrew.]

Broyer, nili R., and Ita Tal-Or. *Take a Seat.* Holon: Holon Institute of Technology, 2004. https://www.youtube.com/watch?v=faGyBWpCW5s (accessed December 23, 2020).

Bruce, La Marr Jurelle. *How to Go Mad Without Losing Your Mind: Madness and Black Radical Creativity.* Durham: Duke University Press, 2021.

Burton, Guy, Imad Sayrafi, and Shatha Abu Srour. "Inclusion or Transformation? An Early Assessment of an Empowerment Project for Disabled People in Occupied Palestine." *Disability & Society* 28, no. 6 (2013): 812–25.

Butler, Judith. *Frames of War: When Is Life Grievable?* New York: Verso, 2009.

———. "Is Kinship Always Already Heterosexual?" In *Left Legalism/Left Critique,* edited by Wendy Brown and Janet Halley, 14–44. Durham: Duke University Press, 2002.

———. "Rethinking Vulnerability and Resistance: Feminism & Social Change." Women Creating Change—Istanbul Workshop, September 16–19, 2013. http://socialdifference.columbia.edu/projects/rethinking-vulnerability -feminism-social-change (no longer available).

———. "Vulnerability and Resistance." *Profession* (2014): 4. http://profession .commons.mla.org/2014/03/19/vulnerability-and-resistance/.

Calvino, Italo. *The Invisible Cities.* New York: Harcourt Brace Jovanovich, 1974.

Cameron, Colin, and Swain, John. "Unless Otherwise Stated: Discourses of Labelling and Identity." In *Disability Discourse*, edited by Mairian Corker and Sally French, 68–78. Philadelphia: Open University Press, 1999.

Campbell, Fiona Kumari. "Geodisability Knowledge Production and International Norms: A Sri Lankan Case Study." *Third World Quarterly* 32, no. 8 (2011): 1455–74.

Carey, Matthew. "*The Mute's House*—Touching Doc on 'Unique, Amazing' Palestinian Boy Contends for Oscar Nomination." *Nonfictionfilm*, January 13, 2017. https://www.nonfictionfilm.com/news/the-mutes-house-touching -doc-on-unique-amazing-palestinian-boy-contends-for-oscar-nomination.

Carlson, Licia. "Cognitive Ableism and Disability Studies: Feminist Reflections on the History of Mental Retardation." *Hypatia* 16, no. 4 (2001): 124–46.

Carroll, Lewis. *Through the Looking-Glass, and What Alice Found There.* Illustrated by John Tenniel. New York: Books of Wonder, 1993. First published in 1872.

Chen, Mel Y. *Animacies: Biopolitics, Racial Mattering, and Queer Affect.* Durham: Duke University Press, 2012.

Chen, Mel Y., Alison Kafer, Eunjung Kim, and Julie Avril Minich, eds. *Crip Genealogies.* Durham: Duke University Press, 2023.

Chesler, Phyllis. *Women and Madness.* San Diego: Harcourt Brace Jovanovich, 1989.

Chivers, Sally, and Nicole Markotic. *The Problem Body: Projecting Disability on Film.* Columbus: Ohio State University Press, 2010.

Clare, Eli. *Brilliant Imperfection: Grappling with Cure.* Durham: Duke University Press, 2017.

———. *Exile and Pride: Disability, Queerness, and Liberation.* Durham: Duke University Press, 2015.

Cohen, Zafrira Lidovsky. *"Loosen the Fetters of Thy Tongue Woman": The Poetry and Poetics of Yona Wallach.* Cincinnati: Hebrew Union College Press, 2003.

Crow, Liz. "Renewing the Social Model of Disability." *Coalition News*: Greater Manchester Coalition of Disabled People, July 1992. https://www.roaring -girl.com/wp-content/uploads/2013/07/Renewing-the-Social-model .Coalition-News.pdf.

Dabashi, Hamid. Introduction to *Dreams of a Nation: On Palestinian Cinema*, edited by Hamid Dabashi, 7–22. London: Verso, 2006.

Dahan Kalev, Henriette. "Made to Be Inept: The Case of Mizrahi Women." *Israeli Sociology* 4 (2002): 265–87. [Hebrew.]

De Certeau, Michel. "Practices of Space." In *On Signs*, edited by Marshall Blonsky, 122–45. Baltimore: Johns Hopkins University Press, 1985.

———. *The Practice of Everyday Life*. Berkeley: University of California Press, 1984.

Deems, Kasey. "'We're All Mad Here': Mental Illness as Social Disruption in *Alice's Adventures in Wonderland*." *SUURJ: Seattle University Undergraduate Research Journal* 1 (2017). https://scholarworks.seattleu.edu/suurj/vol1/iss1/13.

Dekel, Lilach, dir. *Living for Tomorrow: Untold Stories by the Pioneering Women of Israel*. New York: Transformation Films, 2000. DVD.

Deleuze, Gilles. "He Stuttered." In *Gilles Deleuze and the Theater of Philosophy*, edited by Constantin V. Boundas and Dorothea Olkowski, 23–29. New York: Routledge, 1994.

Derrida, Jacques. *Monolingualism of the Other; or, The Prosthesis of Origin*. Translated by Patrick Mensah. Stanford: Stanford University Press, 1998.

———. *Without Alibi*. Translated by Peggy Kamuf. Stanford: Stanford University Press, 2002.

Di Giulio, Marco. "Beyond Silenced Voices: Gender, Power, and Psychiatric Care in Mandatory Palestine." *All of Us*, May 15, 2024. https://allofusdha .org/research/beyond-silenced-voices-gender-power-and-psychiatric-care -in-mandatory-palestine.

———. "Killing out of Compassion: Disability, Care, and the Value of Life in the Early Decades of Israeli Statehood." *Journal of Modern Jewish Studies* 23, no. 2 (2024): 327–47.

———. "Motherhood, Mental Incompetence, and the Denial of Reproductive Autonomy in the Early Years of Israeli Statehood." *Journal of Social History* 57, no. 4 (2024): 550–77.

"Disability, Fetishization of." In *Encyclopedia of Sex and Gender: Culture Society History*. Encyclopedia.com, November 8, 2022. https://www.encyclopedia

.com/social-sciences/encyclopedias-almanacs-transcripts-and-maps/
disability-fetishization.

Dolmage, Jay Timothy. *Disability Rhetoric*. New York: Syracuse University
Press, 2014.

Downey, Anthony, Ruth Gilligan, Rhea Dagher, Yasmin Foqahaa, Mostafa
Attia, and Bobby Beaumont. "Arts and Disability in Lebanon, the Occupied
Palestinian Territories, and Jordan: Literature and Practice Review." Dis-
ability Under Siege: Working Paper, January 2021.

Duvdevani, Shmulik. "*Next to Her*: On Sense and Lots of Sensitivity." *ynet*,
January 11, 2015. https://www.ynet.co.il/articles/0,7340,L-4613005,00.html.
[Hebrew.]

Efrat, Gideon. "On Disability and Formal Utopia in Tamar Getter's Work."
Mitaam 20 (2009): 47–52. [Hebrew.]

Eiesland, Nancy. *The Disabled God: Toward a Liberatory Theology of Disability*.
Nashville: Abingdon: 1994.

Eshel, Ruth. "On the Verge of Amateur." *Haaretz*, November 22, 2003.
[Hebrew.]

——. "To Dance with the Times—The Arab-Israeli Conflict as It Appears in
Israeli Dance." *Israel Dance Quarterly* 10 (1977): 14–21. [Hebrew.]

Eshel Cahansky, Inbal. *Roaring in an Infinite Loop* (*Shoeget belulaat einsof*).
Haifa: Pardes, 2016. [Hebrew.]

——. *Samael My Beloved* (*Samael ahuvi*). Haifa: Pardes, 2013. [Hebrew.]

Estrin, Daniel. "The 'Edgiest' Singer on Israeli Airwaves Is an Orthodox
Mother of Three." *The World*, February 23, 2015. https://theworld.org/
stories/2015/02/23/israeli-singer-doing-alphabet-or-aleph-bet-style.

Feldman, Yael S. *No Room of Their Own: Gender and Nation in Israeli Women's
Fiction*. New York: Columbia University Press, 1999.

Felman, Shoshana. *The Juridical Unconscious: Trials and Traumas in the Twentieth Century*. Cambridge, MA: Harvard University Press, 2002.

Feuerstein, Refael S., ed. *Breaking Through the Glass Wall: Intimacy and Marriage for People with Disabilities* (*Lifrotz et Homat Hazchuchit*). Rishon Le
Zion: Yedioth Ahronoth Books, 2018. [Hebrew.]

Finger, Anne. "Forbidden Fruit." *New Internationalist*, no. 233 (1992): 8–10.

Fink, Jennifer Natalya. *All Our Families: Disability Lineage and the Future of
Kinship*. Boston: Beacon, 2022.

Finkelstein, Vic. "Disabled People and Our Culture Development." *DAIL* (*Disability Arts in London*) *Magazine*, June 8, 1987, 1–4.

Foster, Susan Leigh. "Choreographies of Protest." *Theatre Journal* 55, no. 3 (2003): 395–412.

———. *Reading Dancing: Bodies and Subjects in Contemporary American Dance.* Berkeley: University of California Press, 1986.

Foucault, Michel. *History of Madness.* Translated by Jonathan Murphy and Jean Khalfa. London: Routledge, 2006.

Frank, Arthur W. "An Illness of One's Own: Memoir as Art Form and Research as Witness." *Cogent Arts & Humanities* 4, no. 1 (2017): 1–7.

Fraser, Benjamin. *Cognitive Disability Aesthetics: Visual Culture, Disability Representations, and the (In)Visibility of Cognitive Difference.* Toronto: University of Toronto Press, 2018.

Frazer-Carroll, Micha. *Mad World: The Politics of Mental Health.* London: Pluto, 2023.

Friedes Galili, Deborah. *Contemporary Dance in Israel.* N.p.: Asociación Cultural Danza Getxo, 2012.

Friedman, Michal. "The Beyond Dimension: Female Autobiographies in Israeli Cinema." *Theory and Criticism (Teorya vebikoret)* 8 (2001): 223–36. [Hebrew.]

Friedman, Yael. "The Camera and the National Ethos: The 'Battle of Jenin' in Recent Palestinian Cinema." "On Cinema, Destruction & Trauma," special issue, *South Cinema Notebook* 2 (2007): 125–36. [Hebrew.]

Friend, Robert. *Found in Translation: Modern Hebrew Poets, a Bilingual Edition.* London: Toby, 2006.

Friend, Robert, and Shimon Sandbank. *Flowers of Perhaps.* London: Toby, 2008.

Garland-Thomson, Rosemarie. "The Case for Conserving Disability." *Bioethical Inquiry* 9 (2012): 339–55.

———. *Extraordinary Bodies: Figuring Physical Disability in American Culture and Literature.* New York: Columbia University Press, 1997.

———. "Feminist Disability Studies." *Signs: Journal of Women in Culture and Society* 30, no. 2 (2005): 1557–87.

———. "Misfits: A Feminist Materialist Disability Concept." *Hypatia* 26, no. 3 (2011): 591–609.

———. "Staring Back: Self-Representations of Disabled Performance Artists." *American Quarterly* 52, no. 2 (2000): 334–38.

———. *Staring: How We Look.* Oxford: Oxford University Press, 2009.

Gavriely-Nuri, Dalia. "The Social Construction of 'Jerusalem of Gold' as Israel's Unofficial National Anthem." *Israel Studies* 12, no. 2 (2007): 104–20.

Gefen, Shira, and Kenafayim members. *Spoon of Gold* (*Kapit shel Zahav*). Directed by Rina Padwa. Kenafayim, 2010.

Gelbets, Tamar. *Last One* (*Haaharon*), Tel-Aviv: Modan and Hargol, 2023. [Hebrew.]

Gertz, Nurith, and George Khleifi. *Palestinian Cinema: Landscape, Trauma and Memory*. Bloomington: Indiana University Press, 2008.

Giacaman, Rita. "Reflections on the Meaning of 'Resilience' in the Palestinian Context." *Journal of Public Health* 42, no. 3 (2020): e369–e400. https://doi.org/10.1093/pubmed/fdz118.

Gilbert, Sandra M., and Susan Gubar. *The Madwoman in the Attic: The Woman Writer and the Nineteenth-Century Literary Imagination*. New Haven: Yale University Press, 1984.

Gill, Carol J. "Becoming Visible: Personal Health—Experiences of Women with Disabilities." In *Women with Physical Disabilities: Achieving and Maintaining Health and Well-Being*, edited by Danuta M. Krotoski, Margaret A. Nosek, and Margaret A. Turk, 5–15. Baltimore: Paul H. Brookes, 1996.

———. "A Psychological View of Disability Culture." *Disability Studies Quarterly* 15, no. 4 (1995): 16–19.

Ginat, Gitit. "Gaza Is Nothing." *Bamahane*, February 20, 2004, 36. [Hebrew.]

Gluzman, Michael. *The Zionist Body* (*Ha-guf ha-tsiyoni*). Tel Aviv: Ha-Kibutsz ha-me'uhad, 2007. [Hebrew.]

Goldberg, Leah. *The Courage for the Mundane: Explorations and Insights in Our New Literature* (*Haometz lehulin: behinot vetaamim besafruteynu hahadasha*). Tel Aviv: Sifriat Poalim, 1976. [Hebrew.]

Gordinsky, Natasha. "Essayistic Writing as an Everyday Art: Lea Goldberg's Debate with Russian Culture." *Mikan* 14 (2014): 220–38. [Hebrew.]

Gordon-Chen, Naomi, and Michal Teomi Sela, curators. *Breaking Walls* (*Shovrim homot*). ARTura Gallery Ruppin Academic Center, Hefer Valley, 2021.

Grech, Shaun, and Karen Soldatic, eds. *Disability in the Global South: The Critical Handbook*. Edinburgh: Springer Cham, 2016.

Greenberg, Slava. *Animated Film and Disability: Cripping Spectatorship*. Bloomington: Indiana University Press, 2023.

———. "Embodying Conflict: Representations of Hospitals and Seas in Israeli CinemaAfter the Second Intifada." *Jewish Film & New Media* 7, no. 2 (2019): 214–35.

Greenberg, Slava, and nili Broyer. "Staring Back: Disabled Women Filmmakers Resist Ableism." *Migdar: Journal of Gender and Feminism* 5 (2018): 1–23. [Hebrew.]

Grosz, Elizabeth. *Volatile Bodies: Toward a Corporeal Feminism.* Bloomington: Indiana University Press, 1994.

Hadar, Alon. "Victoria Hanna: 'Me and My Big Mouth.'" *Haaretz*, February 12, 2015. https://www.haaretz.co.il/misc/1.1068772. [Hebrew.]

Hakak, Balfour. "Orit Marton's Poems Are the Victory of Spirit over Matter." *Moznaim* 2, no. 88 (2014): 30–32. [Hebrew.]

Hall, Kim Q., ed. *Feminist Disability Studies.* Bloomington: Indiana University Press, 2011.

Halpern, Roni. *Body and Its Discontent: Israeli Women's Fiction, 1985–2005 (Guf belo nachat—sifrut nashim Israelit 1985–2005).* Tel Aviv: Ha-kibbutz ha-meuhad, 2012. [Hebrew.]

Hamdar, Abir. *The Female Suffering Body: Illness and Disability in Modern Arabic Literature.* Syracuse: Syracuse University Press, 2014.

Hands, Stewart. "An Interview with Israeli Star Hanna Azoulay-Hasfari." *Beyond the Toronto Jewish Film Festival*, November 25, 2009. https://tjff09.blogspot.com/2009/11/interview-with-israeli-star-hanna.html.

Hanna, Victoria. *The Aleph-Bet Song (Hosha'ana).* Directed by Asaf Korman. 2015. https://www.victoriahanna.net/en/85#gallery-2.

———. "Hebrew Vowels Demonstration." Performance at the international conference "Music and Brains: The Surprising Link—An Interface Between Music Cognition and Neuroscience," Jerusalem, February 10–13, 2013. https://www.youtube.com/watch?v=fGliOFFUkoQ.

———. *Twenty-Two Letters.* 2015. https://www.victoriahanna.net/en/85#gallery-3.

Harnett, Alison. "Escaping the 'Evil Avenger' and the 'Supercrip': Images of Disability in Popular Television." *Irish Communications Review* 8 (2000): 21–29.

Hartman, Saidiya. *Wayward Lives, Beautiful Experiments: Intimate Histories of Social Upheaval.* New York: Norton, 2019.

Hasfari, Shmuel, dir. *Sh'Chur.* Israel, 1994.

Hass, Amira. *Drinking the Sea at Gaza: Days and Nights in a Land Under Siege.* New York: Metropolitan Books, 1999.

Hay, Mark. "The Pleasure and Pain of Being Disabled in the BDSM Community." *VICE*, July 25, 2016. https://www.vice.com/en/article/nnkv3d/disabled-bdsm-experiences.

Hedges, Inez. *World Cinema and Cultural Memory*. Basingstoke: Palgrave Macmillan, 2015.

Hedva, Joanna. "Letter to a Young Doctor." January 17, 2018. https://www
.canopycanopycanopy.com/contents/letter-to-a-young-doctor.

———. "Sick Woman Theory." https://topicalcream.org/features/sick-woman
-theory/ (accessed December 4, 2024.)

Heiman, Michal. "The Journey to Pictures Lost by Walter Benjamin." *Haaretz*,
September 18, 2006. [Hebrew.]

Henig. Roni. "Stammering Hebrew: Y. H. Brenner's Deferred Beginnings in the
Novel *Me-Hathala*." *Comparative Literature Studies* 56, no. 2 (2019): 229–59.

Hever, Hannan. "Alone with the Poems" ("Levad im hashirim"). In *Sparks
of Light: Essays About Dahlia Ravikovitch's Oeuvre (Khitmei or)*, edited
by Hamutal Tsamir and Tamar S. Hess, 470–97. Tel Aviv: Hakibbutz
Hameuchad, 2010. [Hebrew.]

———. *Toward the Longed-For Shore: The Sea in Hebrew Culture and Modern
Hebrew Literature (El hahof hamekuve)*. Jerusalem: Van Leer Jerusalem Institute and Hakibbutz Hameuchad, 2007. [Hebrew.]

Hirsch, Eli. "Review of *Dahlia Ravikovitch: The Complete Poems*." *Yediot
Aharonot*, September 24, 2010. https://www.elihirsh.com/?p=2349.
[Hebrew.]

Hirsch, Smadar. "An Angel in a Wheelchair." *Maariv*, January 13, 2004, 19.
[Hebrew.]

Hochberg, Gil Z. *Visual Occupations: Violence and Visibility in a Conflict Zone*.
Durham: Duke University Press, 2015.

Hockenberry, John. *Moving Violations: War Zones, Wheelchairs, and Declarations of Independence*. New York: Hyperion, 1995.

Holmes, Martha Stoddard. "Pain." In *Keywords for Disability Studies*, edited by
Rachel Adams, Benjamin Reiss, and David Serlin, 133–34. New York: NYU
Press, 2015.

Imhoff, Sarah. *The Lives of Jessie Sampter: Queer, Disabled, Zionist*. Durham:
Duke University Press, 2022.

Inbar-Weiss, Nurit. "'That the Pain Not Be Wasted': Combining Personal and
Theoretical Perspectives in Illness Writing." Diss., Ramat Gan: Bar Ilan
University, 2021. [Hebrew.]

Jacobs, Adriana X. "Hebrew Remembers Yiddish: The Poetry of Avot
Yeshurun." In *Choosing Yiddish: Studies in Yiddish Literature, Culture and*

History, edited by Lara Rabinovitch, Shiri Goren, and Hannah Pressman, 296–313. Detroit: Wayne State University Press, 2013.

———. *Strange Cocktail: Translation and the Making of Modern Hebrew Poetry.* Ann Arbor: University of Michigan Press, 2018.

Jacobson, Yotam. "Interview with the Voice Artist Victoria Hanna." Personal blog, n.d. http://www.yotamjacobson.co.il/%D7%96%D7%94-%D7%A7 %D7%95%D7%9C-%D7%94%D7%97%D7%A1%D7%93-%D7%A8%D7%90 %D7%99%D7%95%D7%9F-%D7%A2%D7%9D (accessed March 25, 2020). [Hebrew.]

Jaffee, Laura. "Access Washing at the Imperial University: Militarism, Occupation, and Struggles Toward Disability Justice." PhD diss., Syracuse University, 2020.

Jaffee, Laura Jordan. "Disrupting Global Disability Frameworks: Settler-Colonialism and the Geopolitics of Disability in Palestine/Israel." *Disability & Society* 31, no. 1 (2016): 116–30.

Kafer, Alison. "Amputated Desire/Resistant Desire: Female Amputees in the Devotee Community." Society for Disability Studies Conference, Chicago, July 2000.

———. "Compulsory Bodies: Reflections on Heterosexuality and Able-bodiedness." *Journal of Women's History* 15, no. 3 (2003): 77–89.

———. *Feminist, Queer, Crip.* Bloomington: Indiana University Press, 2013.

Kama, Amit. "Supercrips Versus the Pitiful Handicapped: Reception of Disabling Images by Disabled Audience Members." *Communications* 29, no. 4 (2004): 447–66.

Kaplan, Morris B. *Sexual Justice: Democratic Citizenship and the Politics of Desire.* London: Routledge, 1997.

Kay, Tamar, dir. *Hebron Short Film.* Edited by Erfat Rasner. 2012. https://www .youtube.com/watch?v=_vodlSt8iEo.

———. *The Mute's House.* Jerusalem: Sam Spiegel Film and Television School, 2015.

Kelly, Christine. "Building Bridges with Accessible Care: Disability Studies, Feminist Care Scholarship, and Beyond." *Hypatia* 28, no. 4 (2013): 784–800.

Kett, Maria, and Mark van Ommeren. "Disability, Conflict, and Emergencies." *Lancet* 374 (9704) (2009): 1801–3.

Khanmalek, Tala, and Heidi Andrea Restrepo Rhodes. "A Decolonial Feminist Epistemology of the Bed: A Compendium Incomplete of Sick and Disabled

Queer Brown Femme Bodies of Knowledge." *Frontiers: A Journal of Women Studies* 41, no. 1 (2020): 35–58.

Kim, Eunjung. *Curative Violence: Rehabilitating Disability, Gender, and Sexuality in Modern Korea.* Durham: Duke University Press, 2017.

———. "'A Man, with Same Feelings': Disability, Humanity, and Heterosexual Apparatus in *Breaking the Waves, Born on the Fourth of July, Breathing Lessons*, and *Oasis*." In *The Problem Body: Projecting Disability on Film*, edited by Sally Chivers and Nicole Markotic, 131–58. Columbus: Ohio State University Press, 2010.

Kimmerling, Baruch. *The Israeli State and Society: Boundaries and Frontiers.* Albany: State University of New York Press, 1989.

Kiwan, Dina. "Dis/abled Decolonial Human and Citizen Futures." *Citizenship Studies* 26, nos. 4–5 (2022): 530–38.

Kleege, Georgina. *More Than Meets the Eye: What Blindness Brings to Art.* New York: Oxford University Press, 2017.

Koepnick, Lutz. *Walter Benjamin and the Aesthetics of Power.* Lincoln: University of Nebraska Press, 1999.

Kopit, Alison. "Toward a Queer Crip Aesthetic: Dance, Performance, and the Disabled Bodymind." ProQuest Dissertations, 2017.

Korman, Asaf, dir. *Next to Her (At li Layla).* Israel, 2014.

Kotef, Hagar. *The Colonizing Self; or, Home and Homelessness in Israel/Palestine.* Durham: Duke University Press, 2020.

Krimolovski, Miri, curator. *Selfie in a Limited Edition.* Tel Aviv: Library of Social Sciences, Management, and Education at Tel Aviv University, 2016.

Krymolowski, Miri. "Dancing from the Soul: Tamar Borer—a Dancer in a Wheelchair." *Rokdim* 59 (2002). [Hebrew.]

Kulick, Don, and Jens Rydström. *Loneliness and Its Opposite: Sex, Disability, and the Ethics of Engagement.* Durham: Duke University Press, 2015.

Kuppers, Petra. *The Scar of Visibility: Medical Performances and Contemporary Art.* Minneapolis: University of Minnesota Press, 2007.

Landsberg, Alison. *Prosthetic Memory: The Transformation of American Remembrance in the Age of Mass Culture.* New York: Columbia University Press, 2004.

Lane, Anat. "Gaza." *Telling Pictures* [Mafatal's album], 1994.

Langdridge, Darren. "Speaking the Unspeakable: S/M and the Eroticization of Pain." In *Safe, Sane and Consensual: Contemporary Perspectives of*

Sadomasochism, edited by Meg Barker and Darren Langdridge, 85–97. Basingstoke: Palgrave Mamillan, 2007.

Langdridge, Darren, and Meg Barker. "Situating Sadomasochism." In *Safe, Sane and Consensual: Contemporary Perspectives of Sadomasochism*, edited by Meg Barker and Darren Langdridge, 3–9. Basingstoke: Palgrave Macmillan, 2007.

Lanser, Susan S. "Review of Heather Love's *Feeling Backward: Loss and the Politics of Queer History*." *Modern Language Quarterly* 70, no. 4 (2009): 542–45.

Lauf, Jordan. "Uncovering the Mad Woman." *Tufts Observer*, December 11, 2015. https://tuftsobserver.org/uncovering-the-mad-woman/.

Lev-Aladgem, Shulamith. "History from Below: In Between Professional Theater and Community Theater." *Zmanim* 99 (2007): 64–73. [Hebrew.]

Lev-Ari, Shiri. "Inbal Eshel-Cahansky: 'I Don't Think There Is a God.'" *ynet*, February 26, 2013. https://www.ynet.co.il/articles/0,7340,L-4339463,00.html. [Hebrew.]

Lige, Sara. "Adults with Intellectual Disabilities and the Visual Arts: 'It's NOT Art Therapy!'" Master's thesis, University of British Columbia, 2000.

Lin, Lana. "Freud's Jaw and Other Lost Objects: Psychoanalysis and the Subjectivity of Survival." PhD diss., New York University, 2015.

Linton, Simi. *Claiming Disability: Knowledge and Identity*. New York: New York University Press, 1998.

Livingston, Julie. *Debility and the Moral Imagination in Botswana*. Bloomington: Indiana University Press, 2005.

Longmore, Paul. *Why I Burned My Book*. Philadelphia: Temple University Press, 2003.

Lorde, Audre. *A Burst of Light and Other Essays*. Mineola, NY: Ixia, 1988.

———. *The Cancer Journals*. 2nd ed. San Francisco: Aunt Lute Books, 1990.

Loshitzky, Yosefa. *Identity Politics on the Israeli Screen*. Austin: University of Texas Press, 2002.

Love, Heather. *Feeling Backward: Loss and the Politics of Queer History*. Cambridge, MA: Harvard University Press, 2007.

Lubin, Orly. "Body and Territory: Women in Israeli Cinema." *Israel Studies* 4, no. 1 (1999): 175–87.

———. "Low Gaze, Freed Gaze." In *Igael Shemtov: Low Landscape Low Reality*. Tel Aviv: Loushy Art & Editions, 2004.

———. "On the Way to Mommy: A Journey Toward Femininity." In *Sh'Chur: Screenplay and Seven Readings on the Film (Sh'Chur: Hatasriṭyeshevaḳeriot al haseret*), edited by Hanna Azoulay-Hasfari, 200–219. Tel Aviv: Yedioth Ahronot Books and Chemed Books, 2009. [Hebrew.]

———. "Space and Gaze." In *Where Am I Situated? Gender Perspectives on Space*, edited by Roni Halpern, 17–75. Kefar Sava: Friedrich-Ebert-Stiftung and Beit Berl Academic College, 2013. [Hebrew.]

Maapil Varsano, Hamutal. *A Blue and White Movie: Representation of Sexuality in Israeli Cinema* (*Seret Kachol Lavan*). Tel Aviv: Resling, 2020. [Hebrew.]

Malatino, Hil. *Trans Care*. Minneapolis: University of Minnesota Press, 2020.

Marcus, Ivan G. *Rituals of Childhood: Jewish Acculturation in Medieval Europe*. New Haven: Yale University Press, 1996.

Marie, Mohammad, Sana SaadAdeen, and Maher Battat. "Anxiety Disorders and PTSD in Palestine: A Literature Review." *BMC Psychiatry* 20, no. 1 (2020): 1–18.

Markotic, Nicole. Introduction to *Tessera* 27 (December 1999): 6–15. https://doi .org/10.25071/1923-9408.25168.

Marton, Orit. *To Be Trapped in My Body* (*Lihiyot kluah begufi*). Jerusalem: Pyutit, 2010. [Hebrew.]

———. *A Woman, After All* (*Ishah lamrot hakol*). Jerusalem: Pyutit, 2018. [Hebrew.]

Massad, Joseph. "The Weapon of Culture: Cinema in the Palestinian Liberation Struggle." In *Dreams of a Nation: On Palestinian Cinema*, edited by Hamid Dabashi, 30–42. London: Verso, 2006.

McRuer, Robert. *Crip Theory: Cultural Signs of Queerness and Disability*. New York: New York University Press, 2006.

———. "No Future for Crips: Disorderly Conduct in the New World Order; or, Disability Studies on the Verge of a Nervous Breakdown." In *Culture—Theory—Disability: Encounters Between Disability Studies and Cultural Studies*, edited by Anne Waldschmidt, Hanjo Berressem, and Moritz Ingwersen, 63–78. Bielefeld: Transcript Verlag, 2017.

Meekosha, Helen. "Decolonising Disability: Thinking and Acting Globally." *Disability & Society* 26, no. 6 (2011): 667–82.

Meir, Natan M. *Stepchildren of the Shtetl: The Destitute, Disabled, and Mad of Jewish Eastern Europe, 1800–1939*. Stanford: Stanford University Press, 2020.

Milbern, Stacey Park. "Notes on 'Access Washing.'" The Disability Justice Network of Ontario (DJNO), February 20, 2019. https://www.djno.ca/post/ notes-on-access-washing.

——. "On the Ancestral Plane: Crip Hand Me Downs and the Legacy of Our Movements." *Disability Visibility Project*, March 10, 2019. https:// disabilityvisibilityproject.com/2019/03/10/on-the-ancestral-plane-crip-hand -me-downs-and-the-legacy-of-our-movements/.

Mitchell, David, and Sharon Snyder. "Ablenationalism and the Geo-Politics of Disability." *Journal of Literary & Cultural Disability Studies* 4, no. 2 (2010): 113–25.

——. *Narrative Prosthesis: Disability and the Dependencies of Discourse*. Ann Arbor: University of Michigan Press, 2000.

——, dirs. *Vital Signs: Crip Culture Talks Back*. Boston: Fanlight Collection, 2021.

Mizrachi, Nissim. "On the Social Boundaries of the Critical Discourse on Disability." In *Disability Studies Reader*, edited by Sagit Mor, Neta Ziv, Arlene Kanter, Adva Eichengreen, and Nissim Mizrachi, 332–43. Jerusalem: Hakibbutz Hameuchad and the Van Leer Jerusalem Institute, 2016. [Hebrew.]

——. "Translating Disability in a Muslim Community: A Case of Modular Translation." *Culture, Medicine and Psychiatry* 38, no. 1 (2014): 133–59.

Mor, Liron. *Conflicts: The Poetics and Politics of Palestine-Israel*. New York: Fordham University Press, 2024.

Moser, Nira, curator. *Standard Mark (Tav Teken)* art exhibition. Bat Yam, Notzar Theater, 2016.

Mosleh, Marwan, Koustuv Dalal, Yousef Aljeesh, and Leif Svanström. "The Burden of War-Injury in the Palestinian Health Care Sector in Gaza Strip." *BMC International Health and Human Rights* 18 (2018). https://doi.org/10 .1186/s12914-018-0165-3.

Munk, Yael. "Between Algeria and Palestine: Some Thoughts on Political Cinema." *Ayin Beayin* 1 (2003): 39–49. [Hebrew.]

——. "Fate and Choice in Post-Colonial Feminist Cinema." *Resling* 6 (1999): 21–24. [Hebrew.]

Murphy, Robert F. *The Body Silent: The Different World of the Disabled*. New York: Norton, 2001.

Naaman, Yonit. "'Everyone Knows Yemenites Are Great in Bed': The Correlation Between the Density of a Woman's Skin Pigmentation and the Title 'Bimbo.'" *Theory and Criticism (Teorya vebikoret)* 28 (Spring 2006): 185–91. [Hebrew.]

Nasser, Khaled, Malcolm Maclachlan, and Joanne McVeigh. "Social Inclusion and Mental Health of Children with Physical Disabilities in Gaza, Palestine." *Disability, CBR and Inclusive Development* 27, no. 4 (2016): 5–36.

Naveh, Hannah, ed. *Israeli Family and Community: Women's Time*. London: Vallentine Mitchell, 2003.

———. "Politics of Silencing: The Meaning of Blindness in Jacob Steinberg's Story 'The Blind Woman.'" In *Sefer Yisrael Levin: Kovets mehkarim be-sifrut haivrit ledoroteha*, edited by Tova Rosen and Reuven Tsur, 143–68. Tel-Aviv: Mekhon Kats leheker hasifrut haivrit, Tel-Aviv University, 1994. [Hebrew.]

Nelson, Jack A. *The Disabled, the Media, and the Information Age*. Westport, CT: Greenwood, 1994.

Ngai, Sianne. *Ugly Feelings*. Cambridge, MA: Harvard University Press, 2005.

Nguyen, Xuan Thuy. "Critical Disability Studies at the Edge of Global Development: Why Do We Need to Engage with Southern Theory?" *Canadian Journal of Disability Studies* 7, no. 1 (2018): 1–25.

Nussbaum, Martha C. *Frontiers of Justice: Disability, Nationality, Species Membership*. Cambridge, MA: Harvard University Press, 2006.

Ohno, Kazuo, and Yoshito Ohno. *Kazuo Ohno's World: From Without & Within*. Translated by John Barrett. Middletown: Wesleyan University Press, 2004.

Olmert, Dana. *Predicaments of Writing and Loving: The First Hebrew Women Poets (Bitnuat safa ikeshet: Ktiva ve'ahava be 'shirat ha'meshorerot harishonot)*. Haifa: University of Haifa Press, 2012. [Hebrew.]

Oved, Shiri. *Chiseling My Own (Ehaye li haismel)*. Haifa: Pardes, 2016. [Hebrew.]

Paterson, Kevin. "It's About Time! Understanding the Experience of Speech Impairment." In *Routledge Handbook of Disability Studies*, edited by Nick Watson et al., 181–93. London: Routledge, 2012.

Patinkin, Aran, dir. *Kfar Tikva*. Jerusalem: Israel Film Service, 1983.

Patsavas, Alyson. "Recovering a Cripistemology of Pain: Leaky Bodies, Connective Tissue, and Feeling Discourse." *Journal of Literary & Cultural Disability Studies* 8, no. 2 (2014): 203–18.

Pedaya, Haviva. "Gam-ve-gam (gimgum)" ("Both: Stammer"). *Daka: Journal of Poetry and Criticism* 1 (2007): 32–38. [Hebrew.]

Perske, Robert. "The Dignity of Risk and the Mentally Retarded." *Mental Retardation* 10, no. 1 (February 1972): 24–27.

Pett, Sarah. "Rash Reading: Rethinking Virginia Woolf's 'On Being Ill.'" *Literature and Medicine* 37, no. 1 (2019): 26–66.

Piepzna-Samarasinha, Leah Lakshmi. *Care Work: Dreaming Disability Justice*. Vancouver: Arsenal Pulp, 2018.

———, curator. *Disabled and d/Deaf Poets Anthology*, 2020. https://poets.org/anthology/disabled-and-ddeaf-poets-anthology-curated-leah-lakshmi-piepzna-samarasinha.

Presner, Todd Samuel. *Muscular Judaism: The Jewish Body and the Politics of Regeneration*. New York: Routledge, 2007.

Preston, Jeffrey. *Fantasy of Disability: Images of Loss in Popular Culture*. London: Routledge, 2018.

Price, Margaret. "The Bodymind Problem and the Possibilities of Pain." *Hypatia* 30, no. 1 (2015): 268–84.

Puar, Jasbir K. *The Right to Maim: Debility, Capacity, Disability*. Durham: Duke University Press, 2017.

Pulrang, Andrew. "Disabled People Have Unique Perspectives on Risks and 'Reopening.'" *Forbes*, May 14, 2020. https://www.forbes.com/sites/andrewpulrang/2020/05/14/disabled-people-have-unique-perspectives-on-risks-and-reopening/#7f16542c64a5.

Qedar, Yair, dir. *The Seven Tapes* (*7 haselilim shel Yonah Wallach*). Israel, 2012.

Rattok, Lily. *Angel of Fire: The Poetry of Yona Wallach* (*Malach haesh*). Tel-Aviv: Hakibbutz Hameuchad, 1997. [Hebrew.]

Ravikovitch, Dahlia. *The Complete Poems* (*Kol hashirim*). Edited by Giddon Ticotsky and Uzi Shavit. Tel Aviv: Hakibbutz Hameuchad, 2010. [Hebrew.]

———. *Hovering at a Low Altitude: The Collected Poetry of Dahlia Ravikovitch*. Translated by Chana Bloch and Chana Kronfeld. New York: Norton, 2009.

Reinhart, Tanya. *Palestine/Israel: How to End the War of 1948*. New York: Seven Stories, 2002.

Rice, Carla, Eliza Chandler, Jen Rinaldi, Nadine Changfoot, Kirsty Liddiard, Roxanne Mykitiuk, and Ingrid Mundel. "Imagining Disability Futurities." *Hypatia* 32, no. 2 (2017): 213–29.

Roginsky, Dina. "On the Symbolic and Physical Body: The Representative and Impaired Body in Israeli Folk Dancing." *Israeli Sociology* 13, no. 2 (2011–12): 301–30. [Hebrew.]

Rossen, Rebecca. *Dancing Jewish: Jewish Identity in American Modern and Post-Modern Dance*. Oxford: Oxford University Press, 2014.

Rotman, Yonat. "The Jewish-Arab Conflict in the Works of Amir Kolben, Rami Be'er, and Ohad Naharin—From a Presentation of the Narrative to Its Deconstruction." *Dance Today* 11 (2004): 39–45.

Russo, Jasna, and Angela Sweeney. *Searching for a Rose Garden: Challenging Psychiatry, Fostering Mad Studies*. Monmouth: PCCS Books, 2016.

Sachs, Ben. "Yona Explores the Life of a Poet Who Turned Madness into Verse." *Reader: Chicago's Alternative Nonprofit Newsroom*, October 22, 2015. https://chicagoreader.com/film/yona-explores-the-life-of-a-poet-who -turned-madness-into-verse/.

Samuels, Ellen Jean. "My Body, My Closet: Invisible Disability and the Limits of Coming-Out Discourse." *GLQ: A Journal of Lesbian and Gay Studies* 9, no. 1 (2003): 233–55.

Sandahl, Carrie. "Disability Arts." In *Encyclopedia of Disability*, edited by Gary L. Albrecht, 2. Newbury Park, CA: SAGE, 2006. http://dx.doi.org/10 .4135/9781412950510.n221.

Sandahl, Carrie, and Philip Auslander. "Disability Studies in Commotion with Performance Studies: Introduction." In *Bodies in Commotion: Disability and Performance*, edited by Carrie Sandahl and Philip Auslander, 1–12. Ann Arbor: University of Michigan Press, 2005.

Sarna, Igal. *Yona Wallach: Biography* (*Yona Wallach: biyografyah*). Jerusalem: Keter, 1993. [Hebrew.]

Sayigh, Rosemary. "Silenced Suffering." *Borderlands E-Journal* 14, no. 1 (2015): 1–20.

Schalk, Sami. *Bodyminds Reimagined: (Dis)ability, Race, and Gender in Black Women's Speculative Fiction*. Durham: Duke University Press, 2018.

———. "Reevaluating the Supercrip." *Journal of Literary & Cultural Disability Studies* 10, no. 1 (2016): 71–86.

Segersky, Ofir. "People Don't Realize That a Disabled Person Is Also Sexual." *ynet*, August 31, 2021. https://www.ynet.co.il/dating/sex/article/b1ufzdi11y. [Hebrew.]

Shabat-Nadir, Hadas. "A Boy Without a Face: Blindness in Erez Biton's Poetry." In *Ana min al-Magrab: Reading Erez Bitton's Poetry* (*Ana min al-Magreb: ķeriot beshirat Erez Biṭon*), edited by Yochai Oppenheimer and Ktzia Alon, 115–46. Tel-Aviv: Hakibbutz Hameuchad, 2014. [Hebrew.]

Shakespeare, Tom. "Disabled Sexuality: Toward Rights and Recognition." *Sexuality and Disability* 18 (2000): 159–66.

Shalhoub-Kevorkian, Nadera. *Incarcerated Childhood and the Politics of Unchilding*. Cambridge: Cambridge University Press, 2019.

Shapira, Anita. *Land and Power: The Zionist Resort to Force, 1881–1948*. Oxford: Oxford University Press, 1992.

Shapiro, Joseph. "The Sexual Assault Epidemic No One Talks About." *NPR: All Things Considered*, January 8, 2018. https://www.npr.org/2018/01/08/570224090/the-sexual-assault-epidemic-no-one-talks-about.

Shell, Marc. "Moses' Tongue." *Common Knowledge* 12, no. 1 (2006): 150–76.

Sheppard, Emma. "Using Pain, Living with Pain." *Feminist Review* 120 (2018): 54–69.

Shildrick, Margrit. *Dangerous Discourses of Disability, Subjectivity and Sexuality.* Basingstoke: Palgrave Macmillan, 2009.

———. "Sexual Citizenship, Governance and Disability: From Foucault to Deleuze." In *Beyond Citizenship? Feminism and the Transformation of Belonging*, edited by Sasha Roseneil, 138–159. Basingstoke: Palgrave Macmillan, 2013.

Siebers, Tobin. "Disability, Pain, and the Politics of Minority Identity." In *Culture—Theory—Disability: Encounters Between Disability Studies and Cultural Studies*, edited by Anne Waldschmidt, Hanjo Berressem, and Moritz Ingwersen, 111–36. Bielefeld: Transcript Verlag, 2017.

———. *Disability Theory.* Ann Arbor: University of Michigan Press, 2008.

Sins Invalid. "Disability Justice for Palestine." August 6, 2014. https://static1.squarespace.com/static/5bed3674f8370ad8c02efd9a/t/5fc61ab518e72e5fdba81e43/1606818486004/Disability_Justice_for_Palestine.pdf.

Smilges, J. Logan. *Crip Negativity.* Minneapolis: University of Minnesota Press, 2023.

Smith, Bonnie G., and Beth Hutchison. *Gendering Disability.* New Brunswick: Rutgers University Press, 2004.

Smith, Owen. "Shifting Apollo's Frame: Challenging the Body Aesthetic in Theater Dance." In *Bodies in Commotion: Disability and Performance*, edited by Carrie Sandahl and Philip Auslander, 73–85. Ann Arbor: University of Michigan Press, 2005.

Snounu, Yasmin. "Apartheid, Disability, and the Triple Matrix of Maiming in Palestine." *Peace Review: A Journal of Social Justice* 31 (2019): 459–70.

Soffer, Rona. dir. *Love Davka.* Jerusalem: Sam Spiegel Film and Television School, 2010.

———. *Ms. VeRtigo.* Kokhav Michael: Gesher Multicultural Film Fund and Daroma Production, 2018.

———. *A Redheaded Sheep (Kivsa ktuma).* Tel Aviv: Tel Aviv University, 2014.

———. *Until the Wall Breaks Down: A Film About Rona (Ad shehakir yishaver).* Directed by Uri Harel. Written by Uri Harel and Rona Soffer. 2004. https://www.ronasoffer.com/work.

Soker-Schwager, Hanna. *Excess Thought: Superfluity in Hebrew Literature, 1907–2017 (Mahshavot meyutarot)*. Ramat Gan: Bar Ilan University Press, 2021. [Hebrew.]

Soldatic, Karen. "The Transnational Sphere of Justice: Disability Praxis and the Politics of Impairment." *Disability & Society* 28, no. 6 (2013): 744–55.

Stav, Shira. *Reconstructing Daddy: Fathers and Daughters in Modern Hebrew Poetry (Aba ani koveshet)*. Tel Aviv: Dvir, 2014. [Hebrew.]

Stevens, Bethany. "Structural Barriers to Sexual Autonomy for Disabled People." *GP Solo* 31, no. 2 (2014): 62–63.

St. Pierre, Joshua. "The Construction of the Disabled Speaker: Locating Stuttering in Disability Studies." In *Literature, Speech Disorders, and Disability: Talking Normal*, edited by Christopher Eagle, 9–23. London: Routledge, 2013.

Sufian, Sandra M. *Healing the Land and the Nation: Malaria and the Zionist Project in Palestine, 1920–1947*. Chicago: University of Chicago Press, 2007.

———. "Mental Hygiene and Disability in the Zionist Project." *Disability Studies Quarterly* 27, no. 4 (2007): n.p.

Szobel, Ilana. "Crossing Boundaries: Artist Limor Ashkenazi on Disability and Intimacy." *Lilith*, July 29, 2024. https://lilith.org/articles/crossing-boundaries-artist-limor-ashkenazi-on-disability-and-intimacy/.

———. *Flesh of My Flesh: Sexual Violence in Modern Hebrew Literature*. Albany: State University of New York Press, 2021.

———. *A Poetics of Trauma: The Work of Dahlia Ravikovitch*. Waltham: Brandeis University Press, 2013.

Tausinger, Rona. "Victoria Hanna: Hebrew Is a Working Tool and a Healing Tool." *Israel Hayom*, September 29, 2016. https://www.israelhayom.co.il/magazine/hashavua/article/8764463. [Hebrew.]

Trabelsi, Osnat, producer. "Creation, Protest, and Freedom of Expression in the Wake of *Jenin, Jenin*." Zoom event at the Pluralistic Spiritual Center in Neve Shalom, January 27, 2021. https://www.youtube.com/watch?v=ExTGfWKoBtM.

Tsamir, Hamutal. *In the Name of the Land: Nationalism, Subjectivity, and Gender in the Israeli Poetry of the Statehood Generation (Beshem hanof: Le'umiyut migdar vesobyektiviyut bashirah hayisraelit bishnot hahamishim vehashishim)*. Jerusalem: Keter Books Heksherim Center, 2006. [Hebrew.]

———. "The Pioneers' Sacrifice, the Holy Land, and the Emergence of Women's Poetry in the 1920s" (*Hakorban hahalutsi*). In *A Moment of Birth: Studies in Hebrew and Yiddish Literature in Honor of Dan Miron (Rega shel huledet*), edited by Hannan Hever, 645–73. Jerusalem: Bialik Institute, 2007. [Hebrew.]

Tsoffar, Ruth. "Staging Sexuality, Reading Wallach's Poetry." *Hebrew Studies* 43 (2002): 87–117.

Tugend, Tom. "*Storm* Drifts off Oscar Map, but *Mute's House* Stands Its Ground." *Jewish Journal*, December 21, 2016. https://jewishjournal.com/culture/arts/213244/storm-drifts-off-oscar-map-but-mutes-house-stands-its-ground/.

Usinger, Mike. "Struggles Pay off for Victoria Hanna." *Georgia Straight*, February 17, 2016. https://www.straight.com/music/640691/struggles-pay-victoria-hanna.

Utin, Pablo. *Lessons in Cinema: Conversations with Israeli Filmmakers* (*Shiurim be-ḳolnoa: siḥot im yotsrot ve-yotsrim Yiśreelim*). Ramat ha-Sharon: Asyah, 2017. [Hebrew.]

Valenti-Hein, D., and L. Schwartz. *The Sexual Abuse Interview for Those with Developmental Disabilities*. Santa Barbara: James Stanfield, 1995. https://www.ojp.gov/ncjrs/virtual-library/abstracts/sexual-abuse-interview-those-developmental-disabilities.

Vig, Shoshana. "Being Imprisoned in My Body: Shoshana Vig's Interview with Orit Marton." *News1*, April 21, 2010. https://www.news1.co.il/Archive/0014-D-47320-00.html. [Hebrew.]

Walker-Cornetta, Andrew. "Without the Lord: Eliza Suggs, Religion, and the Good Disabled Subject." *American Religion* 5, no. 1 (2023): 66–92.

Wallach, Yona. *Let the Words: Selected Poems of Yona Wallach*. Translated by Linda Stern Zisquit. New York: Sheep Meadow, 2006.

———. *The Unconscious Unfolds like a Fan: Selected Poems, 1963–1985* (*Tat hakara niftahat kemo menifa*). Tel Aviv: Haakibbutz Hameuchad, 1992. [Hebrew.]

Wasserman, Dan, dir. *Do You Believe in Love?* (*Hashadhanit*). Tel Aviv-Yafo: Heymann Brothers Films, 2013.

Watts Belser, Julia. "Familiarity and Difference: Classical and Contemporary Jewish Thought on Disability." Talk given at the 2013 Summer Institute on Theology and Disability, Dallas. http://bethesdainstitute.org/2013-theology-presentations.

———. "God on Wheels: Disability and Jewish Feminist Theology." *Tikkun* 29, no. 4 (2014): 27–29.

———. *Loving Our Own Bones: Disability Wisdom and the Spiritual Subversiveness of Knowing Ourselves Whole*. Boston: Beacon, 2023.

Weeks, Jeffrey. "The Sexual Citizen." *Theory, Culture & Society* 15, nos. 3–4 (1998): 35–52.

Weiman-Kelman, Zohar. *Queer Expectations: A Genealogy of Jewish Women's Poetry*. Albany: State University of New York Press, 2018.

Weisman, Anat. "After All of This, I Will Have to Muster All of My 'Courage for the Mundane': On Leah Goldberg's Paradigmatic Temperament." *Prooftexts* 33, no. 2 (2013): 222–50.

Weiss, Meira. *The Chosen Body: The Politics of the Body in Israeli Society*. Stanford: Stanford University Press, 2002.

Weiss, Yfaat. "A Man with His Life at Both Ends of Time: Leah Goldberg, Paul Ernst Kahle, and Appreciating the Mundane." *Yad Vashem Studies* 37, no. 1 (2009): 137–78. [Hebrew.]

White, Sara. "Crippling the Archives: Negotiating Notions of Disability in Appraisal and Arrangement and Description." *American Archivist* 75, no. 1 (2012): 109–24.

Wills, David. *Prosthesis*. Stanford: Stanford University Press, 1995.

Wispelwey, Bram, and Yasser Abu Jamei. "The Great March of Return: Lessons from Gaza on Mass Resistance and Mental Health." *Health and Human Rights* 22, no. 1 (2020): 179–86.

Wolpert, Julian. "The Dignity of Risk." *Transactions of the Institute of British Geographers* 5, no. 4 (1980): 391–401.

Woolf, Virginia. *On Being Ill*. Ashfield: Paris, 2012.

Yeshurun, Helit. "Yona Wallach April 1984: An Interview." *Hadarim* 4 (1984): 105–18.

Yosef, Raz. "Conditions of Visibility: Trauma and Contemporary Israeli Women's Cinema." *Signs: Journal of Women in Culture and Society* 42, no. 4 (2017): 919–43.

Yudkoff, Sunny S. *Tubercular Capital: Illness and the Conditions of Modern Jewish Writing*. Redwood City: Stanford University Press, 2019.

Zach, Natan. "Reflections on Alterman's Poetry" (*Hirhurim al shirat Alterman*). In *The Poetry Beyond Words: Critical Essays, 1954–1973* (*Hashira sheme'ever lamilim: teoria vebikoret 1954–1973*), 43–58. Tel Aviv: Hakibbutz Hameuchad, 2011.

Ziv, Amalia. "'Our Virgin Friends and Wives?' Female Sexual Subjectivity in Yona Wallach's Poetry." *Hebrew Studies* 56, no. 1 (2015): 333–56.

Zoanni, Tyler. "The Possibilities of Failure." *Cambridge Anthropology* 36, no. 1 (2018): 61–79.

Zohar, Uri, dir. *Peeping Toms* (*Metzitzim*). Israel, 1972.

Zooaretz, Ruti. *Eaten* (*Ahulot*), Or Yehudah: Kinneret, Zmora-Bittan, Dvir, 2008. [Hebrew.]

Zosto, Revital. "Dance Between Life and Death." *Maariv*, January 23, 2009. https://www.makorrishon.co.il/nrg/online/55/ART1/844/275.html. [Hebrew.]

INDEX